Broken Biscuits

Broken Biscuits

and Other Male Failures

Adam Farrer

Harper North

HarperNorth
Windmill Green
24 Mount Street
Manchester M2 3NX

A division of
HarperCollins*Publishers*
1 London Bridge Street
London SE1 9GF

www.harpercollins.co.uk

HarperCollins*Publishers*
Macken House, 39/40 Mayor Street Upper
Dublin 1, D01 C9W8

First published by HarperNorth in 2025

1 3 5 7 9 10 8 6 4 2

Copyright © Adam Farrer 2025

Adam Farrer asserts the moral right to
be identified as the author of this work

A catalogue record for this book
is available from the British Library

HB ISBN: 978-0-00-871069-9

Printed and bound in the UK using 100%
renewable electricity at CPI Group (UK) Ltd, Croydon

All rights reserved. No part of this publication may be
reproduced, stored in a retrieval system, or transmitted,
in any form or by any means, electronic, mechanical,
photocopying, recording or otherwise, without the prior
permission of the publishers.

This book contains FSC™ certified paper and other controlled
sources to ensure responsible forest management.

For more information visit: www.harpercollins.co.uk/green

For Janet and Ian

'To be The Man you've gotta beat The Man, and I am The Man.'

Ric Flair

'I think God, in creating man, somewhat overestimated his ability.'

Oscar Wilde

'I just don't get why you want to tell people all these personal things.'

Ian Farrer (my father)

Contents

Domesday	1
If I Were Jon	31
The Beautiful Ones	55
The Three Fs	91
Broken Biscuits	127
Taken	161
An Inside Job	185
Bonnie Black Hare	217
This is Your Brain On Drugs	241
Exposures	275
A Picture of Health	313
It's the End of the World As We Know It	335
Acknowledgements	369

Domesday

In 1986, every school child in the UK was obliged to celebrate the 900th anniversary of *The Domesday Book*: a great survey of land and assets demanded by William I following the Norman Conquest. For weeks, classes just like mine learned about the Battle of Hastings, made Norman helmets out of sugar paper and sketched their own versions of the Bayeux Tapestry. During breaks, we'd recreate scenes from the battle, imitating the thrashing, final moments of King Harold, our bodies jolting like fish out of water as we clutched at imagined arrow shafts protruding from our eyes. The entire country seemed to be united in this celebration of its huge, reconfiguring loss. A national demonstration of late-onset Stockholm Syndrome.

The Domesday Book compelled my friends and me, not because we were all great fans of land taxes and census data, but mostly for how the key word was pronounced: *Doomsday*. This made it sound much more

Broken Biscuits

thrilling than it was, like a spell book bound in human skin. We didn't pay attention to the actual contents so much; what child would? While the area of Suffolk where I spent my childhood featured a heavy crop of thick-forearmed aspiring young farmers, none of my friends cared how many sheep a landowner possessed almost 1,000 years ago. What we cared about were the legends that had somehow sprouted up around the book. Or the lies, depending on how you liked to think of them. And most of the lies I heard came from a boy named James.

'What *really* interests me,' he said, as he took a colouring pencil and began drawing a felled Anglo-Saxon having his face trampled by a horse, 'is the treasure.'

'What treasure?' I asked, my interest suddenly piqued.

At this, James put down his pencil and turned to me, vibrating with the kind of excitable pressure you'd expect from a vigorously shaken can of Pepsi.

'Well …' he began, and I braced myself, because James always had a great deal to say. An only child who spent a lot of his time having to make his voice heard among adults, over time he ended up sounding like one. You've met them, those kids who wouldn't seem out of place in a bar, loosening their ties and opening up to you about their disappointing quarterly-sales figures or their harrowing second divorce.

'Wealthy landowners were scared of Norman taxation,' he said. A cold and disappointing start. I didn't know

Domesday

what taxation was back then, but I knew James well enough to trust that, while he might take his sweet time, he'd eventually get to the juice. He explained that these landowners had killed most of their livestock and buried great quantities of their riches to avoid being taxed on it, their hope being that one day soon the Normans would be overthrown, their riches could be dug up again and their status would be restored. But this, 1986 had taught us, did not happen. 'And it's said that some of that treasure is still out there,' James added, 'guarded by the ghosts of the landowners.'

More often than not, 'it's said' is used as scaffolding to bolster a shaky but intoxicating lie. James had used it before, when telling me that Death by Chocolate cake was so named because 'it's said' a single slice was loaded with so much fat and sugar that just one mouthful could fill your arteries with what was essentially toffee, killing you instantly. And now he was using it to tell me exactly the kind of thing I wanted to hear.

The secret to a successful lie is the grain of truth at its core. All of us knew about the Anglo-Saxon treasures found to the far west of our town at Sutton Hoo in the 1930s. We'd seen photos of gold items studded with gems; the ceremonial helmet and weapons. While it was exciting to think wealth of that kind could be discovered so close to our homes, we'd assumed it was a one off. Then our history teacher showed us a photocopied news article

Broken Biscuits

about a nine-year-old boy named Gary Fridd, and a lightbulb came on in my head.

In 1976, Fridd had been playing on the edge of a river in Yorkshire when he discovered a 1,000-year-old Anglo-Saxon chieftain's sword. He'd pulled it from the waters and in doing so briefly became very famous. He appeared in national newspapers and on the popular kid's TV show, *Blue Peter*, posing with what became known as The Gilling sword, which he'd been permitted to keep. Of course, he immediately sold it, just as I would have. For 'a fortune', we were told. This news was confirmation that the treasure at Sutton Hoo had not been a uniquely exciting find. In fact, treasure might be dotted all over the UK. Particularly where I lived in the east of England, the preferred invasion point for waves of wealthy conquerors, all of whom could have dropped precious items on battlefields where they sank into the dirt and swelled with value.

What James told me just added weight to that knowledge by mixing in intentionally buried wealth. Whether he was lying, or simply mixing up information he'd half understood, didn't really matter to me. By that point I was immune to reason, able to think of little else but those storied, undiscovered riches, just waiting for me to find them. Ready to transform my life at a time when that was exactly what I needed.

* * *

Domesday

I spent my early years in Haverhill, a once quaint East Anglian market town that expanded into a sprawling nest of charmless functional housing as part of a 1958 London overspill project. The capital's post-war population growth was causing a social and housing crisis, which a committee decided was best eased by offering Londoners the chance to trade their cramped homes for the clean air of the flat, expansive Suffolk countryside.

Plans were drawn up to triple Haverhill's population, and new houses and factories appeared on the outskirts of the town, which began to spread across the map like a wine stain. The designs for these new buildings looked futuristic and utopian right up until the moment they left the architect's drawing board and were rained upon, at which point they looked as exhausted and miserable as a bus queue of early-morning commuters. To my grandparents, though, they looked like Heaven.

The youngest of my nan and granddad's three kids, my mother was ten years old when her family relocated to Haverhill. Growing up, whenever my siblings and I would complain about access to the bathroom or having to share a bedroom, she'd remind us that she'd been raised in a mildewed two-room flat in south London, where weekly washes were taken in a tin bath in the back yard.

'You don't know you're born,' she'd say. 'Try being soapy and naked outside. The rest of the street knew my arse better than I did.'

Broken Biscuits

So, it was a blessing for her to start a new life in a place with a garden and access to air she could breathe without the threat of inhaling a rat. She would eventually meet my father at Haverhill Meat Products, a huge abattoir and warehouse complex that processed meat for Sainsbury's. Most of my friends' parents met this way, thanks to Haverhill's new factory-led economy, which employed most of the town. There was Winmau, which made the dartboards we'd see on TV. Addis, the producer of toothbrushes, swing-bins and the plastic washing-up bowl that my mother would soak her cracked and swollen feet in after her shift at the abattoir. Then there was International Flavours & Fragrances, which regularly atomised the town with scented clouds of synthetic strawberry and banana. None of my friends knew anyone who worked in this particular factory, or quite what it did, so we pictured a vast Wonka-like space filled with primary-coloured lakes of the fragrances that made our town smell like an eight-year-old girl's pencil case.

But while you might be able to pour concrete over something and call it new, the overspill project couldn't fully erase the history of a town so old that it was referenced in the pages of *The Domesday Book*. I may have grown up in a home that was constructed under the Wilson government, but I could walk out of my front door and roam a land that had previously been enjoyed by witchfinder generals and the Black Death.

Domesday

Those of us born in the area grew up feeling like we were part of a lineage that was impossibly old, every inch of our territory imbued with myths and historical significance. We all knew that a few towns along from us, over in Hadstock, a church was said to have once proudly displayed the flayed skin of a Viking invader on its door. And that in 1690, at Place Farm, on the spot where my primary school would be built 270 years later, a farmer named Killingback had beaten a young orphan boy to death. Upon escaping conviction by claiming a horse had trampled the child, he was said to have been tormented each night by visitations from the boy's spirit.

'*Killingback*?' I'd said years later in disbelief, hearing this farmer's name for the first time. '*Killing ... back?*'

It seemed too on the nose for a murderer. The sort of thing you'd call a character in a bad novel, like a homicide detective named Inspector Corpse. But while I was shocked to learn of the murder, its location didn't surprise me at all. To an outsider it might seem odd that a town planner would stand on the notoriously haunted site of a heartless child-murder and think, *Hey, let's build the classrooms right here.* But the truth was, the region boiled with dark history and it was hard to pick a patch of Haverhill that was *not* the location of a grim legend.

Spot an area of raised earth appearing like a bubble on the otherwise pancake-flat landscape and you could be certain that it already had its own mythology. As a burial

Broken Biscuits

mound, maybe, or perhaps the corpse of a slain giant, grown over with a sheet of grass and mosses. The ghosts of plague victims, peeled Norsemen and trampled children were spoken of by the kids in my school not so much with notes of horror but as if they were local celebrities.

'My brother saw Annie Suckling outside The Red Lion,' someone might say, referencing the ghost of a local highwaywoman we all claimed to have encountered at one time or another. Our reply would not be a gasp or a snort of derision, but a keen, 'Ooh, what was she wearing?'

Because of this, Suffolk has always felt to me like a county bewitched. A folk-horror wonderland, where the spirits and rituals of earlier communities are baked in. Every kid in my school shared a playground with ghosts and walked in the footsteps of treasure-stashing Anglo-Saxons. Each of us part of a continuing narrative that predated every tree we'd ever climbed and would long outlast International Flavours & Fragrances.

When we were very young, my friends and I possessed a particular form of boldness that seems incredible to me now. Each of us fearless in our own peculiar ways. Mark could be convinced to eat anything. Michael enjoyed setting traps; Stephen enjoyed starting fires; Ian could scale a tree swiftly and to great heights, unbothered by the notion that a single rotten branch could have sent him crashing to his death. For my part, I would do anything

Domesday

for attention. If that meant throwing myself into a patch of nettles or cycling at speed into a brick wall, I would do it with a song in my heart and wear my wounds with pride.

There was nothing too dangerous for us to try and each one of us should have died a dozen times. When Stephen suggested we crawl into the concrete drainage pipes on the edge of the reservoir to see where they went, our only response was, 'Me first!' Not a second was wasted on claustrophobic panic or mental images of our bloated corpses bobbing along in the sewer system. There was a raggedy energy to us that could only be burned off by risking our lives or causing trouble. We'd knock on one another's doors after school or at weekends, always ready to present the other members of our gang with a new reckless possibility.

'Do you want to smash up some toy cars with a brick?'

'Do you want to watch me eat a rock?'

'Do you want to set fire to a big pile of ring caps, then run like mad?'

If it could be said that our gang had a territory, it was the Black Path, a tarmacked-over former railway track that ran through our estate and off into the arable distance of East Anglia. It was the foundation for our hastily assembled, arm-breaking BMX ramps. The giant, dark scroll on which we chalked every swear word we knew in the hope of scandalising passers-by. But really, it was the

Broken Biscuits

bold defining line that was drawn through all of our childhood adventures. Running for miles, it was variously banked by dense woods and orchards, sprawling fields and Stour Brook, the river that wriggled its way through the centre of Haverhill. Whatever terrain we wished to imagine ourselves in, the surroundings of the Black Path offered it. This might be the Mekong River Delta, war-torn Endor or whatever South American jungle featured in *Raiders of the Lost Ark*. It was always enough.

Transported to these places and armed with cap guns and rifle-shaped sticks, we shot each other to death on the banks of Stour Brook, our giggling corpses rolling into the shallows. Revived seconds later, we scoured the orchard floors for bruised and half-mulched fruit, damsons, greengages and Bramley apples, which we launched at one another, delighting as they exploded upon impact. Stephen once threw an apple at me so rotten and weather-stewed that when it collided with my head it burst like a water balloon, sending me to the ground dazed, my skull appearing to leak apple sauce.

'Woah! It's like brains!' Stephen said, wide-eyed with awe as he looked down at me. He would go on to join the army straight out of school and spent the majority of his years of service standing in a field in Eastern Europe waiting for something to happen. His military career never presented him with anything as exciting as the sight of my head exploding on the border of the Black Path.

Domesday

Occasionally, something or someone would come along to interrupt our play: another gang of kids we'd have to fight off, or perhaps a mocking, older brother. Other times it was a jutting representation of impending adulthood pressing against our world. When Michael went for a pee in the bushes and discovered a pornographic magazine stashed in a tree stump, he shrieked as if he'd just discovered a corpse.

'Urgh, look at this!' he said, holding a naked centrefold at arm's length, the corner of the magazine pinched between his thumb and forefinger. We all gawped at it, this image of a blonde, smiling woman, her legs spread and her hands gripping her calves. One by one we inched closer, like a group of curious Neanderthals who'd been presented with an iPad.

'Urgh,' we echoed, but the sound left our throats without a note of disgust. We were hypnotised and compelled. Recognising this, Michael began tearing the magazine to pieces, laughing as he tossed the shredded pages into the air. This broke the spell, banishing that kind of imagery back to a world we were not yet ready for. Then we gunned each other down again, our fallen bodies surrounded by a confetti of bare flesh, nipple and hair. Later, I would notice Michael picking up some of these ripped pieces and stuffing them into his pocket.

Our days were spent this way, dirt-caked and screaming, until one of our mothers called out for us and we

Broken Biscuits

reluctantly trudged home from battle to take baths or eat dinner. This was a group of friends that I missed the second they were gone, impatient for my next opportunity to shoot them all in the head then settle down on the riverbank to swap football stickers and new swear words, while Mark extinguished lit matches on his tongue and Michael covertly scanned the bushes for copies of *Razzle*.

When middle school rolled around, though, new alliances were formed and our gang dissolved. Ian moved to Canada. Mark and Michael ended up in different schools. Stephen became much cooler than anything I could keep up with. A page was turned, and on it I was a different character. Unsure of myself in a new environment and increasingly solitary. There were several things I could have blamed for this, but if I had to pinpoint the real difference-maker for me, I'd say it was the glasses.

My teacher, Mrs Blackwell, had noticed a decline in my work, my usual distracted daydreaming during lessons now accompanied by frequent squinting. Not being able to see what was on the blackboard, I'd often guess at what I was being taught and hope for the best.

'Um ... Egypt?' I replied one afternoon, when questioned about the hazy letters she'd written on the blackboard.

'February,' she said, sighing as she tapped the board with a stick of chalk. 'I was asking you how many syllables there are in the word ... *February*.'

Domesday

She sent a note home to my parents that day, advising that I visit an optician. This led to a diagnosis of extreme short-sightedness that soon left me helpless without my new prescription glasses. They were huge, brass-framed things with eye-magnifying lenses that left me looking like I was in a permanent state of having just received some shocking news.

'You look stylish,' my mother told me. 'Like a model.'

This could only have been true if she was comparing me to the kids they used on the back of comic books to advertise *Advanced Dungeons & Dragons*. I may as well have been fitted with a back brace and a note around my neck asking everyone to be kind to me about my chronic bed-wetting. My glasses instantly placed me among the ranks of the helpless, and once it reached the point when no one could remember me without them, middle school was over for me reputationally. Each morning when I put them on, I felt more of the bark of my pre-middle-school boldness being peeled away, exposing a tender, vulnerable flesh. I would never again be impressive. I was a bottom feeder and should learn to like it down there.

Then there was the idea of this treasure. The notion that, with the slurp of a sword pulled from a riverbank, everything could change for me. Glasses don't matter when you're rich and famous, and if there *was* treasure out there, they gave me a better chance of finding it.

* * *

Broken Biscuits

On Sundays, I'd often help my elder brother, Robert, with his paper round; his delivery bag on that day so burdened with broadsheets and supplements, it felt to me as if we were transporting an anvil. He'd heave it onto the seat of his bike and wheel it along his round, handing me newspapers to shove through doors. I'd run up driveways and grind them through finger-snapping, spring-loaded letter boxes, agreeing to this labour for the chance to hang out with Robert, but also because his route took in my favourite house in town.

Located on the rural edge of Haverhill, it looked to me back then like a stately home, the imposing mass of it set out on a huge plot lined with immaculate gardens and a gravel driveway dotted with nimble-looking cars. The privilege of this house was that it wasn't overlooked by anything, the view behind it just trees and fields stretching into the uninterrupted distance. Its privacy punctured only by me, snooping.

'They're Americans,' Robert had said of the owners the first time we'd delivered there, which elevated the whole setup for me.

For most of my life I've found the idea of America intoxicating. My TV had taught me that glamour was born there, along with steroid muscles, the concept of cool and cars so impractically wide they could only be power dressing. It was a land where everything seemed better and brighter, and this house was a little

Domesday

patch of it in my town – the owners living a life I aspired to.

That first visit, I cautiously crunched across the gravel and peered through the ground-floor windows into the set of *Antiques Roadshow*. There were plump, richly upholstered sofas, antique furniture, oil paintings and, most excitingly, a huge television. When I dreamed of what I'd spend my treasure riches on, this was it. One day, I would sit in a house just like it, having friends over, eating snacks in front of my snooker-table sized TV and doing whatever else I felt like. No need for school, no one to tell me what to do. I would be free. Little Lord Fuckyouall.

'Oi!' Robert said, cuffing me across the back of the head. My nose doinked against the living room window. 'Fucking peeping Tom.'

He posted the paper through the door then kicked me back down the drive, but I treasured the memory of this house long afterwards.

One day ...

Whenever we finished Robert's round, we'd head back to the newsagents to drop off his newspaper bag, taking a shortcut across a patch of waste ground that bordered the Black Path. I always enjoyed this route, particularly during the days of hosepipe-ban summers, when the long grasses around us were sun-parched and you could fool yourself that you were walking through the bristles of an

Broken Biscuits

upturned push broom. We were making this journey after his round one morning when Robert stopped abruptly and drew my attention to a long branch staked into the ground among the golden grasses, a small, dark object impaled on its end. As we edged closer, we saw that this object was a shrew, its velvety fur tenting around the sharp end of the branch. It was not all that bloody a scene; the contents of a shrew are pretty minimal. Still, it was a ghastly thing to find. So, naturally Robert leaned in close to examine it.

'Satanists …' he said, peering at the shrew's tiny, leaking head, the tone of his words familiar to me from countless numbers of westerns that I'd watched with my father. The kind of line issued by leather-skinned cowboys as they crouched to analyse the tracks around a scorched circle of wagons. 'Injuns …'

Robert was obsessed with the idea of Satanists back then, in the same way that my friends' sisters seemed to be obsessed with pastel leg warmers and the career of Simon Le Bon. Back in the mid-80s, Satanic panic was tearing across the American psyche like a forest fire, and it generated a heat that could be felt across the Atlantic. Satanists were blamed for corrupting America's youth by Bible-thumping preachers and lurid news reports. We'd hear stories of ritual abuse, animal sacrifice and murder, most of it reportedly encouraged by the kind of heavy-metal that Robert enjoyed listening to. By the time Satanic

Domesday

panic arrived in the scrubby wilds of Suffolk it had been reduced to rumours of bloody sacrifices, which fitted right in alongside entrenched, local notions of grisly folklore.

'They do it out in the woods,' Robert told me, settling down beside me on my bed later that day. 'Down near that path where you lot play.'

I felt a plunge then, somewhere between my heart and my stomach. A nauseous reminder of the way my life had been reconfigured. *Where we used to play*, I thought.

More pressing, though, was the information Robert was delivering about the blood-drenched tree stumps he claimed to have seen, makeshift altars where chickens and stray animals were ritually beheaded. The Satanists drank the blood straight from the necks of these animals, he said, 'like they were downing a bottle of beer'. Over the course of a few minutes, Robert managed to redraw the map of my childhood, filling it with scenes that wouldn't have seemed out of place in a video nasty. My jaw dropped lower with every sentence. But *he* hadn't been scared. If anything scared Robert, I was not aware of it.

'They wouldn't fuck with me,' he told me cockily, leaning back on my bed. 'Even the devil has to be afraid of something.'

While he had no interest in Satanism as a belief system, he enjoyed the shock value of the imagery. The devil screamed down from the posters on his bedroom walls and out of the speakers on his record player. He owned albums by Venom, Iron Maiden and Mercyful Fate that I was afraid to listen to, fearful that the needle would dislodge the demons I felt certain had settled into the grooves of the vinyl.

'Adam, quick! Come here!' Robert would call out, summoning me to his room. As I bounded eagerly to the doorway he'd drop the stylus onto a Black Sabbath album, his laughter blending with the music as I darted back to my own room, my hands clapped over my ears.

While I had my suspicions that Robert was lying about what he'd seen near the Black Path, I couldn't take any chances. I'd seen pentagram graffiti sprayed onto pavements and carved into the flanks of trees. There was evidence of fires in the woods. And then there was that shrew. It seemed to me that if Satanists *were* out there, it could only be a matter of time before they graduated from tiny mammals to child-sized ones. I pictured myself impaled on a stick, my blood being glugged from a geyser in my neck, and I didn't much fancy it. But if I was going to find my treasure, I might just have to risk encountering the occasional devil worshipper along the way.

One thing I knew about Satanists is that they only acted out their rituals at night. Even back then, as scared as I was, I was aware that creeping about in robes and muttering incantations was something that would look goofy in the fierce light of the summer sun. Robert's album sleeves and the horror movies he liked to show me

Domesday

had taught me that those practices require darkness and flickering candlelight to be truly effective. But while Satanists might operate in the dark, I was always in bed by 9 pm: we worked different shifts. As long as I was careful and kept my eye out, our worlds need never collide, and I'd be free to seek my fortune. So, as the summer rolled around, I made a plan.

The summer holidays offered me six weeks of long days. I'd have the light to protect me and plenty of time. So, I traced a map of Haverhill from my dad's road atlas and marked out areas on it that I wanted to cover. The fields and waste grounds, the woods, but firstly the river. This seemed to me like a good starting point. I pictured Gary Fridd reaching into the water and pulling out The Gilling sword. Then I imagined myself the same way, grabbing hold of a jewelled hilt and heaving it out of the stagnant banks of Stour Brook. I saw everything that would follow it, too: fame, impossible wealth, status. This was a reward so tantalising it made me hungry.

Each day before setting off, I packed a satchel with my map, some snacks, a trowel and a four-inch wooden knife that my Uncle Tony had brought me back from a safari holiday in South Africa, the handle carved to resemble a human head. I carried this for protection, wary of bumping into a Satanist who might have grown sick of working nights. While I was not the fearless child I once was, I still had some of my bullish pre-glasses confidence left. If I

Broken Biscuits

was going down, then I'd go down swinging a blunt memento from the Kruger National Park gift shop.

That first day, I followed the route of Stour Brook as far as daylight hours would allow, walking its banks and poking a stick into the shallows, feeling for anything substantial. When the river got deeper, I waded in, bending over and raking my hands across the slime-covered beds, my chin just above the shimmering, insect-buzzed surface, always hopeful that just one more plunge and my fingers would be rewarded with the touch of something precious. And if it didn't happen that day, I felt confident it might happen on the next day, or the one after that. I had time on my hands, and the small but comforting thrill that still came from risking my life.

My parents never asked me where I was going or what I was doing that summer. Leaving the house, I'd yell 'I'm playing out!' and that was my sole obligation, free at that point to go wherever I liked. These days, when my daughter leaves the house, my brain can only think in worst-case scenarios, never fully settling until she walks back through the door or texts me to say she's arrived safely at her destination. But she's my only child, and maybe that's different. I was one of four kids to parents who both worked full-time. It was probably a relief whenever one of us left the house. And had I taken them to one side and explained what I was doing, I feel certain they would have only heard the higher-octave

Domesday

version of the sound characters in Charlie Brown cartoons hear when an adult speaks. I did once try to tell my father what I was up to, but only because I had no other choice.

'What the bloody hell are you doing?' he asked, catching me in our back garden digging about in his lovingly tended flowerbeds, a hopeful look on my face. Caught off-guard, I was forced to explain myself.

'You won't find anything here,' he said. 'If there was treasure in the garden, they would have found it when they built the house.'

That was the extent of his interest. He wasn't the type to grab a spade and say, 'But come on, son. Let's head out into the fields anyway and see what we can find!' My father and I never had that kind of relationship, and I didn't mourn it. None of my friends were buddies with their dads, either; it was nothing personal. What it really came down to was that grown-ups are the great forgetters. They don't remember a time when they might have believed in the promise of dusty treasure maps. Or if they do, they don't often dwell on it. Between work, bills and the varying bullshit that children are trying to tell them, they barely have enough time to eat before they fall asleep in front of the TV and everything starts all over again. So, I wandered the countryside for twelve hours a day without them ever stopping to wonder if I'd been abducted or murdered.

Broken Biscuits

'Why would anyone kidnap Adam?' I could imagine my parents saying, answering the door to the police. 'He's not even the cute one.'

The one person who did take an interest in what I was doing, though, was Robert; monitoring my behaviour was his ongoing hobby.

'What the fuck are you doing?' he asked, catching me standing in Stour Brook one afternoon, my hands stained tar-black with reeking mud.

I looked up at him, trying to work out if I wanted to share my treasure. In my head I saw my American dream house halving in size.

'Nothing,' I replied.

'No one stands in a river for nothing.'

He had a good point, so I told him the truth.

'You know *The Domesday Book* ...'

I don't know how long I stood there, up to my waist in water, explaining to him what James had told me. My theories. How I'd been spending my summer. But however long it was, it was too long for Robert.

'If there was treasure,' he said, cutting me off, 'don't you think I would have found it already?'

'Not if you didn't know where to look for it.'

Robert's expression darkened. I should have known better than to suggest I knew more than him. He jumped down into the shallows, waded toward me in one purposeful stride and shoved my head under the water,

Domesday

holding it there for long enough to make me think he might actually kill me. But he let go, as he always did when threatening my life, laughing as I bobbed violently to the surface, spluttering. Then he slopped back to the bank and left me to it, this idiotic childish fantasy. He'd turned sixteen that summer, and while Satanists were one thing, buried treasure was kid's stuff. A few weeks earlier he'd scored a job on a government work-placement scheme organised by Manpower Services. He was an adult now. Already forgetting.

I squelched home that day, more determined than ever. There *would* be treasure for me. There *would* be fame. And there *would* be paying Geoff Capes, The World's Strongest Man, to repeatedly dunk Robert in the river until he apologised to me and kissed my brand new solid-gold boots.

When Stour Brook offered me nothing, I turned my attention to the fields and began setting off down the Black Path. I walked for hours, my fortifying snacks consumed within the first ten minutes. And because no one thought of hydration back then, I didn't consider bringing water. In time I would suffer for this as the rising effects of sunstroke came for me. But until then I paced my route, methodically lacing my way across each ploughed field like a scene-of-crime officer studying the location of a murder. Back and forth, kicking at clods of churned up mud as I went, gritty sweat greasing my armpits and the small of my back. Once in a while, I'd gasp with excitement, stooping to chip at the dry earth with my trowel and paw at a glinting object that caught my eye. I rejected drinks cans, spent shotgun shells, nails and engine parts while sheets of gauzy cloud shifted overhead, and the sky turned from blue to tobacco. I thought of how this area might have looked 1,000 years earlier and the people who might have passed that way and what they might have dropped. Spurred on by the hope that some of them might have been as clumsy as me.

But as the shadows of the trees grew, taking on towering, cloaked shapes as they stretched across the ground, I would be reminded of the time when this would become Satan's territory. Once the afternoon edged into the evening, I'd set off home, keeping an eye on the woods as I went.

It was here, as the trees closed in around the Black Path and my route of escape grew limited, that I felt a presence. Heard Robert's words in my head, so clear and certain: 'Satanists …' I could have sworn I saw them then, skulking in the shadows and grinning, their robes shivering between the trees. The evening breeze brushed its fingers through the branches, creating a sound that could have easily been hissed chanting. And I might have been wrong, but I was sure, out of the corner of my eye, I'd witnessed the flash of a sacrificial blade catching the last of the dying sunlight.

Domesday

Worked up into a panic and bracketed by threat-concealing trees, it was at this point that I often started running, my wooden knife clenched in my fist and my satchel batting against my hip as my feet slapped along the Black Path. I didn't dare to look behind me, I just ran, swallowing great gulps of air as I went, my chest ready to explode from the effort and my head pounding from sun exposure. I only gave myself leave to slow down when I reached the safety of the streetlights on the edge of our estate.

'Where have you been?' my little brother, Ben, would ask, looking up from the TV as I'd clatter through the door, still panting.

'Just out,' I'd say. Then I'd catch the smell of dinner and feel the punch of a hunger that had been suppressed until this point by the adrenaline of fear and anticipation.

I'd throw myself into a chair at the dinner table and wolf down fish fingers, mash and beans, my forehead thudding and my eyes puffy from hay fever but my plan for the next day already bubbling away. Later, getting into the bath, I'd wince as the water made contact with my sunburned skin. My legs so heavily scored by bramble thorns and brittle grasses they looked as if they'd been beaten with a headmaster's cane. Then I'd lie there in the water, a film of sweat and grime peeling away from me, and think of peril and ritual sacrifices. Another bloody practice in a part of the country so familiar with these

Broken Biscuits

things. But mostly what I thought about was the treasure, and the coming days of making my way through fields, woods and river slush, taking risks until I found it. I wanted more than my life was offering: I wanted a fortune; I wanted to be on *Blue Peter*; I wanted to buy my school and on the first day of term hear everyone cheer for me as I had it knocked to the fucking ground.

* * *

I'd like to tell you that I eventually encountered the Satanists, who circled me as I walked the fields and marked my little map, having stayed out just that little bit too long. That I fought them off using the jewelled shield and sword that I'd managed to wrench from the earth, then ran down the Black Path toward home, cloaked hands reaching for me from the wooded shadows as I went. I would love to recount the moment I called out to Michael, Stephen, Mark and, unaccountably, Ian, who all rushed to my aid with hurled rocks, burning sticks and rotten apples – raining them down on my pursuers until they were dispersed into the woods like smoke, never to return. And finally, that we all then made our way, chanting victoriously and sword aloft, to the nearest auction house.

But I am not writing this from the east wing of my stately home. Instead of a fleet of muscle cars outside the window of my ex-council house, there is a damp-smelling

Domesday

2007 Jetta. My TV is a thirty-eight-inch Samsung that I bought from a supermarket eight years ago, just after my divorce. All I had to show for that summer of digging was sunburn, heatstroke and an intimate understanding that effort does not always equal success.

Often these days, when friends see me out walking, my head down and my brow furrowed, they'll tell me that I look grumpy and ask what's wrong. It's hard to explain to them that what I'm doing, what I've always been doing, is searching. Scuffing at the ground with the toe of my shoe then squinting into the dirt as I go, always hopeful that this will be the day when I'll see that glint of something great. Playing the pavement lottery. It's a practice that has drawn my adult body into a shape that now cannot be altered. I have ground-studying wrinkles, a shuffling gait and a stoop that has left me looking not unlike a fishing rod that has hooked a big catch. But almost forty years in, I see no point in stopping now. Not when that catch could be just a few steps further.

While I no longer believe in Satanist conspiracies and am on the fence about ghosts, I do still believe in lost treasure. And not just that, I still believe in the possibility that I'll find it. A discovery so spectacular, its glow so unavoidable and potent, that it'll eclipse me entirely.

If I Were Jon

When I heard the news, I rushed home to tell my mother. She was in the kitchen, preparing potatoes and tossing them into a bucket-sized pan on the stove.

'Jon's coming back from Australia!' I said, the words bursting from me as if I'd spent the previous ten minutes holding my breath underwater.

'Oh, here we go again,' she said with a sigh, not looking up from her peeling. She'd been here before. 'If I were Jon and Jon were Me,' she said, her voice singsong and as loaded as a playground taunt as she recited an old A.A. Milne poem. 'Then he'd be six and I'd be three. If Jon were me and I were Jon, I shouldn't have these trousers on.'

'Mum,' I moaned, 'can you not?'

'I'm sorry,' she said, dropping a potato into the pan with a dull clang. 'Just don't be so weird about him this time, okay? You know how you get.'

* * *

Broken Biscuits

I must have been about eight years old when my friend Ian first told me about Jon. The two of them had been buddies for years, he explained, and his family had just moved in down the road, so he was coming over to play with us.

'You'll really like him,' he assured me. 'Everyone does.'

Who the hell is this Jon kid? I thought. I'd known Ian for three years by that point and he had never once mentioned Jon to me. Now here he was, this stranger arriving out of nowhere to unsettle the balance of our friendship group. So, I decided, sight unseen, to despise him.

At that point in my life I was a scrapper, always getting into fights and trouble. I had a little gang, and we went around causing low-level disruption on our estate. But I always felt that my status in that group was uncertain, so I was threatened by the arrival of this boy who'd been given the big sell and whose presence could alter my standing.

'Okay, does he have a BMX?' I asked, wondering how I might conspire to nudge him off it and into a bush full of brambles. To send him on his way. Or, if he insisted on sticking around, show him his place. But then I met Jon and all I could think about was how much I wanted him to like me.

He was, to me, perfect. Good-looking, fashionably dressed, his hair the kind of Midwich Cuckoo blond I was

If I Were Jon

only used to seeing on the beautiful people they hired to star in shampoo commercials. And he laughed easily, charming us all with a laid-back charisma; winning over each member of our gang in turn as if he'd performed a piece of close-up magic that only they could see. I'd never encountered anyone like him. And when he led us down the road to show us his home, I saw the world he inhabited and fell for it completely.

When I told my mother about him that evening during dinner, I was effusive. Waving my fork around and talking at a bumbling, feverish pace, my mouth incapable of both eating and getting out all the things I wanted to say about Jon.

'He's really cool. He can run really fast and he's funny and he has loads of Star Wars figures and lives over near Arrandene Road, so we can play all the time.'

I told her all about Jon's house, which was so much newer and nicer than ours. About his big, toy-filled bedroom where he'd given me a rubber Gremlins figure simply because I said I liked it. And I spoke enthusiastically of his mother, who was kind and pretty like the mothers I'd seen on US sitcoms and who'd told me I could come over for tea one day.

'Well, maybe you should move in there,' my mother said, feeling the jab of the verbal knife I'd unintentionally slipped under her ribs. The inference that a much better home and family than our own was just down the road,

Broken Biscuits

waiting for me in a glimmering new build. 'I'm sure you'll be very happy.'

'No! I didn't mean that,' I said, apologetic then. 'It's just that he's really nice and he's got all this … stuff.'

'If I were Jon,' she said, 'and Jon were Me …'

While I instinctively knew to stop short of pointing out that Jon was handsome, my mother had recognised what was happening before I did. There wasn't the terminology back then to label a boy crush, but that's obviously what was happening. I had experienced for the first time someone whose life seemed so desirable to me that I didn't know what to do with myself. So, I reacted like a fan. A cheerleader. And more than that, I was overcome by the uncomfortable sensation of wanting to be someone else entirely. Wishing myself away.

In time, Ian and his family would leave the country and Jon would fill his place in our gang. Joining us as we stormed through the estate and the nearby woods, causing mayhem. When Jon moved from his school to mine, we hung out there, too. And when it was just the two of us, we bonded over more sedate pursuits. Each of us confessed to a love of comic books and drawing. He'd quietly noticed that his family was better off than mine and was quick to share his things with me. Pressing comics into my hands as I was leaving his house; explaining that I could bring them back whenever I liked. He knew I couldn't afford them myself, but would never have

If I Were Jon

said so. The generosity that seemed to come so easily to him was alien to me. With three siblings, everything I had was fought for and closely guarded. But Jon only had one brother and actually seemed to enjoy the novelty of sharing what he had, seeing the pleasure that unselfishness delivered. *Imagine that*, I'd think, walking home with a wad of X-Men comics in my hand. *Imagine not having to care.*

It was acts like this that kept elevating Jon for me, enhancing his status to such a degree that my appreciation would eventually go a little too far. One Saturday afternoon, the two of us were lying on the grass near the woods, catching our breath after a running race that Jon had won by a huge and easy margin. I looked across at him as he stared up at the clouds, his cheeks flushed, the grass cradling his immaculate head. A thought burst out of me before I could stop it.

'You should have your own TV show,' I said.

I'm not sure what kind of show I had in mind exactly. I guess I was picturing a camera crew that just followed him around as he showed off his new trainers and attempted backflips in his garden. Or simply filmed him as he looked directly into the camera, allowing viewers the opportunity to experience the sensation of being in his company. He just seemed too good looking and charismatic to *not* be broadcasted into everyone's homes, and it felt almost offensive to me that he wasn't. So, I blurted

Broken Biscuits

this idea out, regretting the words the moment they left me.

'What?' Jon said, his head snapping around to face me, perplexed.

'I said, "We should probably go".'

I got to my feet, blushing. Wishing I could grab the words from the air between us and stuff them back into my mouth.

'No, that's not what you said.'

'Yeah, it was.'

'Okay,' Jon said finally, rolling his eyes. Giving in.

But we both knew what I'd said, this mortifying thing that revealed so much. I was terrified that I had ruined something between us, having externalised what must have felt to him in that moment like a stalker's fascination. To his credit, Jon didn't try to embarrass me with it. He just smiled and acted like it hadn't happened. Maybe he was used to it. Maybe people told him that he should have his own TV show all the time. While we never spoke of it again, I held this moment inside me like a burning coa of embarrassment and a reminder of that unfulfilled ache I felt. Of how I wished someone would say that sort of thing to me, look at me the way I looked at Jon. To live a life so wonderful that another kid might meet me, then run home to tell their mother all about it.

'*If I were Adam and Adam were me …*'

If I Were Jon

When I learned a couple of months later that Jon and his family were leaving the country to start a new life in Australia, I was almost relieved. While I was sad to see him go, I tried to look at the positives. Once I was out of his orbit, maybe I'd feel a little better about myself. Maybe I wouldn't have to see everything I wasn't reflected back at me whenever I was around him. But when he returned barely a year or so later, the move to the other side of the world having not really worked out, the difference between us became even more profound.

Some adolescent boys blossom from grotesque little snotballs into fine-looking young men, while others are transformed from cute kids into looking as if they'd been redesigned by David Cronenberg. But Jon skipped past all that. There was no disruption to his good looks. He was a cute kid and he stayed that way. If there was a change in him, it was only an upgrade. He returned to the UK sporting a head of thick golden locks, a Hulk Hogan tan and the residual twang of an Australian accent at a time when the country was still in the throes of a cultural obsession with Crocodile Dundee and Grundy soap operas. His ascension to pin-up status in our school was as rapid as it was unsurprising.

'Stop them!' he begged, rushing up to me and grabbing my arm one breaktime during his first week back at school. He looked over his shoulder and I turned to see half a dozen girls rounding the corner of the playing fields and racing towards him. 'Please?'

I did what he'd asked and stepped into the path of a girl named Alison, her cheeks flushing beneath a towering privet of crimped hair.

'Leave him alone,' I shouted, waving my arms in front of her as if attempting to calm a wayward horse.

'I can't,' she said, shoving me aside. 'He's *too* good looking.'

I couldn't argue with her, so I just watched in silent awe as these girls ran after him and into the distance, the squealing tail to Jon's darting comet. His vibrant celebrity very much back in my life.

During those days immediately following his return, Jon walked the corridors of our school with the air of a visiting dignitary. Kids in our class would ask him what Australia was like and he'd hold court from his desk, telling exaggerated stories about his time over there. I marvelled at the reaction in the room as he detailed his encounter with a nest of black widow spiders in his bathroom and bravely mashing them to death with a toothbrush. While it was understandable that the other children would be enraptured, it was surprising to see that our teacher, Mrs Carter, was also reeled in by Jon. She leaned back against her desk, smiling and rapt, his impromptu lecture a more than acceptable delay to her lesson plan because we were all learning something important about the cult of personality.

If I Were Jon

Seriously, I thought, as Jon moved on to a story about fending off a venomous snake. *Is everyone buying this shit?*

But I knew the answer to this question because I was buying this shit, too. You just wanted in on people like Jon, to experience the glow of their special energy. The rare quality I had experienced in his company, one on one, was now being spread around the whole school, and it was intoxicating. And even if he *was* exaggerating these stories, the important thing was that he didn't need to. Kids with his gifts didn't have to lie out of necessity. If they did it, it was purely for fun, not because they had any deficiencies to cover up. The truth of Jon was more than good enough. Anything he added was just an ornamental flourish.

One thing that hadn't changed in his absence was that he and I were still friends, our relationship clicking back into place as if his time in Australia had just been a weekend away in Cromer. While I was still envious of him, I enjoyed being in his company as much as I always had, and he seemed to enjoy mine too. Which I was glad of, as at the time I needed all the friends I could get.

While Jon had only gained layers of gilding while he'd been away, puberty had taken me by surprise and launched a vicious, unprovoked attack. It dimmed my eyesight, tripped up my tongue and left my physique struggling through that monstrous mid-point between

Broken Biscuits

chubby and adolescently gangly. So, I retreated into a solitary world of fiction. Rather than head out of the house and risk doing anything embarrassing, I increasingly chose to stay at home, where I'd read comics and fantasy novels filled with escapist adventures and extraordinary lives. I was touching the spectacular from a distance.

So, it surprised me to still be included in Jon's friendship group, albeit on the periphery. I seemed to fulfil in him a need that other, cooler kids couldn't. This was the part of him that still enjoyed the same dweebish things I did. Once in a while, I'd find myself being invited over to sleep at his house, where most other people couldn't see us socialising or enthusiastically talking about Batman. I didn't take offence to the covert nature of our friendship, I was simply grateful that it existed at all.

Still, it was unexpected when Jon collared me between classes to invite me to his fourteenth birthday party. There would be a lot of people there, he told me. Other boys from school. It would be a fun time. But for me this invitation was a very public acknowledgement.

'It's no big deal,' he said, registering my obvious excitement at the invite and recognising a need to rein it in. 'Just a bunch of us hanging out.'

'Rad!' I replied. 'I'll be there.'

'Yeah,' he said protectively, his voice low. 'Don't say rad. No one says rad anymore.'

If I Were Jon

'Okay,' I said. 'Wicked.'

Jon sighed heavily then. Seemingly aware that, despite his great and obvious powers, he was unable to save me from myself.

Though the party might not have seemed a big deal to Jon, I had not taken it lightly. I'd not had an invite to a party in years. The last time I'd received one, it was written on Spider-Man headed paper and the party itself had ended with a game of pass the parcel and everyone being sent home with a slice of cake and a plastic whistle. I understood that this party was something different, though. My opportunity to come in from the social cold.

While a single invite did wonders for my self-esteem, it sadly did nothing to improve my popularity, underscoring so many of the reasons why I should never have been invited in the first place. I would advertise my attendance to anyone who would listen, leaning into the words with heavy emphasis as if I was speaking euphemistically about a secret society.

'See you at *Jon's party*!'

'Sorry, can't talk right now. I'll tell you all about it at *Jon's party*.'

'Yes, of course I'm going to *Jon's party*! Why wouldn't I be?'

Anyone meeting me for the first time might have assumed it was some sort of vocal tick. Yet another unfortunate defect in my repertoire. And when opportunities to talk about the party didn't naturally present themselves, I found a way to create them.

'Did you say *Jon's party*?' I replied, when a boy named Kevin tapped me on my sleeve in History class to ask me something.

'No, I said could you lend me a pen.'

'Oh, okay. Well, I'm going to *Jon's party* anyway, so I guess I'll see you there?'

'Yeah, all right. So, about this pen …'

I marked off the days in my page-a-day diary, edging closer to the night of the party. I might never be Jon, but I would be closer than ever to leaving my old self behind.

'Get your things together,' my mother said, on the morning of the party. 'We're going to Clacton.'

'What?!' I said. 'Why today?'

But I knew why. My father worked long night shifts for British Gas – four on, four off – and when the stars aligned and we'd hit a Saturday with decent weather, our family always made the most of it and hit the coast. My mother would transform a Sunblest loaf, a block of cheese and half a Polony sausage into a meal we'd all resent once we reached the seafront and smelled the fish and chips. But what I really cared about during these trips was the sea. When I was in that water, it felt as if heaven had descended onto the earth. Usually, I lived for days like

If I Were Jon

this, my desire to be in and near the sea pathological by the time I hit my teens. So, I was annoyed at this situation, at being taken to one of my favourite places then forced to resent it.

I knelt on the kitchen lino, moodily rolling my trunks up inside a towel and squeezing them into a carrier bag, while my mother slapped margarine onto white bread.

'Well, we need to be back by five,' I snapped, scowling up at her. 'Six at the latest.'

'Oh, of course,' she said, mimicking my voice, and the words my home had echoed with over the previous fortnight. 'We won't let you miss *Jon's Party*.' But she knew what it meant to me. Recognised the high stakes. She traded the mockery for something softer. 'We'll be back in good time, I promise.'

She handed me some clothes from the ironing pile, and I headed upstairs to dress for the beach, grateful for the opportunity to sneak one last look at the outfit I'd laid out for the party. I didn't really own any fashionable clothing, mostly wearing hand-me-downs from my brother or my older cousins. But I'd managed to pull together something that looked a little like the things other kids wore: a pair of black jeans that I'd been keeping pristine, a knock-off Lacoste sweater and a pair of white and purple, non-brand high tops, their tongues fat like doll-sized duvets. All this stood in stark contrast to

Broken Biscuits

the beach clothes my mother had picked out for me: a Garfield T-shirt and a pair of shorts depicting bananas and strawberries lancing through a bundle of acid green fronds. From a distance, I looked as if I'd stepped into a fruit bowl and hoisted it up to my waist. But I didn't care so much about that, because in a few hours I'd be walking into a party and leaving as someone else entirely.

'Come on!' my mother shouted up the stairs. 'If you're not in the car by the time I count to five you're not going to *Jon's Party*.'

'Okay, okay!' I shouted, racing downstairs and lumping sullenly into the car alongside my younger brother, Ben. I sulked for most of the journey but as we got closer to our destination and I could see it coming into view, the sea played its usual tricks on me. As always happened when I visited the coast, time became slippery. Once I was in the water, I completely gave myself over to it, splashing Ben and bobbing about on the rolling waves. Diving deep and clawing my fingers into the slithering sands in an effort to hold myself in that underwater world for as long as possible. When I finally emerged, I was exhilarated and so sunburnt you'd think I'd just come fresh from witnessing a nuclear blast. I padded up the beach to the spot where my parents were sunbathing.

'What time is it?' I asked.

'Five-thirty,' my father said, opening his eyes and squinting at his watch. He closed them again. 'Ish.'

If I Were Jon

'What?!' I yelled, feeling suddenly queasy. 'We have to leave *right* now!'

'It'll be fine,' he said, unhurried as I flapped my hands and fussed everyone into action. 'You can be fashionably late.'

He didn't understand that I wasn't fashionably anything. I didn't have that luxury. And it wasn't fine. It was almost six by the time we'd got everything together and reached the car. Then there was the drive home, the traffic. By the time we hit the outskirts of town it had already gone 7 p.m.

'It's okay,' my mother said, trying to be blasé about it, hopeful that her attitude would carry across to me. 'We'll just drop you there on the way home.'

'But I can't go like this!' I said, gesturing at my obnoxiously zesty clothes, at my limbs the colour of freshly plucked rhubarb. I thought of my chosen outfit laying forlorn on my bed. This clothing that I'd tried on, posed with, practised things to say while wearing. The armour I'd assembled for myself.

'You look like you've been surfing,' my mother said, and the confidence in her delivery was so convincing that I found myself falling for it. Believing that the fresh, salted glow of my sun-scorched body might suggest something cool and Bondi Beach-adjacent about me. A vibe that Jon, an honorary Australian, would surely recognise and appreciate. I stepped out of the car and headed up his

Broken Biscuits

drive, turning to look as my family drove away. Ben was laughing at me through the rear window.

The front door of Jon's home was ajar, and I could hear music and laughter from inside. Though I'd been there often, the house felt new and uncertain to me. Foreign territory that would require the immediate learning of a new language. I headed through into the living room, where a dozen or so boys were milling around. Crucially, none of them was wearing shorts. Everyone seemed to be in baggy jeans and Stussy T-shirts. The occasional Global Hypercolor. Kevin from History was changing a cassette on the stereo and as I passed him he stopped what he was doing to look my way.

'Nice shorts!' he said.

My reflex was to thank him but, having once been badly injured by a medicine ball, I knew that words could sometimes be deceptive. This was not a compliment, and I realised then what an error I'd made by walking into that house at all, instinctively moving my hands to cover my waist. I was Adam, suddenly naked in the garden of Eden. Adam, suddenly a figure of fun in Jon's living room. Had my skin not been so sunburnt, Kevin would have been able to see me blushing.

I scurried on past him and through into the kitchen, where Jon stood cramming a fistful of snacks into his mouth.

'Hey!' he said, then looked down, spraying a ticker tape of crisp shards at the sight of me. 'Nice shorts!'

If I Were Jon

I needn't have bothered practising things to say. It seemed that my shorts were providing a conversational buffet that could keep everyone going all night. But Jon appeared to recognise the vulnerability of my situation and typically decided not to capitalise on it. Instead, he directed me to the sideboard, which was laden with drinks and salty snacks. Telling me to help myself.

Because Jon's parents were unlike anyone else's, they had made themselves scarce that evening and trusted him with the run of the house. In practice this meant that, in addition to the soft drinks and nibbles, there was also a selection of alcohol and the TV in the living room was broadcasting a pornographic movie. A group of boys were sitting around the screen, transfixed and tensely gripping cans of lager. Others sat on the sofa, crossing and recrossing their legs with the vigorous persistence of knitting needles. I had never seen a film like that before and wanted to stick around and watch, but knew that if there was one thing that could make this evening worse for me it was an erection announcing itself from the leg of my nice shorts. So, I grabbed a Coke off the sideboard and headed out to the back garden, where the risks seemed lower, and my clothing felt like a more logical fashion choice.

'What the fuck are you wearing?' a boy named Colin asked as I stepped out onto the lawn, laughing hard as he headed towards me. 'You look like a ...' he paused,

Broken Biscuits

searching for a simile and coming up dry, '… a fucking idiot.'

Colin and I had been friends in primary school. There is a photo somewhere of us smiling together at one of my own cake-and-whistle birthday parties. So, I tried to laugh off his comment, hoping our shared history would stop this from going any further. Colin towered over me, over pretty much every kid in our school, and had picked up a reputation for enjoying the physical advantage his size gave him over other people. For making good use of arms that were the size of my legs. I could do without a bloody nose, not needing any additional colour on my outfit. So, I was relieved when he took this no further, walking past me and into the kitchen.

I remained in the garden, holding my can for support and lurking on the fringes of someone else's conversation, acting as if I was involved in it. Mimicking the other boys' behaviour and laughing at a joke someone was telling. I was just reaching a point where I thought I might be able to turn this evening around, when I noticed Colin marching purposely towards me, an egg held in his giant paw.

In school the following Monday, witness statements would be conflicting about what happened next. Some swore Colin had thrown the egg at me. Others claimed that he'd cracked it over my head and an excitable few added that I'd pissed my shorts in fear. But the one detail everyone agreed upon was that I had shrieked and run

If I Were Jon

from Colin, my hands held proactively over my head as I exited through the garden gate. And in doing so, had initiated a chase.

Colin followed me and shouted my name, another egg in his hand. I darted into the trees behind Jon's house. While Colin's long legs gave him a speed advantage, I knew these woods well. I traced the familiar paths that my gang and I had once ruled, the branches whipping at my raw legs in the cool, late-summer evening air. Colin was audibly stumbling through the silt and fallen leaves. I don't know how long I ran for, but in time his voice ebbed away. There's a chance that I outfoxed him, but it's more likely that he'd simply given up, remembering that in chasing me he was running from a party where there was alcohol, pornography and social interactions. I had overplayed my importance. Not the prize I'd mistaken myself for.

At that point I had options. I could have re-entered the party and owned what had happened, headed back into the kitchen and gamely cracked an egg over my own head. Or strutted into the garden to make fun of myself before anyone else could, giving it jazz hands and wisecracks.

'Is that a banana on my shorts or am I just pleased to see you?'

But the one thing I was certain about was my inability to read a room, so instead I slipped out of the tree line

Broken Biscuits

and headed for home, taking my time so as not to arrive back suspiciously early and raise uncomfortable questions.

'How was the party?' my mother called out from the living room, hearing me coming in through the front door.

'Yeah, it was good,' I said, quickly climbing the stairs to wash the spattered egg off my legs.

When I finally reached my bedroom, I closed the door and swatted my party clothes off the bed, kicking them across the floor. They were part of the alternate reality where things had worked out for me, and I couldn't bear to look at them. I sat down on my bed and thought about how much Jon might have seen of what happened. In the coming days and weeks, I would guess that he saw a lot of it. Close to everything in fact; and what he hadn't seen, I'm sure he heard about. Because a distance grew between us after the party. He wasn't unfriendly to me, but I don't recall any more invites to his house. No more time with just the two of us. When I stopped him during break to tell him that I'd come over to return some comics he'd lent me, he was politely dismissive.

'It's okay,' he said, looking away from me as if distracted by someone calling his name. 'You can keep them.'

It could have been the natural order of things, friendships just fading away and people moving on as they sometimes do. But I suspected that Jon had finally reached his limit. That the intensity of my focus on his life had

If I Were Jon

grown too uncomfortable to be around. But the pain of that realisation was still to come. At the time, all I knew for certain was that if I were Jon, I wouldn't have had those shorts on. So, I undressed and hid them at the back of my wardrobe, hoping never to see them again. Then I climbed into bed and reached for a book, looking for the comfort that only really came from imagining lives other than my own.

The Beautiful Ones

My brother Robert and I were walking home from my sister's house when he brought us to a stop outside a pub.

'Fancy a pint?' he asked, not waiting for my answer before heading inside to order us some drinks. 'Wait here.'

I was fifteen at the time, and too young to drink alcohol, but I was flattered that Robert's talk of 'a pint' had included me. He didn't take me to the pub often, but when he did it felt special. A public admission that I, so unlike him, so much his opposite, was his brother. At these times it felt like I belonged to him, and him to me.

Waiting outside for him to return, I tried not to think of how I had always been terrified of this particular pub, which sat on the corner of the recreation ground that separated a 1960s housing estate and my secondary school. As squat and menacing as a poisonous toad, the pub's brickwork was the uneasy colour of soot and dried blood, giving it the appearance of a building that had

Broken Biscuits

hosted both a gutting fire and a grisly murder. Across its largest exterior wall, above a flowerbed blooming with nothing but broken glass and spent condoms, was an array of graffiti. The centrepiece of this was a huge cock and balls daubed in white paint that arced from one end of the wall to the other, its scale and ambition rivalled only by the Cerne Abbas giant.

Alone, I would always hurry past this pub, fearful of running into some of the kids from my school who I knew drank underage there. But I tried not to think about any of that, because Robert was inside and if I was with him I was protected. In his company, nothing could go wrong.

'Fuck's sake,' Robert said, sloshing some of his pint onto his hands and down his jeans as he backed out of the pub, bumping the door open with his shoulder. He handed me a stubby bottle of Coke, a candy-striped paper straw bobbing from its mouth. 'Here,' he said. 'Don't say I don't give you nothing.'

He placed his pint on the floor, flicked the spilt beer from his fingers and began fishing his cigarettes out of his biker jacket, the leather creaking like a therapist's chair. I watched admiringly as he leaned back against the metal railing opposite me, took a cheek-hollowing drag and issued a series of smoke rings into the air between us. At this last move, I let out a light, high-pitched gasp, as impressed as if he'd just breathed fire. Robert shot me a curious look. A frown crossed with what I guessed was concern. And something else, too. He took a deep, deciding breath and I knew that he was about to say something important to me. I took the straw into my mouth and sipped at my Coke, waiting.

'You know that if I found out you were gay,' he said, his tone flat and controlled, 'I'd disown you.'

There was no ambiguity to be found in this sentence. It was a cold, hard statement and as his words landed my ankles felt suddenly soft and buttery, as if they might fail me and send me crashing to the floor.

'I'm not!' I said, sputtering my straw with a light pop. 'I like girls!'

'Good,' he said firmly, returning to the comfort of his cigarette. He turned to look off across the housing estate as if something had caught his attention while I blushed, nauseous and self-conscious, waiting for him to look back at me. What I needed from him most of all in that moment was the reassurance that my answer had been sufficient, and this subject had now been fully resolved. I needed to know that our relationship hadn't changed. That we would still go to the pub together. That I was still his and he was still mine.

I couldn't bear that he wouldn't look back at me, the inference being that he couldn't bring himself to. So, I turned away too, quietly drinking from my Coke and searching for a different point of focus. My eyes fell upon the graffiti. Then there we were, two brothers looking away from one another. Robert towards the tungsten streetlights, hissing cigarette smoke, his thoughts a mystery. And me, sucking on my straw as I stared at a ten-foot cock and balls, thinking, *I definitely like girls … I definitely like girls …*

* * *

The thing about having your sexuality questioned is that if it happens often enough you begin to question it yourself. And by the time Robert brought it up with me I was getting pretty used to thinking of answers.

During my first year at secondary school, a rumour got started that I was gay, and it spread with the speed and efficiency of an airborne virus. In 1989, there was no Pride, no queerness, no place for allyship or understanding. The UK was a year into Section 28, a period when 'gay' was used only as a punchline or a grenade to be tossed at someone if you wanted to wound and reduce them, or draw attention away from yourself. It was not a time when I could have pointed out that the few gay people I'd met had been nothing but kind to me, or confidently responded that I didn't think there was anything wrong with being gay. In 1980s rural Suffolk there was nothing more damaging. So, I pushed back against it as if I was fighting off a lion.

'I'm not gay!' I yelled on my way to a morning lesson, pushed into this broadcasting reaction by David, the boy

The Beautiful Ones

who had started the rumour in the first place and loved goading me into fighting back.

'Did you just say you were gay?' he said, treating the 'not' as if it were silent.

'*No*! I said I'm *NOT* gay!'

'Yeah,' David said, turning to the other kids my shouting had attracted. 'He definitely said it.'

The other obvious targets in my school, those with the lisps, the flouncing gaits and the shrieking laughs, were smarter than I was. Wise enough to stay in their seats and keep their mouths shut when these kinds of accusations came their way. Waiting for the storm to pass. To bring in excuse notes for PE so that no one witnessed them running. So, it was much more fun for these kids to come for me, a victim who always gave them something to play with.

My main problem with all this was that I was straight. This I knew with absolute certainty. I *did* like girls. But then, if everyone was so keen to tell me otherwise, maybe they recognised something about me that I didn't? I'd never gone through burgeoning sexuality before. I had no idea how it worked. Maybe it starts off with you being directed towards the opposite sex because society expects it of you until, at some point, you're sitting in front of *Baywatch* and realise that you're staring at a different swimsuit.

The thing that really helped this rumour to persist, though, seemed to be the air of plausibility it carried. The

Broken Biscuits

things I did that made people hear 'Adam's gay' and think, *Oh yeah, I can totally see that.*

There were those anecdotes of my mother's that I was so fond of repeating at school. The ones that had her friends in stitches but were lost on a teenage peer group that did not welcome or understand jokes about periods and childbirth-related haemorrhoids. Then there were the pink socks I'd worn when we were allowed to dress in our own clothes on the last day of term. The way I flapped my hands whenever I talked, as if conducting an orchestra through a feisty rendition of 'The Deadwood Stage' from *Calamity Jane*. The fact that I knew all the words to 'The Deadwood Stage'. I was the defence witness who simply could not stop handing damning evidence to the prosecution. My downfall cheered on by a packed, public gallery.

But there was also the quiet evidence. The things I never gave air to that made me question even myself. The thoughts that had me wondering if I was simply the last to know, my sexuality written on my forehead and presented to everyone except me.

It's true that there were certain boys in my school I found impossibly compelling to look at and I was concerned about what this represented. Fearful of the can of worms it could open. Did straight boys stare at each other like this? Did they lose themselves in the dinner hall during lunchbreak by admiring Nick's bee stung lips, the

The Beautiful Ones

perfection of Simon's philtrum or the effortless way that Adrian moved his hand through his hair and angled his head when someone asked him a question? Did they agonise over whether this was behaviour more associated with attraction than envious admiration?

It seemed to me that most other boys in my school did *not* think about these things. When they talked about girls, they were cartoonishly horny about it. A girl might walk past a group of boys and they'd howl at her like the stalk-eyed wolf in Tex Avery animations, or else they'd relentlessly pursue her, a mob of Pepé Le Pews in school uniform. And when they weren't talking about girls or football, they were looking my way and discussing how truly terrible it must be to be gay. The evidence I presented to them proving this theory absolutely.

But what if I questioned them and closely monitored their behaviours? Was all their exaggerated action and coarse talk just decoration? A cover-up. Was everyone, in fact, *incredibly* gay and just lying to themselves, their overt heterosexuality a masterful mask for their forbidden homosexuality? Again, this seemed unlikely.

Perhaps the most unfair part of all this was that *no one* was interested in me, so it seemed absurd to be forced into making a declaration of my sexual orientation. Does loudly insisting 'I'm straight!' really matter if you're attracting no one at all? Only, it seems, to the kids who needed a target. Because there was one demographic I had

Broken Biscuits

no problem attracting. No one got hot for me quite like a bully.

If it could be said that a nickname qualifies by the frequency of its usage, then my school nickname was, by a country mile, Queer. Closely followed by Poof. Poof is a quaint, gentle-sounding word. The type of sound-effect bubble you'd add to a comic book if you wanted to illustrate the impact of someone being struck with a feather pillow. But when it was thrown my way, it landed against me like a brick. And because I was straight and these words were not mine to reclaim and repurpose, I couldn't use them to fortify an identity. To cushion myself even slightly. I heard them shouted at me in corridors or read them scrawled in chalk across the back of my coat and school bag. They were written on paper aeroplanes and thrown at me in class. If I fought against it, I was protesting too much; if I didn't, I was passively admitting it. I was trapped and beginning to believe there was no way out.

* * *

On the walk home from the pub, Robert and I didn't talk. I wasn't sure what was going on in his head, but what I'd been thinking about was what had initiated his statement. It hadn't just been the gentle, girlish noise of delight I'd made at the sight of his smoke rings, but something much bigger. A problem he felt he needed to find a solution for. To quash.

The Beautiful Ones

I'd thought I'd been doing a pretty good job of separating church and state, my school dramas kept well away from the sanctuary of my home. But it seemed like Robert had either heard about those rumours or, more likely, had spotted the same kinds of things about me that the kids at school had. And just like at school, I planned to fight my corner.

'Would a gay boy have posters of Kylie Minogue on his wall?' I wanted to ask him, using a defence that would protect me around the time of 'Better the Devil You Know', but would become redundant by the release of 'Confide in Me'. Or I could have referred him to the biker magazines he'd once caught me looking at in his bedroom, which contained photos of topless women straddling Harley-Davidsons and feverishly misspelt erotic stories set in female prisons. But they also featured, it had to be said, big hairy guys in black leather. It wouldn't have been the difference maker I'd thought it was to shake a copy of *Outlaw Biker* in Robert's face and insist 'This magazine gives me an erection!' There are smoking guns and there is watching someone take the incriminating shot into their own foot. The witness for the defence rests, all out of options.

Besides, I knew what had been bothering him. Any other reason was just grasping at straws. And it was something that had started in his bedroom. More specifically, it was something that had started with Prince.

Broken Biscuits

Robert's bedroom was hallowed ground, both to him and to me. It was his domain alone, as private and forbidden to me as a hurtfully exclusionary gentleman's club. I was allowed as far as the doorway, and then only by invitation. From here I was permitted to admire him wrestling the notes of AC/DC's 'Thunderstruck' from his electric guitar, or watch him lying on his bed, louchely smoking while he gave me his opinions on the world. But if I stood there for too long, the novelty of my adoration would pass and the door would be closed in my face with a soft but certain click.

Still, nothing tastes quite as good as the forbidden, so I'd wait until Robert left the house, roaring away on his motorbike or shambling with his friends towards the pub, then head to his room. Cracking open his door, I was always cautious. As if he might somehow hear or get a tingling in his Spidey senses and rush back. The room smelled of trapped cigarette smoke, joss sticks, soap and something yeasty from the home-brew kit he stored in his wardrobe. It's a smell that I often catch a note of these days, in bars or old shops, and it snaps me back into his room and the moment of standing on his carpet, feeling the anticipatory thrill of being about to poke through his possessions and discover something new.

While everything in Robert's room held a magic for me, the contents of his wardrobe, those biker magazines under his bed, it was increasingly his record collection that drew

The Beautiful Ones

me in. It was kept pristine and orderly within faux-leather storage boxes, which gave it a private and precious energy. Over time, I'd been working my way through his vinyl, methodically slipping each disc from its box and marvelling at the artwork, the liner notes. If a record grew too enticing for me to cope with just looking at it, I'd risk placing it on his player and dropping the needle, the volume turned as low as possible and my ear pressed against the speaker. Record by record, song by song, trespass by trespass, I was connecting with his world and working out my own.

I was snooping in his room one Saturday morning, knowing he was safely at the garage where he worked, when I reached a section at the back of one of these vinyl boxes. Unlike the rest of his collection, these records were not alphabetised. The artists unusual, not marrying up with the meticulously arranged heavy metal and ska that had preceded them. Instead, there was a Tracy Chapman album, another by Sade and two records by Prince.

I pulled out one of these records – a twelve-inch single of '1999' – and flipped it over. On the back cover was a photo of Prince lying on satin sheets, naked except for purple gloves and working on a watercolour painting. His eyes stared directly into the camera. At me. It felt like a lascivious look. An invitation.

If you google this photo and take a look yourself, you might stop to wonder about what kind of person takes all

Broken Biscuits

of their clothes off, hops into bed then grabs a brush and starts daubing on an A2 flip pad. Or you may wonder, as I did, about Prince's exceptional bottom. The curve of it, his skin lightly oiled and shining under neon lighting, disappearing beneath those sheets. I wasn't sure how I felt about it. The sweep of his flesh so deceptively soft and feminine, so pleasing to my sensibilities, but attached to a man with a moustache. So, what exactly did that make me?

I was so focused on this photo that I didn't notice Robert entering the house, having rushed back home from work to collect something he'd forgotten. Nor did I hear the door opening behind me or the advance of his steps. I was only aware of his presence when his solid hand grabbed a fistful of my hair and pulled my head backwards. The shock causing my hands to clamp around the record.

'You *little* bastard!'

I expected to be yanked to my feet. To feel a flurry of punches and the lurching experience of weightlessness as he threw me from his room. Instead, I looked up to find him staring down at me and at what I'd been so captivated by. At his teenage brother kneeling on the floor with a naked image of Prince in front of him, so lost in that image that the rest of the world had stopped existing. Robert's expression shifted from fury into what I now believe was one of brooding calculation. He was adding two and two together and realising he had a problem.

The Beautiful Ones

'Go on,' he said, snatching the record from my hands as I scrabbled to my feet. 'Fuck off.'

There was something changed in his tone. Still angry but a touch defeated, as if some of the air had been let out of him. I didn't think about his reaction too much at the time. I was just grateful he hadn't hit me. So I ran, thinking about my close shave but also about Prince looking back at me from that record. And what his music must sound like.

I didn't get much in the way of pocket money, so buying his music and finding out for myself was not an option. But a couple of weeks after catching me in his room, Robert and I were watching Top of the Pops together, and Prince got a mention on the Top 40 chart rundown. I sat forward on the sofa then, hopeful for a snippet of music or a performance. For something more. Wanting to know what he looked like with clothes on. Robert saw this response and tossed a small explosive my way.

'He's gay,' he said, dismissively pointing with his toe at the image of Prince on the screen, up six places to 14 with 'Alphabet Street'. 'It's girl's music.'

'But you've got his records,' I said, realising the danger of my response as the words left me. I waited for Robert to reach over and punch me in the leg, but he didn't rise to this.

'That's cause girls like him,' he said.

Broken Biscuits

The Tracy Chapman, the Sade, the Prince, he explained, was the music he put on when he had girls in his room. Something gentle and yielding that Anthrax and Iron Maiden couldn't provide. But if he had intended to curb my enthusiasm, he'd failed. Usually, Robert's opinion would be enough for me, and I'd happily adopt his words as if they were my own. But while the gay part of what he'd said had landed with me as a warning, a message reading, *I caught you staring at a photo of a gay man for too long*, he didn't put me off. By that point I was too curious to give up.

At the next opportunity I had, I crept back into Robert's room. Choosing a weekend when I knew I'd be safe from him. He'd gone on a camping trip to Thetford Forest with his friends, somewhere too far away for him to just nip back. Leaving me way out of range of his senses. So, I slipped through his door and headed straight to his record box, pulling out his other piece of Prince vinyl. It was a copy of the album *Purple Rain*, where again Prince stared from the cover under atmospheric lighting, this time with his bottom safely concealed by a motorbike and black leggings. Bordering this image were bands of wildflowers, giving the album the gentle quality of a scrapbook. But I got a sense that there was something special about it. I suspect it was fear. That if I listened to it, I would be a different person by the end than I had been at the start. Most likely a gay person. Still, I fed it from the sleeve, placed it on Robert's player and dropped the needle, my ear held beside the speakers. Wanting whatever I was about to hear.

A swooning gospel organ played. A voice spoke.

'*Dearly beloved* …'

Forty-three minutes and fifty-five seconds later, I *had* changed. Because I had never heard anything like it before. It was the first time I felt something close to what I would later recognise as love. This music that in time would become part of the safe and comforting world I sent myself to when the rest of my life became too much. And, in time, I would find someone else I could share that world with.

* * *

Tim had moved to our town from Cheshire during the second year of secondary school, arriving in my form with an unfamiliar accent, a commitment to veganism and a *Dr Who* obsession that burned bright despite the show's cancellation two years earlier.

Most kids would arrive in a new school and immediately try to adapt to their environment, concealing who they were and adopting the social costume most likely to suit the prevailing wind. But Tim made no concessions, appearing fully defined as the person he'd decided to be when the rest of us were all still attempting to work ourselves out. He was a character decidedly and strangely

Broken Biscuits

himself. I'd never met anyone quite like that before, someone so unbothered by the opinions of others. None of us had. So, he was immediately treated as a peculiarity. Not bullied in any obvious way, but not accepted either. Far from a square peg attempting to fit into a round hole, he was a brand-new shape that didn't fit anywhere and didn't want to, so was left to inhabit the same margins I was. And in the way that the unwanted naturally gravitate towards one another, Tim and I would begin spending a lot of our time together. Often thrown into the same hopeless teams during PE, or when classes required pupils to work in pairs and no one wanted to share a table with the poof or that weird fucking northern kid who was afraid of beef burgers.

In time, we fell into the habit of sharing our breaks together in a spot on the outer edge of the school playing fields, far away from the main building. It was, physically and metaphorically, a safe space. We knew that no one could be bothered to come all that way to pick on us. Not when there was the football pitch at the opposite end of the school grounds, its white lines bordered by dense trees that the cooler boys could melt into, where they could smoke or get off with girls. Tim and I couldn't hope to compete with any of that behaviour, which belonged to a world we barely existed in. So there, at the farthest point of the school grounds, we could retreat to without being accused of truancy, Tim and I would sit and talk about

The Beautiful Ones

books and comic art and Tom Baker. Temporarily safe, our words not judged or wilfully misinterpreted.

'Adam,' he asked me one lunchbreak, peeling open a Tupperware box containing cold, glistening leftovers of nut loaf. 'Do you like Prince?'

Tim often spoke like this with me. Preceding his questions by using my first name. From anyone else, I'd have considered this particular question a set-up. If one of my bullies had asked me this, a reply of 'Yes' would have been treated as if I'd climbed onto a chair and belted out a tearful rendition of 'I Will Survive'. But as much as I trusted Tim, I still paused before answering, thinking of Robert.

He's gay. It's music for girls.

My brain translated Tim's question to a more familiar one: '*Adam, are you gay?*'

But because there was no artifice about Tim, no threat, I decided that he'd asked this question because he actually wanted to know the answer. He had no interest in using it as a weapon. Because, when I told him that I *did* like Prince, he was overjoyed. He liked him, too. Adored him, in fact. So, whatever Prince was, whatever he might be seen as by anyone else, it seemed that he was music for the two of us.

'Adam, have you heard *Dirty Mind*?'

I told Tim that I hadn't, but I had seen it in record shops, the cover showing Prince looking defiant, as if daring someone to ask him why he was wearing nothing but a bolero jacket and black underpants.

'It's very rude,' Tim said, smiling as he told me all about it. His knowledge of Prince, it turned out, was encyclopaedic – and it was clear that he was excited to share that knowledge with me. He pulled a Walkman out of his bag and got to his feet. 'Here, listen.'

He pressed play, cranked up the volume and set the Walkman down on the grass. Tinny drums played and Tim began to dance, demonstrating an approximation of a routine he'd seen Prince doing on MTV. It was twitchy and squirming, like James Brown strutting on a hotplate. Tim's body convulsed, seeming to connect directly with the thin, distorted beat and shrieking voice leaking from the headphones.

Watching him, I was jealous. I wished that I cared that little about what anyone else thought. As far away from the other kids as we were, they would spot the kinds of movements Tim was indulging in. His spinning and jolting. They'd hear the sound of his Walkman carrying on the breeze. I didn't need any more negative attention, but Tim didn't care, caught up in the music, the dancing, the sharing of this thing he loved with someone else who loved it too. There was something so beautiful and admirable about the way he could let himself go. And while the rumours about me refused to die and the pressure of the bullying continued to build, I now had Prince to turn to

The Beautiful Ones

and someone to share him with. It felt like I had a new line of defence.

'So, what's your favourite song?' Tim asked, as he pressed the stop button and sat down on the grass beside me, getting his breath back.

My reply came without hesitation.

* * *

When staying in school all day started to get too much for me, I took to heading home for my lunch. I'd take this journey quickly, wanting to get home before I gave in to the growing urge to throw myself in front of passing cars. Most days I would compose myself and return for classes in the afternoon, but often I would conspire to remain in my bedroom, hoping that no one would notice my absence in classes or my presence in the house. If I made a success of this, I could avoid afternoon registration in my form room, where most of the kids who singled me out would be. My school was pretty lax when it came to absences. They didn't chase them up unless they hit extreme levels, so I knew my parents would never get a call alerting them to mine. While it made me sad to think of Tim sitting in our faraway spot, snacking alone on vegetable batons, I wasn't as strong as he was, and I knew he'd understand.

If my parents were around when I got home, I would slip into my room and sit on my bed, staying as quiet as possible and occupying myself with near silent pursuits, reading or drawing in the hope that I'd go unnoticed. But what I enjoyed most of all were those times when I got home and found that I had the house completely to myself. Once I'd made certain that no one else was around, I could head to my room, close my curtains and switch on my record player. The arm of the stylus left raised as it always was, above the A-side of my own second-hand copy of *Purple Rain*. Positioned eight minutes and thirty-one seconds in, ready to be lowered directly onto track three: 'The Beautiful Ones'.

I'd close my door and place the needle on the record before swaying to the slow, echoing drum-machine intro. Then there were the soft, insistent keyboards letting me know it was time to bring an invisible microphone up to my lips. And here I would begin to sing along with Prince as his voice cut in, high and melodic.

'Baby, baby, baby ...'

These days I sound as if I read continuity announcements on Radio 4 but back at the turn of the 90s, when my voice was breaking and puberty was still an incomplete process, I could hit notes like a piccolo. So, I duetted with Prince, my shaky falsetto concealed by the strength of his powerful, elegant one. As the song swelled and the passion in Prince's voice grew to a scream that was far beyond my reach, I'd switch to miming and close my eyes, a howling solo pouring from the air guitar that had appeared in my hands. Falling to my knees and rolling

The Beautiful Ones

around on my floor with the guitar in my arms, I'd imagine the impressed audience that I'd see before me should I open my eyes. By the time the song was done, I was light-headed, having travelled somewhere private and blissful. Five minutes and thirteen seconds where no one could touch me. But there was one person who could reach me in that place.

Robert had arrived home on one of those days when the house had been empty, and I'd thought myself safe. Attracted by the unexpected sound of music blaring from my room when he knew no one else should have been home, he headed upstairs and threw open my bedroom door.

'What the fucking hell are you doing?' he barked.

My eyes unscrewed and I squealed like a rat in a trap, my sprawled body bunching up protectively as if to undo what Robert had seen. Desperate to reverse the sight of me being transported by this 'girl's music', eyes closed, writhing and vamping. Prince howled, *'Do you want him or do you want me?'* as I scrambled to the record player to switch him off. The song suddenly unbearable to me.

'Fucking hell, man,' Robert said, drawing in a deep breath, looking oddly sick as his hand gripped the door handle. It hadn't been a simple embarrassing case of him catching me miming along to music. That was a thing most kids did once in a while, when they didn't think anyone would be around to see them. I'm sure he would

Broken Biscuits

have just laughed had he walked in and caught me jumping around to 'Welcome to the Jungle' or 'Ace of Spades'. Maybe blackmailed me into doing chores for him under threat that he'd reveal what he'd seen. But he'd caught me indulging in an act that, to his sensibilities, was monumentally, off-the-charts gay. And what's more, I'd been clearly loving it, having the time of my life as this music washed over me. Drenching me.

'Fucking hell ...'

Of course, I'd not considered any of that at the time, too busy dealing with the immediate sense of embarrassment and exposure. My truth, the private version of me, had been given full and exposing light. The vulnerability left me shuddering.

These days this kind of exposing and shame-inducing stuff happens to people all the time. A clip emerges online of them hungrily picking their nose or having their public marriage proposal rejected, it goes viral and they are done for. The truth of someone can be suddenly known to other people in a way that they'd never expected. But I was hiding this truth and Robert was the last person I ever wanted to see it.

He walked out of my room, and I ran over to the door, slamming it behind him. I needed him safely away from me. Then I sat there on my bed, catching my breath and waiting to see what he would do next.

* * *

The Beautiful Ones

Tim and I soon began trading Prince albums, buying cheap, blank cassette tapes from the market and sharing our small collections with each other. But while I would just copy him albums, then maybe use the blank spaces to add other songs I liked, Tim would fill that excess tape with stories, comedy skits and dispatches from the special little world he inhabited when we weren't together. These might detail his trips to the library, what he'd seen from his window or analyses of his recording process.

'I do hope you appreciate the effort I'm going to here,' he said in the space at the end of his copy of 'Controversy'. 'It's quite the caper, putting these together.'

These homely words were jarring, coming hot on the heels of songs with titles like 'Jack U Off' and 'Do Me, Baby'.

On the way home from school one afternoon he handed me the latest tape, this time the promised copy of *Dirty Mind*. On the card insert, using felt tip, he'd drawn a portrait of Prince pouting, and beneath it had written the words, *Dirty Mind* plus 'God Hump U Baby'.

'What's "God Hump U Baby"?' I asked.

'It's a surprise,' he said, smiling broadly.

I assumed it was an obscure Prince song that he'd uncovered. Even more music for me to love. So, I thanked him and placed it in my bag, telling him as we splintered off towards our respective homes how much I was looking forward to hearing it.

* * *

Broken Biscuits

Robert knocked on my bedroom door and called my name, something he'd been doing a lot since bursting in on me – giving it a few firm taps and telling me that dinner was ready or that our mother wanted me for something. Before that he'd always just strolled in, as if my bedroom was his spare. I'd been wary of him after he'd caught me, waiting for the hammer to fall. For him to rinse me in front of other people.

'You won't believe what I caught Adam doing …'

But he surprised me by not talking about it at all. Instead, there had been sheepish looks; tense, thin-lipped smiles. And now this respectful door knocking. I told him to come in.

'Here,' he said, handing me a compilation tape he'd made for me, the track listing carefully written out in biro. 'Don't say I don't give you nothing.'

'Thanks,' I said, looking at the songs, all of them hard rock and heavy metal. This was the fourth of these tapes he'd handed me in recent weeks. The first one had been presented to me with the justification that it would stop me going through his records. If I wanted to listen to them so badly, he said, then here they were.

But these were his curated cuts. The songs he wanted me to hear. On this latest tape there was 'Slide It In' by Whitesnake. 'Pearl Necklace' by ZZ Top. 'Girls, Girls, Girls' by Mötley Crüe. This kind of music was okay. I liked the pace of it, the guitar solos. But none of it moved

The Beautiful Ones

me. None of it made me want to sway. These were not songs I could live inside.

That, of course, had been the point. All the songs Robert was presenting me with were pounding and stridently heterosexual, about men having sex with women. Many of the tracks were harvested from albums with semi-clad ladies on the covers. From records that practically levitated with gravity-defying breasts and hairspray. These tapes were a reminder of the correct path. This was not girl's music. This was boy's music about girls, and that's what I should be spending my time with. I had learned by this point that Prince wasn't gay and that his music was mostly about sleeping with women, but that had been lost on Robert. For him, it all fell down on the presentation. Prince was too much like girl's music for him to fully engage with the fact that it was made by a straight man who fancied women as much as Robert did – maybe even more so. But just as the real Prince was lost on him, the gestures Robert was making were lost on me. I'd interpreted them as apologies for barging in on me. As gifts. Because it hadn't just been the tapes. There had also been the magazines.

'I thought you might like these,' he said, placing a few copies of *Knave* and *Mayfair* on my duvet. Women pouted at me from the covers, and I flicked through them the moment Robert left my room. They were a step up from his biker magazines, containing photos of women removing their underwear in office settings or sprawled across cars while making O shapes with their mouths. These were images that made me feel dizzy and wish, not for the first time, that I had a lock on my bedroom door.

But all this attention, the tapes, the respectful knocking, these magazines, had been part of something bigger. Robert's reminder of which swimsuit I should be concentrating on.

I put Robert's latest tape on my stereo then sat down on the edge of my bed to play Ghosts 'n Goblins on my computer, pounding heterosexuality blasting from my speakers. I'd rather have been listening to my copy of *Dirty Mind*, but I was trying not to play Prince when Robert was around, knowing that it made him think less of me. So, I saved that one for best. Besides, Robert was being nice to me, and I wanted to enjoy the spotlight of that attention for as long as it lasted. I didn't want to do anything to interrupt the warmth of that.

There was a tap on my bedroom door, and I turned down the music.

'I've got someone here who wants to meet you,' Robert said, his mouth held close to the jamb.

I couldn't think who this someone might be. No one wanted to meet me. Still, I was curious and told him to come in. When he opened the door, he was with his girlfriend, Debbie, and her younger sister, Rochelle. I'd seen her a few times, tagging along with Debbie. A short, moodily pretty brunette, Rochelle was a couple of years older than me. I'd never got the sense that she'd ever looked at my gawky body and Coke-bottle specs in a way that suggested: *I have to know more.* I'd believed myself to be invisible to her and was grateful for it. Now here she was, wanting to meet.

'You two have a chat,' Robert said, as Debbie nudged Rochelle into my room then closed the door behind her.

She offered me an awkward, 'Hi,' then sat down beside me on the bed. I didn't really know what to do with this, so I offered her my controller.

'Do you want a go?' I asked. She said no thank you, she was fine. So, I started a game and we sat in uncomfortable silence, her sitting with her hands in her lap, occasionally yawning as I made a knight in armour repeatedly die on screen. After about ten minutes of this, she got to her feet.

'I think I'm going to go now,' she said.

'Oh, okay,' I replied, a little sad but relieved. On the screen, pixelated zombies overwhelmed my character, stripping him down to his skeleton.

'It was nice to meet you,' she said, then left the room, closing the door behind her before I had a chance to say, 'You too'.

I was about to restart the game when I heard her voice on the landing, murmuring something in a hushed tone. This was followed by Robert, issuing a muted but still audible swear.

Broken Biscuits

'For fuck's sake,' he said. 'Nothing? He didn't try anything?'

'I don't think he was interested,' Rochelle said.

'Oh, fucking hell.'

Just as with everything Robert had been doing around me lately, I was confused by what was going on. So, I restarted my game and focused on killing zombies. Unaware that there had just been a test, and I had failed it.

* * *

Before heading to school the next morning, I'd borrowed my mother's Walkman and slipped the *Dirty Mind* cassette into it. Clicking play as I left the house and looking forward to finally getting some alone time with the music I loved.

The album was, as promised, very rude. The songs matched up with the images in the magazines Robert had given me. As the final track ended, there was a dull click. The sound of the recording being paused then restarted. It was familiar to me as the one that preceded all of Tim's audio letters. So, I readied myself to hear his latest updates, but instead what I got was a steady, rhythmic beat. A clapping sound clearly recorded into his tape deck. Then there was Tim's voice, not talking but singing breathily. And not just that, he was singing something filthy.

His musical paean to Sarah, Alison and Marie – three girls in our class he had crushes on – it was clearly inspired by the album that preceded it. Each girl was named and paid tribute to with feverish, impassioned whoops and graphic intentions. There were barks and sing-song gasps, backed by that persistent beat, reaching a panting crescendo with his urgent plea just as the tape was running out.

'*I want you, I want you, I want you …*'

This, it seemed, was 'God Hump U Baby'. I rewound the tape and listened to it again as I headed across the grounds of the school. Unable to quite believe what I was hearing.

Reaching my classroom, I'd hoped to see Tim sitting at his desk so I could talk to him about it. but learned he was at home sick that day. So, I sat at my own desk in the far corner of the classroom to think about what I'd heard. I considered that insistent beat. Imagined him dancing to it on the edge of the playing fields. The twirls and thrusting. What snapped me out of this image was the familiar jab of a paper aeroplane striking me on the side of the head. I looked across the room to see three boys from my form smirking at me. I unfolded the plane, knowing what it would say before I read it. The letters written in an angry scrawl.

FUCKING QUEER

Broken Biscuits

My response to this was instinctive, and I knew it was wrong even as I was doing it. I had a choice, but it also seemed in that moment that I didn't. I couldn't bear another day of this, of being singled out and pushed into a lonely and desperate place. My desk positioned out of necessity to be so far away from everyone else's that the next logical step was to climb out of the window. It didn't occur to me that high school was temporary and that within a year I would be free from it all. Instead, I felt impossibly, permanently trapped. And Tim had presented me with a way out.

I grabbed my Walkman and headed over to Sarah's desk, experiencing that feeling you get when you know what you're about to do is wrong but you're incapable of stopping it.

'I think you should listen to this,' I said, handing her the Walkman.

She put the headphones over her ears and clicked play, her eyes growing immediately wide. Cheeks glowing. She played it to Alison and Marie. Someone overheard and asked to listen to it. Within the hour there wasn't a child in our year who didn't know what Tim had done and I was no longer the focus of negative attention. In sharing that song, this gift intended only for me, I'd lit a fire that was so much bigger than the one I represented. My sexuality was old news. I had become something new and intoxicating; the laughed with, not the laughed at.

The Beautiful Ones

When Tim walked into class the next day, oblivious to what everyone knew, he smiled warmly at me just as he always did, and I felt a lurch of sickness, knowing what was coming for him. For my friend. The laughter, the taunting, the humiliation of a private self broadly shared. It had been understandable when other kids had thrown me to the wolves in this way, because we weren't friends. But what I'd done with Tim was different. So much worse. It had been a betrayal.

'Fucking hell, Tim,' a boy's voice yelled across the classroom. 'You dirty bastard!'

I watched Tim's face as confusion turned to realisation. He looked across at me, understanding what I must have done. His face put on a demonstration of hurt that stopped just short of crying, but I knew he wanted to. I wanted to as well. So, I lowered my head, the shame seeming to drain from my stomach and into my shoes.

To his credit, he took everything that followed in his stride. When people teased him and made remarks, he didn't shout or try to redirect the focus onto some other patsy. Didn't fight like a wild animal was taking him down. Instead, he took his lumps stoically and found a way to laugh them off. He didn't even seem angry with me. But I'd wounded him and sold him out. There was no way of undoing that.

'Adam, that was just meant for you,' he said later on when I tried to apologise. 'You shouldn't have done that.'

Broken Biscuits

What I wanted was for him to hit me. Really hit me. For once, I was ready to not fight back. But violence was never in him, so his response, that cold, mild chastisement, hurt even more. By being kinder and better than me, and by not meaning to, Tim had left me to burn and I can still feel the blisters more than thirty years later.

In time, the radiation of his notoriety faded, and people moved on. Things returned to relative normality and before the week was out I would feel the familiar sharpness of a paper aeroplane stinging my cheek.

* * *

During the run up to Christmas, when I knew Robert was been out drinking with friends from his work, I went back into his room for a snoop. I was no longer that bothered about his records, now much more interested in seeing if he had any more copies of *Knave*.

I examined his wardrobe, rooted through his sock draw and the boxes he kept under his bed then turned my attention to the small sideboard under his window. I opened the sliding door on the front and pawed around inside, then crouched down fully so I could get a better look. I found a stack of magazines and was lifting them out to flick through, hopeful of what I might find, when I saw it. Up against the back panel and still in its shrink wrap. A copy of Prince's *Sign O' The Times*. The double album I'd never heard because it was too expensive for me or Tim to buy, so had been regularly dropping hints about it to my parents over the preceding months.

You don't hide records that you're planning on playing for girls, those have their own special place. This one, I knew, was for me. Well-hidden because, short of installing a razor-wire fence, Robert knew I'd find myself in his room at some point, poking around. I lifted out the record, flipping it over in my hands and reading the information on the back. At the top of the track listing, it read: *Produced, Arranged, Composed and Performed by Prince* – a line that could have easily been used to describe my life at that point. But I didn't consider this at the time. Instead, I placed everything back as I'd found it then headed to my own room, closing Robert's bedroom door behind me with a soft and certain click.

A few days later, there was an album-shaped gift under the tree. In lieu of a gift tag, the dedication had been written in biro across the wrapping paper, in the blank space between holly and bells.

To Adam the Madam, it read, *from Rob*.

As Christmas approached, I stared at this gift as if I had X-ray vision, the image of the record inside seeming to burn through the paper. What my vision didn't pick up on was what this gesture from Robert really meant. It was an album I desperately wanted but it was also an acceptance that I could have Prince and whatever else I needed to make me happy. Because there had been a softening in Robert since that evening outside the pub. Perhaps an understanding that he had gone too far.

I'll disown you.

What would disowning mean? For him and me, for our broader family. Would it involve crossing the street to avoid me? No longer protecting me? Not sharing a Christmas together? There would have been a cost in any case, and he'd apparently deemed it to be too great. So, however uncomfortable I might make him, whatever I was, he'd decided that he would still be mine and I would still be his.

Still, when he handed this gift to me on Christmas morning, he wouldn't meet my eye, meaning he didn't see my practised look of happy surprise as I tore open the paper and looked at the record inside. He also missed that moment of joyful anticipation, this music I was so excited to hear and already knew I would love, along with the realisation that I'd lost the only other person I could really share that love with.

'Thank you so much,' I said, stuffing down any thoughts of Tim.

'Don't say I don't give you nothing,' Robert said, finally able to look at me.

And I replied, sincerely, that I wouldn't.

The Three Fs

It's hard to pinpoint those times where a different decision would have changed everything. Some call them 'sliding doors' moments. Others, particularly those who hate the movie *Sliding Doors*, prefer to talk of parallel universes. These infinite worlds we live alongside, where a single choice or hesitation could be the difference between crossing the road to buy a winning lottery ticket and crossing that same road to get tangled under the wheels of an articulated lorry. But I can identify one of mine, and it happened while I was sneaking out of a party. Someone reached out, grabbed my arm and placed me on a set of tracks that I'm not sure I'd have found my way onto otherwise.

The party was being held at my friend Jay's house during my second month at university. At the time, he was living in a large, Victorian semi-detached with rooms across three floors, his landlord having made sure that every space big enough to squeeze a bed into was set up

Broken Biscuits

with a lockable door and a weekly rental charge. In this way, he'd found it possible to cram close to a dozen students into the place at any one time, informing the house with the bloated, infested quality of a rat's nest. It was always busy and always loud. People forever coming and going, the kitchen and shared bathrooms becoming squalid places, forever teetering on the brink of appearing vandalised. It quickly picked up a reputation as 'the party house', though parties were never planned there. No advance notice given. They just started out of nowhere. Like a fire, or a fight. Someone would begin playing music in the kitchen during the afternoon, start rolling a joint and by the evening this would have somehow transformed into a party that would end at around 4 a.m. following neighbour complaints and a police intervention.

Whenever I visited Jay, I'd marvel at the scars of these events. The hall carpet was a Jackson Pollock of spilled drinks and cigarette burns, evidencing countless nights of young people staggering about in altered states and having a greater time than I'd ever known. I had never been to a party as an adult, having never had the opportunity or, I suspected, the stomach for it. But I was visiting Jay one evening, some music began playing downstairs and before I knew it there I was, a guy at a party.

'We need some booze,' Jay said as the music increased in volume and the building thrummed to the sound of several dozen simultaneous conversations. We heard

The Three Fs

something shatter, followed by a cheer. A bottle or perhaps a window.

'I ... I can get some booze,' I found myself saying, the words as uncomfortable in my mouth as a handful of Lego. I had rarely bought alcohol at this point, never once referring to it as 'booze'. Whenever I *had* bought it, the act felt as furtive as shoplifting. But I was accidentally at a party in 'the party house', and sensed it would be good for me if I could hold my nerve and get through it. I just needed to make it to the off-licence and back. The returning hero, entering the house to a fanfare as I held up an unbranded carrier bag containing two dozen discounted Czech lagers. 'I'll be back in ten,' I said.

If I'd known the word bacchanalian back then, I would have used it describe what I saw as I left Jay's room and descended the stairs into the guts of the party. With the vocabulary available to me at the time, though, I simply thought of it as too much for me to handle. The party was in its infancy but already there were staggering drunks and yelled conversations edging towards arguments. Looking into the kitchen, I saw a girl crying and being comforted by a friend, while beside her a couple made out and a guy with a Beatles mop-top leaned forward to snort something off the table. Everything smelled of weed, spilt beer and the sharp insistence of fresh vomit.

I wasn't comfortable with any of this. The noise, the sight of it all. I wanted to be a part of it so badly, but it

Broken Biscuits

was too much too soon. I needed to dip my toe into this world, not belly-flop from a great height. So, while I *would* be heading out of the door, I decided that I would not be returning – as a hero or otherwise. Instead, I would go home and listen to my Jeff Buckley album, thinking about what I was missing out on and trying to be grateful for having avoided everything that could and would have gone wrong for me had I stayed. What stopped me was Louise.

She was leaning against the banister at the foot of the stairs and rifling through a toddler-sized handbag, her platinum hair swishing like a grass skirt. A careworn leather jacket was slung over her shoulders in a slovenly, precarious manner, the way a coatstand looks when you casually toss something onto it. There was something windblown and chaotic about her, as if she'd arrived at the house seeking refuge from a hurricane. As completely appropriate in this scene as I wasn't.

Because I was looking at her and not where I was going, I stumbled on the bottom step and almost fell, bracing myself on the banister and hissing a swear. At this, she looked up at me and smiled. Not mockingly, but something warm. The kind of smile you'd offer if someone presented you with a kitten. I smiled back, feeling myself blush, then focused on the door. My way out of all this.

'Have you got a light?' she asked, reaching out to grab my arm. At her words, her attention, I was suddenly

The Three Fs

aware of myself. My legs felt uncertain, like I'd missed another step. But I tried to sound confident.

'Yeah,' I quacked, patting my pockets in search of the lighter I'd recently taken to carrying. I didn't smoke, but before heading to university my brother Robert had handed it to me, adding that it was a good way to meet people.

'Someone will always want a light,' he said.

By *someone* he meant girls.

I passed her the lighter, and as I did she took my hand, pulling me closer to her and raising her voice above the music.

'I've seen you around,' she said.

'I've seen you around, too,' I replied.

It was impossible to have not noticed Louise on campus. I'd often see her in the corridor on the way to classes or standing in the refectory queue. She was hard to not look at. Part of this was down to the effect she had on the people in her presence. She seemed to make everyone around her feel interesting and special just by entering her orbit. Students I otherwise knew as quiet and reserved would blossom with unusual confidence when speaking to her, becoming suddenly loud and gregarious. Now I felt this superpower being directed at me and found that I could not stop talking. About art, music, anything but explain that whenever I looked at her my heart began beating so hard I could feel it pounding at the top of my

Broken Biscuits

skull. While I spoke, she lit her cigarette, smoked it halfway then mercifully raised a hand to stop me talking about Joseph Beuys. Saving me from myself.

'Have you got a girlfriend?' she asked.

'No,' I replied. This, I believed, was obvious. A fact so blatant I could have been wearing it as a pin badge on my jacket alongside *Yes, I am a virgin* and *My mother still buys my underwear*.

Louise fixed me with a stare, took a deep pull on her cigarette, her cheeks hollowing, then exhaled smoke up and to one side. Her gaze never breaking. She was working me out, I guessed.

'Good,' she said finally, grinding the cigarette out onto a door frame and letting the butt drop onto the hall carpet, where she scuffed it with a swift chicken scratch of her foot. 'Come on.'

She took my hand again and led me upstairs, where we stopped on the landing, off which doors led to a warren of rooms. Jay was in one of them, waiting in a now distant and insignificant past for his booze. My skin buzzed with fear and excitement, wondering what was coming next. If this might be the set-up for a cruel trick. I shouldn't have even been talking to someone like Louise, let alone being led somewhere by her.

She leaned against a wall beside one of the doors and gave me another searching look, one that made me wonder hard about what my face was doing. I knew that

The Three Fs

I was blushing again, and wondered if I was also doing that daydreaming expression that got me in so much trouble with teachers and bosses. The one that made me look stupid and bored.

'Okay, then,' she said, 'kiss me.'

This felt like the practical in a job interview for a role I was woefully unqualified for. But I did what I was told and hoped for the best.

I'd had my first kiss just a few months earlier, aged nineteen. So late in the day I'd feared it would never happen. Twenty had been the deadline I'd internally decided upon. If I'd reached that age before it happened, then I was done for. A failed male project. Kaput. I wasn't sure exactly what I'd do, but I know that I'd mulled over suicide, always comforted by having it as an option. But then there was a woman in Bridlington during the summer, a kiss after a club night that only happened thanks to her initiative and three pints of Fosters. A life-saving move that sent me off to university with the seal at last partially broken on my purity.

My lips met Louise's clumsily, but our energy matched. While I was scared of everything that was happening, I was also nineteen and horny, which has a power all of its own. Still, I was profoundly aware of my every move. Of where I was, how her body felt in my arms, of her hands in my hair and digging into my back. I hoped I wasn't getting this wrong and opened my eyes to look at what

Broken Biscuits

Louise was doing. Hers were closed and she seemed to be into what was happening. People were walking past us, drinking, staggering off on their own missions. A couple with matching purple dreadlocks gave me a smile and a thumbs-up. I closed my eyes and tried to focus on Louise, but found that I couldn't completely give myself over to the experience, my internal monologue blaring like a tannoy announcement.

I AM KISSING A WOMAN I HAVE ONLY JUST MET. I AM JUST LIKE OTHER MEN.

Louise's tongue tasted of tobacco and something zesty and alcoholic. I was trying to work out exactly what that was when she stepped back, wiping her lips, and studied me again. Her lipstick had left a tiny claret-coloured swoosh at the side of her mouth. It was my reflex to apologise for this, for the mess I'd made. But before I could, she spoke, seeming to answer a question that I hadn't asked.

'Okay,' she said, then pulled me through the door behind us and into a small, shabby room. It had no curtains and was lit by the amber of the streetlamp outside the window. On the floor lay a single mattress, draped in a greying summer-weight duvet. Pinned up on the wall above the pillow was a large poster showing a naked Harvey Keitel in a still from the movie *Bad Lieutenant*. Louise crouched to mess with the stereo beside the mattress. A song by Portishead began to play. The room

The Three Fs

wasn't hers, she said. It was a friend's, but they were away. They wouldn't mind.

'Mind what?' I asked.

'You fucking me.'

'*Oh*,' I said.

'"*Oh*", he says,' Louise replied, laughing as she began to undress.

This felt like one of the dreams I'd often have as a teenager and wake from suddenly in the night. In these, there was none of the courtship or romance that I expected sex to require in real life. Just the act. Now here I was in the real world, having been decided upon and picked, like an item in a fruit bowl. A cherry, I thought much later.

While Louise removed her clothes, I half averted my gaze, looking to naked Harvey Keitel as if he had the answers for how to handle this. When I looked over at Louise's gradually revealing body I felt the same sensation of jelly-legged uncertainty I got whenever I squared up for a fight. Except this time it was different, because I had an erection, and I didn't want either of us to lose.

'Jesus Christ,' Louise said, standing naked in front of me. 'Take your fucking clothes off.'

She lowered herself onto the mattress and climbed under the duvet, watching me.

Nothing prepares you for the moment of being naked in front of another person for the first time, but it helped that I was being ordered around and couldn't retreat into

Broken Biscuits

my natural reticence. Still, there was a moment when I considered giving in to a small and potentially life detonating thought.

Should I do ... a little dance?

Instead, uncertain about the merits of my body and how it compared to Keitel's, I frantically undressed then joined Louise under the duvet. She moved in to kiss me, pressing her soft, cool skin against mine. My penis batted stupidly against her thigh, while a song called 'Wandering Star' played at low volume. The booming music downstairs seeming to fade into the distance. As we kissed, I frantically tried to access all of the untested sex tips I'd picked up over the years, thinking of the advice on female anatomy offered to my friends and me at middle school by a boy in the year above us.

'Women have this kind of switch between their legs called a clitoris,' he'd told us, his tone weighty with knowledge. 'Find it, rub it and don't stop.'

'What will happen if I stop?' one of my friends had asked.

'Just don't.'

And now there I was, a naked woman in my arms, wondering about that switch.

'You're shaking,' Louise said.

'Am I?'

'Or you're vibrating,' she said, laughing. 'But I can work with that.'

The Three Fs

Whether she was laughing with me or at me, I didn't much care. She was having fun and she was beautiful and she was still in bed with me. Then she was on top of me, looking down, smiling, her hair tickling my face. I took in the smell of her; alcohol, tobacco and light, fresh sweat mixed with a fragrance I would later learn was Issey Miyake's *L'Eau d'Issey*. It was the smell of the adult world finally coming to get me.

Oh fuck, I thought. *This is it.*

By *it*, I meant the moment when I would become a man. It would also be the moment when something unexpected happened.

Louise had just reached down between my legs and was leaning forward to kiss me when she leapt back, a loud crashing noise causing her to recoil and look sharply behind her, covering her breasts as she did. The bedroom door had burst open and the couple with the purple dreadlocks tumbled into the room, the two of them collapsing onto the carpet like a stack of dumped laundry. They were kissing hard at one another, biting really, like each was trying to steal a mouthful of food from the other. The sounds of the party roared into the room, a sudden cacophony. Louise scooted around beside me, and I held her. I was just trying to work out how to handle this situation, whether to prove my worth to Louise by standing up and confronting the two of them while fully naked, when a guy wandered in, a can of Carling in his hand. Presumably he'd been curious about the noise and had come to check it out. Neither he nor the couple acknowledged mine or Louise's presence, and as if to underscore their presumed privacy, the guy with the dreads slithered down the woman's body and pressed his face between her legs. At this, Carling Guy lowered himself down on the floor to watch, casually swigging from his can as if he'd just settled down in front of the TV for the cup final.

I AM AT A STUDENT PARTY, I thought. *PEOPLE ARE HAVING SEX IN FRONT OF ME AND I AM NAKED. THIS IS JUST LIKE IN THE FILMS.*

This thought was broken by a yell, as the woman spotted Carling Guy watching her. She struggled to her feet, swearing hard, raised a dinner plate above her head and, before I had a chance to work out where this plate had come from, brought it down with force over his skull. White shards of crockery exploded across the room, Louise grabbed at me, and I came. Two weeks later she moved in with me, and we started shopping for a puppy.

From the earliest days of our relationship, I was playing catch-up. Making up for lost time. I knew that Louise was experienced, but initially that made me feel better about myself. That she could have been with any number of people, but she'd chosen me, this novice. Her attention made me bold, and the first few weeks were exciting, as I

The Three Fs

threw myself into this new adult life with the kind of aplomb I'd previously only reserved for unlimited buffet access. Louise and I were both studying art and we quickly fell into a lifestyle of drinking cheap red wine, working on our projects then, spattered with clay and acrylics, falling into bed together. My art history teacher knew it was an attention grabber to tell us about the debauched lives of artists and it felt as if I was now just like them, having gone from timid virgin to roaring Bohemian at the smash of a plate. But I could only play that role for so long, the real me soon burning through this costume I was wearing and reminding me that l wasn't cool enough to be wearing it.

Sitting with friends in the student bar a few weeks after she moved in with me, Louise responded to something Jay said.

'God, I must have had ten thousand shags.'

She was exaggerating, and I'm not sure exactly what Jay's comment had been, but I was as impressed by Louise's response as I would have been if I'd heard a writer claiming, 'I've written ten thousand novels.' I didn't know enough to understand that if you've had that many sexual experiences, or written that many words, there's a good chance that most of them will be dreadful. At the time, I laughed along with everyone but as Louise and I wheeled our way home and towards our bed I grew concerned. I interpreted what she said as confirmation that she was an expert in her field and that being with her came with a sense of responsibility. She'd had all of this passionate, atmospherically lit, tremendously satisfying sex and now there was I, her new boyfriend with oil paint in his hair pawing at her body in the dark and asking, 'Is that okay?' She'd soon realise the mistake she'd made and I'd be on my own again. The idea of being alone, of having to resort to my own company again having waited so long, seemed worse than anything. So, I decided to learn everything about sex before it was too late.

I had never been given the birds and bees chat. My father had handled the tricky issue of explaining sex to me by simply avoiding the conversation entirely, figuring that, in time, I would work it out for myself. This was his way with most things, his few instructional lectures tending to stick to safe, practical topics. Like how to eat hot soup or avoid pissing on the bathroom floor.

'Just hold it steady,' he'd told me when I was very young, readying myself as I stood in front of the toilet bowl, my shorts and underwear around my ankles as if I'd just been pantsed. 'Aim for the centre and try not to make a mess.'

Had he offered it, I'm sure his sex advice would have been pretty much identical. He likes to share information in a brisk and economical manner, offering basic information that relies on common sense to fill in the blanks when

The Three Fs

it comes to finesse and technique. A conversation he didn't want to have would have been no different. Besides, it seemed like a lot of embarrassment and effort to put in for a boy who, it seemed increasingly likely, would die a virgin. Just like the offside rule or the size of Mount Everest in cubic metres, sex advice was knowledge that I just couldn't envision ever having a use for. Had my father decided to take me to one side and educate me, it seemed he would have been wasting both my time and his. For my part, I would rather he'd pinned me down and chipped out my teeth with an icepick. Anything but have him attempt to explain to me the operation of the vagina in ten words or fewer.

But now I was feeling stupid. I should have asked for that talk, if not from my father, then at least from Robert, who lost his virginity during his first year in secondary school and as far as I could tell had not stopped fucking since. He'd have loved to have given me that talk, surely enhanced with a series of sordid mimes. But lacking that option, I would begin seeking out and devouring sex advice as if I was cramming for an exam.

These days, I could have just googled for answers and within seconds been presented with a host of practical information along with a step-by-step HD video. But back in 1995, looking for guidance on how to navigate sex was an act closer to foraging. I was clueless and grateful for any information I could lay my hands on. I didn't

Broken Biscuits

care whether that advice came from an agony aunt or a toilet wall, I was prepared to pay attention.

In the university library, I found books containing erotic artwork by Namio Harukawa and Eric Stanton that made me clutch my pearls and look over my shoulder as I carried them to the photocopier. In the campus refectory, I'd pay close attention as other students gossiped, dissecting their sex lives over cheesy chips and cans of Tango. Tales of both disasters and successes, each detailed in bug-eyed awe. And frequently, there would be bragging. Most of this came from a guy on my course named Aaron, who'd drop the wisdom he'd claimed to have earned from 'banging birds', adjusting his crotch while he spoke as if worried he'd worn away his penis in the process. Reassuring himself that it was all still there.

'Women are like dogs,' he once said with a wink. 'Throw them a bone and they'll be loyal to you whatever you do.'

While I didn't know much, I knew enough to ignore Aaron. Much more useful to me were the copies of *Cosmopolitan* and *More!* I'd often find abandoned on the refectory tables. They featured extensive lovemaking tips and 'Position of the Fortnight' articles that made sex look like the late stages of a game of Twister. I'd study these pages as if they were peer-reviewed medical papers, then head home to ask Louise how confident she felt about standing in the shower with one foot behind her ear.

The Three Fs

Catching the bus home one afternoon, I spotted a flat-roofed industrial unit on the edge of town, its windows blacked out and a sign above the door reading PRIVATE SHOP. Words I had interpreted as SEX LIBRARY. If there was one place I was sure to get answers, it was here. So, I got off at the next stop and slipped inside this shop. It was dimly lit and desolate-looking, like one of those hurriedly assembled businesses that sell fireworks out of bankrupt retail spaces. On every available wall, images of women looked my way and pretended to want me. There was a smell, too, a lingering aroma that mixed warm polythene with dog breath, which I tried not to inhale while I rocked on my heels in front of a display of pornographic magazines and variously nobbled sex toys. The guy behind the counter had long salt-and-pepper hair and a push broom moustache, which he picked at as he watched me squinting at a product named The Triple Ripple.

'Do you need any help?' he asked.

'*God*,' I wanted to say, '*you don't know how much.*' But instead, I told him I was okay and made for the door, adding that I'd come back with my girlfriend another day. A line that must have broken his heart every time he heard it.

'Course you will, son,' he said, as I headed out into the suddenly stark sunlight and gasped for air, my cheeks blushing the colour of the Turkish flag.

Broken Biscuits

Too embarrassed to turn to my friends for help, I wrote a letter to the Dear Deirdre column in *The Sun* newspaper, asking her for advice. While I would never buy that paper, I wasn't above reading it for free in the shop. But after a couple of weeks of my letter going unprinted and my newsagent shouting at me that his shop wasn't a library, I finally built up the courage to talk to my friend Susan, a mature student who spoke about sex more than anyone I knew. To spend more than a few minutes in her company was to learn of the time she and an ex once had sex fourteen times in the space of a single day.

'Thirteen would have been unlucky,' she'd explain. 'I wouldn't say it was agony until about the ninth time,' she'd add, a smile of wistful reminiscence on her face. 'But you push through that. God, though, I couldn't walk the next day.'

I didn't want this. I didn't want agony. I wanted Louise to fall in love with me, and I didn't believe that the way to go about this was to send her limping to the hospital, her legs bowed like a wishbone. Still, I felt certain Susan would have some answers, and came at her obliquely at first, asking her what she thought women wanted.

'They want the three Fs,' she said, decisively and without hesitation, counting them off on her fingers. 'Food, fucking and flowers. The one F they don't want is feelings.'

My problem was that I was full of feelings, so what was I supposed to do with them? I knew that feelings

The Three Fs

were seen as girlish things, women's things, like wearing an Alice band or listening to Wet Wet Wet. But this was the 90s; things were supposed to be changing. People kept talking about a sensitive kind of masculinity called 'the New Man', and I wondered if that meant my feelings were permissible now. Maybe *I* was a new man and there was a place for me.

'Don't be fooled by all that,' Susan said. 'If you show your feelings to a woman, you're done for.'

I considered the three Fs.

'Why flowers?' I asked, thinking it was a pretty clichéd option to make the big three.

'Because women like to be apologised to. It reminds them they're right.'

This sounded to me like something Aaron would say.

'What do I do about my feelings?'

'I don't know,' Susan said. 'Have a fight or something. Or put the effort into fucking. That's the key. You have to really put your shoulder into it.'

This sounded like great advice if I was thinking of pushing a car up a hill or helping someone move a piano, but I got the sense that listening to Susan would do me way more harm than good. Still, I bought Louise a bunch of chrysanthemums on the way home from campus that day. She eyed them suspiciously.

'What have you got to apologise for?'

Broken Biscuits

'Nothing,' I replied, knowing that every part of me screamed with apology whenever we were together. My every action one of contrition. Always sorry for not being the kind of man I was sure she needed me to be. What was really worrying me though, was that all the advice I'd thought would help me become that kind of man seemed to involve tricks and psychology. I just wanted someone to tell me how to be great in bed, and now I was caught up in the science of mind games.

One afternoon, as we were making our way across campus after a lecture, I decided to open up to Jay, explaining that, until a few weeks earlier, I had never slept with anyone before.

'What, never?' he said, smirking. His eyes wide and lit with humour, as if I'd just revealed to him that I still wrote heartfelt letters to Santa. I brushed aside the humiliation, telling him that I needed help. 'I'm not sure what I should be doing.'

I mentioned the three Fs.

'Have you been speaking to Susan?' he asked. Then he reset, taking me seriously. 'Look, you're asking the wrong person. It takes me hours.'

To me, this sounded like I was asking *exactly* the right person. It wouldn't be until a few years later, when Jay would break up with his girlfriend and express his love for a man named Gary, that I would put this in context. But at the time I wished I'd had his way with women.

The Three Fs

'Honestly,' he said. 'I think you're worrying too much. She moved in with you, for fuck's sake. You can't be that bad. Just enjoy it and work it out. Stop overthinking it. You'll ruin things.'

This was without a doubt the best piece of relationship advice I would receive from anyone, so of course I'd paid no attention to it.

The same things that can bond you to someone, their quirks and idiosyncrasies, can be the same things that erode affection. These behaviours that go from being acts that elicit gooey looks of adoration to ones that can make someone want to place a pillow over your face until you stop wriggling. One of these things, it seems, was my cloying niceness. My desperation to make Louise happy, making sure she wanted for nothing. A behaviour that would become smothering. I grew aware of a new look that she would sometimes give me. The one that you get when someone is beginning to regret buying a puppy with you. I sensed that I was losing her, and that it would take more than sex to fix it. I was starting to realise that it was about much more than that, and I'd been focusing on the wrong thing. Eroding the qualities that made her want to go to bed with me in the first place.

Shopping in Asda one afternoon, I saw an affectionate couple in the produce aisle, so bound up in each other's bodies you'd think they were conjoined at the crotch.

Broken Biscuits

'I can't believe you're mine,' the guy said, slipping his arm around his partner's waist and kissing her gently on the nose.

'I can't believe you're mine,' she echoed, looking up at him dolefully.

'I'm yours.'

'And I'm yours.'

Some people would have witnessed this then looked around for the camera crew that must surely be filming this poorly written Hallmark movie, but what I heard was everything I wanted from my own relationship. A mutual and equal bond of love and commitment. I wanted to belong to someone.

Later that evening, eating a bowl of grated cheese and pasta on the sofa beside Louise, I chanced my arm.

'I can't believe you're mine,' I said.

'You've got cheese on your chin,' she replied, gesturing to the same spot on her own face. 'Right there.' I wiped it away and tried again.

'Really, though, I can't believe I'm yours.'

'That's nice,' she said, spearing a fusilli with her fork and twirling a dangling cheese strand.

'Are you mine?' I risked.

'I'm not anyone's,' she said, her brow crinkling.

'I didn't mean …' I took a composing breath, forgetting the three Fs entirely. Focusing on the forbidden fourth. 'I just love you.'

The Three Fs

'I know,' she said, kissing me on the lips then getting up to scrape the rest of her dinner into the bin.

I told myself that she'd been too cool to say the words out loud but that her kiss had been the answer I'd wanted.

Louise and I were sharing a pint in the student bar a few days later when she slid the glass towards me and sighed heavily.

'This doesn't feel right,' she said.

I looked down into the glass.

'No,' she said, 'I mean *things*.'

'What things?' I said, then took a sip from the pint. My mouth suddenly very dry.

'I'm not sure,' she said, looking into my eyes then away over my shoulder. Towards the exit. 'I just feel like I need a new direction. I don't know what, just not *this*,' she gestured around the bar, a sweeping movement of her arm that I tried to ignore had also included me. I reached over and held her hand, not knowing what to say but hoping it would be enough.

'I think I need to be on my own,' she said.

I felt as if I'd been hit in three difference places with one punch.

'Are you breaking up with me?'

'No,' she said awkwardly. 'I just need ... some space. I don't know.'

Broken Biscuits

She looked into my eyes again, holding a hard, focused expression. I braced myself for her to say something else that hurt, but whatever she saw when she looked at me, it caused her features to soften. She hooked her arm through mine, pulling me in close, then kissed me gently on the head. While I would not realise it at the time, it seemed I did have the glue to hold a relationship together and that glue was pity.

'I'll give you all the space you need,' I said, leaning into her.

'I know, baby,' she said. 'I know.'

Had a TV audience been watching this, they would have known that the ball had already started rolling. Shouting at their screens like I was a low-ranking dating show contestant, my fate obvious to everyone except me. *'God, I can't wait for her to dump that guy!'* But Louise just couldn't go through with it. It was another month or so before she tried again, when I was bringing her a mug of tea she hadn't asked for.

'I've applied for a new course,' she said, taking the mug from me and setting it down on the coffee table.

'Oh, cool,' I said.

'In Norwich.'

'Oh.'

Oh, he says.

There was something resigned about her tone, amplified by the composing breath that had preceded her

The Three Fs

words. Something I didn't pick up on at the time but would grow familiar with over the years.

It's not working out.

I can't do this anymore.

But because Louise struggled to say the most difficult part, and I had yet to experience a break-up, I'd entirely missed the point of what was being said to me. I was in need of a translation app. Something that would convert 'I've applied for a new course in Norwich' to 'I am breaking up with you and moving 150 miles away. I'm sorry, but this is what the audience wants.'

While I'd been attempting to hold on to our relationship with crowd-sourced sex tips and desperate gestures, Louise had been making plans to relocate to the other end of the country. She wanted to move down there during the summer, she said, to get settled in before the course started in a few months. So, I made a suggestion that must have seemed to Louise like one last tragic attempt to hold onto her.

'Okay, well, I'll move down there with you,' I said. 'Get you settled in. Then I can visit at weekends.'

Louise had seen the advantages in this, though likely not the same ones I saw. I believed that, with no other distractions, just the two of us, we would get closer again. She would stop giving me those sad, uncomfortable looks and I would never have to be without her again. Never alone again.

Broken Biscuits

That July, Louise and I drove her possessions down to Norwich from Yorkshire. We paid for two months' rent on a small, top-floor studio flat in a converted hotel, its single, large window overlooking the River Yare. The place was cheap and well lit, and the landlord didn't care that Louise had a dog as long as the rent was paid on time.

Back in Barnsley, I put a deposit on a room in a house share with Jay and still had another year of study to complete on my course, so would need to return there in September. Until then, we were out of money. My deposit and Louise's rent had wiped out our cash reserves and her grant wouldn't come through until the autumn, so I took on a part-time job as a kitchen porter in a nearby hotel. While I chopped vegetables, monitored an industrial dishwasher and discreetly stole food from the pantry, Louise stayed in the flat working on her art projects. After my shifts I would return home, delighting the dog with the sausages I'd pilfered from the hotel's carvery. Louise always looked relieved to see me.

'Come here,' she'd say, undressing in a way that suggested she was in fact dressing. Putting on a necessary work uniform. A tabard, say. Or grubby overalls. 'I'm bored.'

As come-ons go, it ranks pretty low, but this was the pattern we had fallen into. I was yet to fully understand that, for some people, sex could be disconnected from

The Three Fs

love or even affection. It could be as functional as using the bathroom or eating a sandwich. People didn't have to like each other to enjoy and use one another. But it was a long time before I learned this, the idea of future relationships incalculable to me in the summer of '96. At that time there was just me and Louise, in this forever. What would also occur to me much later was that the reason we had so much sex back then was because it was free, and we didn't own a TV. Had circumstances been different, I suspect I'd have found myself replaced by a well-circled copy of the TV guide. But during those times, my body being demanded of after a day spent scrubbing pans and doubting the stability of our relationship, it felt like love.

'Do you think we should get married?' I asked as we were lying in bed after work one evening.

Louise laughed at this with shocked and sudden force.

'No!' she said, appalled. 'Why would we want to do that?'

Like most of the things I knew about relationships, this was something I'd picked up from TV. Marriage is the end goal, the ultimate aim of the relationship story arc. You make a woman an offer of marriage, she is delighted and leaps into your arms and you spin her around, smiling and kissing. Cut to the wedding scene, your tearful relatives looking on as you kiss the bride. A full-throated power ballad begins to play. This weird distance I'd felt

Broken Biscuits

between us over the last few months was perhaps my fault, because she was waiting for me to pop the question. But I didn't tell her any of that.

'Because we love each other?' I said.

I let that hang in the air for a few seconds. It felt like I was waiting for her to show me her half of a heart pendant. She got out of bed and walked over to the window, her naked body silhouetted by the streetlights as she looked down towards the river below.

'Who gets married these days?' she said.

When September rolled around, I packed my essentials into a rucksack and caught the National Express coach back to Barnsley. A nine-hour journey with two changes and a chemical toilet that broadcast its contents through the coach with a thoroughness that suggested it was a considered design choice. But this didn't deter me from getting back on board each Friday and making my way to Louise, spending the Saturday with her then jumping back on the coach to spend a third of my Sunday trying not to inhale.

After my first few visits, Louise had walked with me to the station and kissed me goodbye. Increasingly, though, we said farewell at her front door, always with a hug, not always a kiss. I'd walk to grab my coach, making excuses for her in my head. She'd meant to kiss me but was distracted by thoughts of her coursework. That the dog

The Three Fs

had been acting up. I could make any circumstance fit into a comforting narrative.

Back in Barnsley, we'd talk on the phone every day but with a growing remoteness in her voice that had nothing to do with geographical distance. Her words hesitant and distracted. Calls became shorter.

The last of these came while I was standing in my bathtub doing laundry. Because my house didn't have a washing machine, we washed our clothes in the tub, treading them as if crushing grapes for wine. Jay called up the stairs, telling me that Louise was on the phone. I was excited, this rare call from her to me rather than vice versa. I grabbed the receiver from him and sat on the stairs, my bare feet still damp and unpleasantly fragrant from dirt and detergent, listening as she pulled the trigger.

'I don't think you should visit anymore.'

The stairs felt as if they'd given way beneath me. It took a long time for me to say anything, my words caught in my windpipe like a chunk of apple.

'Why?' I asked.

'Look …' she said. 'It's just not working anymore.'

'I think it is.'

'Do you?'

I tried to think of an answer that wasn't a lie.

'It could,' I said.

'It couldn't.'

Broken Biscuits

'Why?'

Another sigh. Silence. Breathing.

'I thought you loved me,' I said.

'I didn't say love.'

'You said I was yours.'

'That's different.'

She must have sensed this was too much, too wounding, because she threw me a bone.

'I don't know,' she sighed. 'Look, it's just too far. The distance.'

'Okay, well I'll quit my course and move down there …'

'Right,' she said, firm again. Her words dropped like heavy bags she'd been carrying around. 'I've been seeing Barry.'

She'd mentioned this name a few times on the phone. Her landlord's son, always turning up to fix things around the flat. A great guy, I was told. Really helpful. Couldn't do enough. I tried to picture him, this anonymous, capable man who, without visual reference, was every handsome, muscular, sexually confident thing I was not. The thought of him lying on the sheets I'd bought in the Habitat sale, petting my dog, it was too much. I slammed the phone into the cradle and cut the call, like I was snapping a book shut. I thought she might call me back out of concern, but she didn't. It must have been a relief to get me off the phone. To have finally put an end to this. Somewhere, an audience applauded.

The Three Fs

I spent the next couple of weeks ducking classes and calling in sick so I could stay in bed listening to Kate Bush albums on repeat and making pathetic noises. I was convinced I'd used up my one shot at love and that no one would ever touch me again. I barely ate, only leaving my room to tromp downstairs and make mugs of tea then cry *'WHY?!'* out loud, my words masked from my housemates by the roar of the kettle. Then I'd head back to bed and squirm pitifully in the clothes I'd been wearing for more days than I could remember.

Louise and I never spoke again, but a week or so after that last call she sent me a letter. In it, she told me a lot of things. That she was sorry. That I would find a woman who was right for me. But most interestingly, that someone had bitten off the end of Barry's nose during a pub fight and he would require surgery to build him a new one. This last piece of information was complex to process, as I tried to picture a man I'd only ever imagined and hated, and then what that man might look like with a gory new hole in his face. While I'd have loved to, I couldn't take any real pleasure in that. And because the letter didn't say anything comforting like, 'I want you back, Barry has too many holes!' it gave me something else to cry about.

What snapped me out of this was Jay, who barged into my room one evening to perform both an intervention and an act of self-preservation.

Broken Biscuits

'You need a new girlfriend!' he yelled. 'Seriously, man. This is killing me. If I hear fucking "The Saxophone Song" again, I swear …' He stopped then, his nose wrinkling. 'Jesus,' he said, throwing open my window. 'Have a fucking shower.'

Jay had seen me for what I was, a contemptible puddle of wah wah, every inch someone who deserved to be broken up with. But not a lost cause. He yanked the duvet off me and kicked the side of my bed until I rolled out of it and got in the shower.

I stood under the seething water, blasting the indulgent crust off my body, feeling better for it but still a long way from the revelation that I'd been holding onto Louise beyond all reason. Past the departure of real tenderness and affection. My need for her, the unbearable thought of being alone again, had come to resemble love. But the truth was, Louise and I had not been in a relationship for months, not in any way that had mattered. She'd never told me it would be a long-term thing. Had made none of the declarations that lived in my head. She wasn't responsible for everything I freighted our relationship with. Her only misstep had been in not kicking me harder and sooner.

These were all realisations that came in increments, over years. In that time, I've been the nice guy, the wrong guy, the fling and the bastard. The transitional relationship, the one that got away and the one that couldn't go

The Three Fs

away fast enough. I've been a fiancé, a husband, a divorcee and a husband all over again. Had I hesitated at the top of those stairs, Louise may have asked someone else for that light and I might have been none of these things. I'd have gone home to my virginity and my Jeff Buckley and Barry might still have his original nose. But instead, she reached out, brought me to the party and taught me the first few steps of a dance that, thirty years on, I'm still trying to get right. It's possible that, in one of those infinite universes, I master the steps. But I suspect not. Because, while the possibilities might be endless, there are limits to everything.

Broken Biscuits

My mother and I were sitting in her living room discussing Nico, the stripper she'd met the previous evening.

'He had a woman with him, looking after his clothes and things, and she was really young,' she said, pausing to dunk the tip of a penis-shaped biscuit into her tea. 'And I thought "Well, that's a bit inappropriate."'

She tapped her biscuit against the rim of her mug then bit off a rough inch.

'But it gets worse,' she continued, speaking through her mouthful. 'Turns out the woman was his daughter!'

'Oh God!' I replied, and almost dropped my own penis biscuit.

On the coffee table between us sat an open, square tin, its lid to one side, bearing an embossed illustration of a fluffy kitten surrounded by flowers. The tin was full of these biscuits, made by my mother to be handed out the previous night at The Ozone Club, a small entertainment

Broken Biscuits

venue tucked away on a residential street just a two-minute walk from the beach. It was there that she had appeared as the warm-up act for Nico as part of a combination burlesque, bingo and strip show simply called *Ladies Night*.

These sorts of circumstances are not unusual for my mother, who for the last decade has been the eldest member of the Ruby Red Performers, a mature-aged burlesque troupe based in my hometown of Withernsea on the East Yorkshire coast. This late-life career has seen her dance on primetime TV, at festivals and once as the after-dinner act at a business conference in Birmingham that she prefers not to talk about. *Ladies Night* was just the latest in a long list of invitations for her to dance the can-can while dressed in her underwear. She's never been happier, and I have never been happier for her. Still, when she was asked to share a stage with Nico, I grew concerned that she might have entered troubling new frontiers. Her own concerns, though, lay elsewhere.

Not one to resist a theme, she'd struck upon the idea of making phallic biscuits to hand out to patrons during the bingo portion of the evening. The ones we were eating had been her failed first drafts, hand cut, formed and baked the day before she'd managed to source a penis-shaped cookie cutter from a friend, of whom she'd asked no follow-up questions. The biscuits in the tin between us were the defects. Short, long, fat, thin, a galaxy of shapes

Broken Biscuits

much closer to the array you'd see if you stopped a random group of men in the street and asked them to drop their underwear. But for *Ladies Night*, they were simply not good enough.

'I couldn't hand those out,' she told me. 'What would people think?'

What *I* was thinking about at that moment was my then seventy-year-old mother, diligently shaping penises from cookie dough, popping them in the oven then critiquing the results like a judge on *Bake Off*. I was also thinking of my father who, too self-conscious to eat them while anyone else was watching and in contravention of his diabetes, had already covertly grabbed a handful and taken them upstairs where he sat in bed, snacking on them while listening to *Sounds of the Sixties* on Radio 2.

It's true that penises, like biscuits, come in all different shapes and sizes and that each, for the most part, has its place. As far as I know, my own is not alarming from either end of the spectrum. No one has ever gasped at it in shock and awe. But then, no one has laughed at it or sighed in disappointment, either. It's just a penis, neither so small nor so monstrously large that anyone has ever felt compelled to rush from a bedroom and phone a friend for advice on how to handle it. But as I finished off a cookie and selected another that very much dressed to the left, I thought of how the best days of my penis might have been over.

* * *

Broken Biscuits

Up until the age of forty, my penis had been, if nothing else, at least dependable. Then I injured it and everything changed. I could go into details, and if we ever meet and you ask me for specifics, I'll tell you whatever you'd like to know. But for narrative purposes, what's important is that I tore my foreskin while having sex and my reaction to this was so extreme you'd have thought I'd been shot in the stomach. Anguished, bloodied and sore, I gathered up my wounded penis and made an urgent appointment with my GP, Dr Kay.

I have never been afraid of removing my clothes in front of Dr Kay. He gets a salary large enough to enjoy a nice house in the better part of town, and in exchange for that he must occasionally examine my naked body. And he's efficient about it, too, appointments with him often done and dusted in under two minutes, leaving his patients feeling as if they've just been subjected to the rigours of a small, localised tornado.

Over the years he has prodded me, squeezed me and, a few times, referred me to hospitals for further tests, where I have been swabbed, internally examined and, once, had my testicles subjected to an ultrasound. As a result of Dr Kay's attention, I have lowered my trousers and hoped for the best before a parade of doctors, nurses and trainees, none of whom, I felt confident, would be likely to pick me out from a line-up, trousered or otherwise. With a medical professional, you are very much in the company of

Broken Biscuits

people who have seen it all before and only remember the remarkable few.

'Honestly,' a doctor I met at a party once drunkenly told me, leaning against me for support, 'you'd have to be a sideshow exhibit for anyone to remember you thirty seconds after you left the room. We're too busy for …' he paused to lightly burp, his lips heavy with drink, '… too busy for the mundane.'

But this time was different. Nothing about my situation felt mundane. Everything about it was new and exposing. Because it didn't feel like I was there to discuss an illness, but a weakness. I might not have been physically memorable, but I wasn't interested in securing my place in Dr Kay's memoirs. What I wanted was for him to fix an injury that had left me feeling like a victim of war, the walking wounded, and once a man starts talking about his personal struggles in military terms, it is clear that there is going to be trouble.

'What seems to be the problem?' Dr Kay asked, as I sat down opposite him.

It's a subtle question and doctors use it all the time. It broadly asks, 'What do *you* think is wrong with you?'– providing them with enough information to completely flip your self-diagnosis on its head and leave you feeling foolish but relieved. I might walk into Dr Kay's surgery having been convinced by Google that I have cancer of the buttocks then leave with a prescription for antibiotics or a topical ointment along with the sense that all was right with the world. But sitting with him that day and explaining what had happened to me, there was no 'seems to be' about it. There was just 'the problem'.

When I was done detailing my circumstances, Dr Kay snapped on a pair of latex gloves, asked me to lower my trousers then knelt before me as if in proposal. But instead of presenting me with a diamond ring in a velvet box, it would have appeared to an onlooker that he was presenting me with my own penis, which lay on the flat of his hand in as sorry a state as it had ever been.

'I don't see anything wrong with that,' he said, prodding at it with his finger, and I found myself thinking of an old joke that my brother, Robert was fond of telling.

'This bloke goes to his doctors, right, and he says "I *urgently* need you to look at my penis! Seriously, it's important. I *absolutely* need you to look at it, RIGHT NOW!" The doctor hurries the bloke into his office, who pulls down his trousers to reveal a three-foot long, six-inch wide penis. The doctor examines it and says, "Well, I can't see anything wrong with that," and the bloke says, "I know, fucking *magnificent*, isn't it?"'

At this, Robert would always laugh as if it was the first time he'd told this joke, and I would laugh as if it was the first time I'd heard it. But Dr Kay did not seem to be in this for laughs. He was too busy lifting up my penis, turning it over and inspecting the wound, hmming to himself as if he was deciding to put in an offer.

'Okay,' I expected him to say, 'I'll give you a hundred quid for it. Ninety for cash.'

Instead, he told me I didn't need it. I took a sharp intake of breath, my eyes widening in shock.

'The foreskin,' he clarified. 'No one needs it.'

I need it, I thought, suddenly possessive about a part of my body that, like my chin or my ears, I'd barely spent any time thinking about during the preceding four decades. But now, just like those parts of me, I desperately wanted to keep it.

'Basically,' Dr Kay said, getting to his feet and removing his gloves, 'you have three options here: deal with it, try to have it repaired or cut it off.'

I gasped again. He rolled his eyes.

'The *foreskin*,' he said, exasperated with me this time, his clock ticking. I knew I was being absurd, but I couldn't work with ambiguity. Clarity of language is important when someone is holding your dick in their hand and deciding its fate.

As much as I didn't want things to change, just dealing with it didn't feel like an option. At that moment, living with my injury made as much sense as trying to 'walk off' a compound fracture of the tibia. Repairing it was, Dr Kay warned, unreliable and would likely lead to another tear and further surgery, the value of my penis dropping with each procedure. So, seemingly left with no real choice, I opted to cut it off, having for the third time made absolutely certain exactly what he was advocating the cutting of.

Dr Kay rolled his eyes again, tossed his gloves into a medical waste bin and told me I'd soon receive a letter where I'd get *everything* in writing. Then he opened his office door and ushered me into the hallway with just enough time for me to zip up my trousers. I passed through the waiting room and out into the street in a daze.

My usual reflex after a medical appointment is to phone my mother, my confidante in all things. But I didn't feel able to share this just yet. This injury had come with a new level of vulnerability that I wasn't quite ready or able to articulate. So, I headed back to my flat to consider my new situation, which was that, heading into middle age, I would be having the kind of operation most commonly experienced by children. But it was more than that, because a part of my body would be completely different. Forever changed. I'd had operations before, my body over the years becoming branded with a legion of permanent scars. The difference was that the prospect of this one had left me with an unsettling sense of imbalance and fear.

Stepping through my front door, I felt a sense of trepidation. My flat was not a place of comfort or solace at that time. My then-girlfriend and I were in the process of an amicable but painful break-up, my injury having occurred during what, beforehand at least, could have accurately been described as 'a last hurrah'. So, the flat did not feel like a home. Instead, it was in disarray, most of my girlfriend's things packed up in transparent, plastic storage boxes, which offered a diffused view of the books, crockery and ornaments that had once been part of our shared life. That coming weekend I planned to drive her with these boxes from Manchester to her mother's flat in London. So I saw a symbolism in our relationship, one I dramatically vowed would be my last, ending with the bloody finality of a ripped penis. This wasn't just the end of our relationship but the end of me as a man. Of course, I didn't admit any of these thoughts to her. I just told her how my appointment had gone.

'You'll be okay,' she said, hugging me then pulling me in close for a kiss. This was part of the reason we were breaking up. Sex was our reflex action and the only thing about our relationship that had ever really worked, which meant it was no kind of relationship to be a part of. More importantly, though, her embrace highlighted something else that wasn't working. Despite the heat of her body against mine, the charge of the kiss, my penis was unresponsive.

A man is a basic bit of machinery. We can be turned on in the grip of despair, sickness and torment. I've had sex while suffering from the flu, while suicidal and once while still heavily bandaged and woozy following knee surgery. A man could find himself pinned under the wheels of a forty-ton truck but if an offer of sex was made then God damn it, he'd find a way to give it a try. So, the fact that this part of me was dormant left me concerned. Still, I tried my best to shove that thought down, telling myself that I was actually being true to my emotions and respectful of the situation, my body seemingly accepting that this was truly the end for us. That she was no longer my girlfriend but my ex. Besides, I was wounded. What had I expected? So, I wriggled from her arms and began stacking boxes next to the front door ready to load into the car.

The next day at work, I asked for a quiet chat with my boss, Amina. We slipped into a meeting room, where I explained that I'd need a couple of weeks off for the operation and my recovery, giving her only the necessary headlines. She was understanding and sympathetic about it, explaining that I could take all the time I needed. Then I proved how much I didn't deserve that level of sympathy by heading back into the office and regaling my colleague Denis with the details of why I required the operation.

'Oh God,' he said, involuntarily crossing his legs as he pictured the circumstances and the wound itself. I was aware of what was going on even as I spoke. That I was peacocking. A sex injury comes with at least the confirmation that sex had taken place and there was a cachet in that. And by engaging with the storytelling, I could obscure the trauma at the heart of it and temporarily reduce the terror I felt. But it was more than that: I was recounting a story that spoke to the worst male fears.

Men share tales of sexual calamity with the prolonged excitement of a fireside horror story. Knowing they have you on the hook, they will draw out every detail, building to a grim finale. The master of this was an old retail colleague of mine named Martin, who delighted in telling new members of staff about the catastrophic sexual mishap suffered by one of his friends. He'd take an innocent situation, someone painfully stubbing their toe in the stockroom for example, and find a way to pivot to his story.

'You think that hurts?' he'd say. 'I knew a guy who broke his dick.'

The conversational equivalent of a 'SEX! Now I've got your attention' small ad, this line guaranteed Martin an invested audience. He'd then hold court, a grisly smile splitting his face as he detailed his friend's drunken, passionate liaison. After a couple of minutes of scene setting, he'd shift into the disaster itself. 'He heard a pop, like a firework going off, and that …' Martin would pause for effect, echoing the moment before a rollercoaster suddenly descends, 'was the sound of his *tunica albuginea* snapping.'

Broken Biscuits

He'd take a moment then to delight in our flinches and groans, none of us having any idea what a *tunica albuginea* was but instinctively knowing that breaking one couldn't be a good thing. Then he'd add a final flourish.

'Couldn't walk for *months*,' he'd say, these words released like the sigh that follows a big and satisfying meal. 'Pure. Agony.'

I have lost count of the tales I've heard like this over the years. Stories of men whose penises were shredded by vacuum-cleaner hoses. Motorcycle accidents that resulted in genitals transferred from bodies and onto tarmac in a devastating instant. The man whose virulent urethra infection led to an operation where his penis was bisected like a hot-dog bun. I've been subjected to an anthology of severings, tearings and life-ruining experiences shared for entertainment and with little sympathy, like tales of triple murders on true-crime podcasts. As a result of these stories, I know the terms 'degloving', 'penile strangulation' and, of course, *tunica albuginea*. These stories exist to offer the vicarious thrill of a situation that, but for the grace of God, could happen to any one of us and ruin our lives completely. But driving home from work that evening, freed from the oxygen of conversation and with only my injury for company, it was *my* life that was about to become one of these cautionary tales. God, I feared, had shown me none of his grace.

Broken Biscuits

That weekend I packed my ex-girlfriend's things into my car and drove her with them back to London, where I spent a depressed and fitful night's sleep on her mother's sofa before returning to a flat that was now a space full of new spaces. Rooms where there were missing objects, furniture voids and the complete absence of intimacy. Even under normal circumstances this would be unbearable but especially so given my situation. So, I busied myself looking for a new home.

During the weeks when I wasn't trawling Rightmove for properties or staring into estate agent windows, I was worrying about my penis. What bothered me was that, since the injury, it had remained inactive. It was still sore, but I expected something from it. A stirring, at least. I could no longer fool myself that this was out of respect for my lost relationship. That my genitals were simply as sad as I was and not really in the mood right now. It was becoming clear to me that there was a bigger problem, and once I acknowledged that, it became increasingly difficult to think clearly about Victorian semis and south-facing gardens.

Penises are dreadful things really, constantly expanding and contracting based on stimuli. And that stimulus is everywhere to some degree. In movies, on TV shows, in adverts designed to get you so apishly titillated that you'll immediately go out and buy whatever yoghurt or inkjet printer they're trying to sell you. My problem was that

Broken Biscuits

none of this was having an effect on me anymore. It sounds pathetic, I know, but without the shifting, reassuring weight of my penis, I felt lessened as a man. I considered all the times I'd taken it for granted. Had cursed those troublesome erections during my teens that sprang into action on bus journeys just before I had to get off at my stop. Or while working my first job in a supermarket and happened to read the word 'breasts' on a pack of chicken. This unwelcome presence that I felt everyone was aware of, as if it had arrived in my underpants with the resonant clang of a church bell.

Now there was an emptiness, this part of me that no longer had a mind of its own. That perhaps no longer had a mind at all. It had been the thing that sent me into this latest ultimately damaging relationship and now here I was, sitting in an apartment I could no longer afford on a single salary, staring glumly at my crotch. My kingdom for a resonant clang.

In time I put in a successful offer on a house and, on the day that I'd arranged to exchange contracts, I received a letter informing me that my circumcision had been scheduled for one week after my move-in date. This, I felt certain, was a sign. A new home and, shortly thereafter, a new penis, courtesy of the operation that would make everything better. During those first few days in the house, I set about redecorating as if I was preparing for the arrival of a baby. Fretful but excited about my fresh start.

Broken Biscuits

The following week, I took a taxi to the hospital urology department where I was taken through a pre-op discussion with my surgeon, Dr Patel. He mentioned a lot of the risks, reeled off to me in the dull, perfunctory manner of a waitress repeating your order back to you on the day she'd finally decided to quit. To Dr Patel it was an everyday conversation but what I heard was yet another horror story. I could suffer erectile dysfunction, he said; disruption to my urinary tract; everything up to, but hopefully not including, death. Still, he seemed pretty chill about the whole thing, assuring me the risks were low. And really, what choice did I have? So, I put my faith in him and signed the consent paperwork. I was then ushered into a room and asked to change into surgical robes then climb onto a gurney to await the arrival of Peter, my anaesthesiologist.

Peter arrived in the room with the effervescent energy of a game show host, chatty and jovial as if he wasn't about to knock me unconscious and let someone take a scalpel to the tip of my penis. I attempted to meet this energy with light conversation, compelled to act unconcerned, like I got circumcisions all the time.

'So, how many of these do you do a day?' I asked.

'Guess,' he said.

'A thousand?'

'Well, that's just silly.'

He fitted an IV into the back of my hand, injected a milky-looking fluid and told me to count backwards from ten. I was aware of nothing between slurring the number seven and coming to in a recovery room under harsh lights, my mouth as furred and pillowy as a cat's bed.

'Hello!' a nurse said, appearing at my side. 'Do you want a cup of tea?'

'My mum's ... a burlesque dancer,' I croaked.

'Well, that's the first time someone's woken up and said that.'

'She was on ... *Britain's Got ... Talent.*'

'Okay, love. Do you want a cup of tea?'

'Yes, please.'

'And a biscuit?'

'Two ... please,' I said, rubbing at my face with clumsy, drugged hands as I tried to work out if I was wearing my glasses or not.

Because I could not be trusted to leave the hospital in this state, I arranged for my friend Kate to drive me home and keep an eye on me while the drugs wore off. She arrived to pick me up, helping me get my things together while, still spaced and groggy, I sipped my tea and smilingly listened to a nurse as she explained how I should care for my stitches and apply fresh dressings over the days that followed.

'Kate might like to help you with that,' she said, mistaking her for my partner.

'Kate might *not* like to help with that,' Kate said, as we headed out to her car.

Broken Biscuits

The painkillers were strong, and I felt nothing during the bumpy drive out of the car park and along the pothole-addled streets that led to my house, my entire body feeling as if it was bound in bubble wrap. Everything seemed beyond okay.

I levitated through my front door and onto the sofa, where I sat dopily blinking while Kate made me a coffee. She stayed with me until my head cleared, and I was able to reassure her I was fine. Felt great, even.

'Well, call me if you need anything,' she said as she climbed into her car.

'I will,' I replied. 'But don't worry. I'm fine.'

Then I closed the front door, sat back down on the sofa and felt the first painful suggestions of the drugs wearing off. I swallowed a couple of painkillers and, as advised by the nurse, resisted the temptation to unwrap the bandage and examine my scars. Instead, I sat open-legged on the sofa, re-watching *Louis Theroux's Weird Weekends* and trying not to think about my penis, which hung between my thighs as cumbersome and unsettling as a mummified baguette.

I waited until the third day before taking a bath and removing my bandage, using the same level of care I would have applied had I been defusing a bomb. Unwinding the dressings, I surprised myself by not being distressed by what I saw. My penis had a new appearance, but the sight of it wasn't upsetting to me. Bruised and swollen, it had clearly been in quite the fight, but it was still recognisably that part of me. The only things that gave me pause were the numerous black stitches along the incisions, which had left it looking as if it was being attacked by spiders. This felt like one of the few circumstances that could have made the whole situation worse for me. Then I tested out exactly how bad things could get by turning to the internet for advice on what would happen next.

The hopeful, naive part of me liked to assume that my penis would just re-enter the world with a new look, like a *Real Housewives* cast member returning for the latest season largely unchanged except for a different nose, or the telltale signs of buccal fat removal. But the dominant part of my brain, always tuned to worst-case scenarios, wanted to know how long the discomfort would persist and when my penis would regain consciousness. So, I typed 'how long recovery circumcision' into Google and found dozens of forums where men were talking about the fallout of their procedures. If there's one thing that can be guaranteed on the internet it's that if you put in the effort, you'll find answers. Invariably they will not be the answers you're looking for, but you'll find them all the same.

On every message board and thread that I checked, I found the same thing: men in distress, each of them looking for the same kinds of reassurances that I wanted.

Broken Biscuits

Many were in far worse states than I was. These were men who, post-circumcision, were now insisting their penises were misshapen. That the scar tissue had tightened, leading to painful erections or disruptions to the healing process. Some claimed that their penises had dramatically reduced in size. These were men who, like me, had placed their faith in operations they believed would make things better and now had doubts.

Following links from these posts, I went down a deep rabbit hole of male anguish. Stories of procedures designed to repair and enhance, which led to more drama and tortured testimony. Men who believed they had undersized penises and sought the extensions and implants that would change their lives had instead had them ruined by them. Everywhere I looked, I found guys in toxic relationships with their genitalia, and I was no exception. We were the saddest of oxymorons; a solitary collective, each of us plaintively wandering the forums alone and wailing for answers from folks who couldn't really offer much beyond additional fear.

So, I backed away from the internet, knowing I was doing myself no good. Instead, I focused on my recovery and, following hospital guidance, eventually removed the bandage completely to allow for the next healing stage. What followed was pain. A lot of it. The sensation of my clothing touching my penis felt like a blade was being dragged across it. On necessary trips to the supermarket,

Broken Biscuits

my movements were so shuffling and elderly that I considered asking to use the store's mobility scooter. I returned home each time sweating, my jaw aching from clenching my teeth. When I was alone in the house, I kept my curtains drawn, sparing myself the pain caused by my underwear and walking around naked from the waist down, like a giant toddler who'd escaped a nappy change.

I'd not been warned about this, so I risked checking the forums where someone recommended the application of Vaseline to ease the friction of contact with clothing. I slathered myself with it and the discomfort immediately became bearable, allowing me the luxury of being able to make my way around the supermarket without anyone assuming I'd shat my pants. In time the bruising and swelling reduced and my penis would eventually become something I was pretty happy with. I returned to work, making light of what I'd been through, and tried not to think about the fact that, while there had been some activity during a YouTube advert for yoga pants, I hadn't experienced a proper erection since my surgery. But this, I told myself, was *all part of the process*.

My surgeon had advised me to refrain from sex for six to eight weeks. This would be my recovery time, during which my penis would surely completely repair itself. I just had to give it time. Two months and I'd be back. I wasn't like those other guys on the forums. I'd avoided the disfigurement and all the risks Dr Patel had warned me about. Dodged a bullet. I was going to be fine. By the eighth week, I felt hopeful enough about my future to sign up for a dating app.

I'd never used online dating before, but I went out for drinks with a few women and began feeling pretty good about my new beginning. Occasionally, I would go to bed with someone and, just as I'd hoped, my body behaved like its old self, the excitement of the new overcoming my intrusive thoughts about injuries or that troubling dormancy. Increasingly, though, it failed me completely. And the more it failed, the greater my fear of failure, creating a self-fulfilling prophecy. In those times when the conditions were correct, when I wasn't thinking too much and was relaxed or distracted, everything returned to how it had always been, and I could allow myself to believe that things might be back to normal. More often, there were long periods of emptiness, where I was left waiting for erections with the same level of patience some people apply to sitting out the arrival of rare migratory birds. My love life became slowly dominated by apology and the dwindling light of my confidence.

Because fragile masculinity is a billion-dollar industry, I knew there were ways to tackle problems like this. Viagra, Cialis, a gum called Blue Chew that I'd heard ads for on podcasts. They seemed to be just the thing to restore my self-belief. I just needed to get my head around the injury and required a little chemical boost, that was

Broken Biscuits

all. So, I placed an order and a box of plain-packaged ED medication arrived in the post, which I confidently took, expecting the instant arrival of an erection so robust I could have used it to prise up a floorboard. But nothing I tried had any effect. I may as well have been eating Skittles for all the good they did me. So, I returned to the forums to find out if anyone else was experiencing the same issues as me. What I found were legions of men who felt similarly lost and emasculated after their procedures.

I regret my circumcision every day, one post read. *It ruined my life. My penis doesn't even feel mine anymore.*

This was increasingly how I felt. My penis no longer looked or felt like the autonomous organ that had urged me on through life. Had made me socialise despite my lack of inclination, made me talk to women, dance, get on stage and play guitar. If I followed every achievement of my adult life back to its source, my penis was right there, willing me on.

'Go on, son,' it seemed to say. 'Trust me, this is good for us.'

The problem was that it was increasingly saying nothing at all, and without its voice I didn't know who I was. It's been said that the penis is the antenna to a man's soul, and I had thought myself somehow better than that. But it seemed my masculinity was just as precarious as every other guy's. Until my injury, I'd not realised how centred I was on my genitals, how vital they were, and this discov-

Broken Biscuits

ery was embarrassing. Now I was reading forum posts by men much further down the recovery road than me, who felt the same way. For whom things were not getting better and whose situations were not only embarrassing, they had become desperate.

Honestly, I'm not sure I can go on like this, one post read, echoing so many others I found. *I feel like ending it all.*

And the more I read posts like this, the more I found myself thinking about my brother, Robert.

Not long after the birth of his fourth child, which arrived just ten months after his third, Robert had elected to get a vasectomy. Logistically, it made sense. In an era of low infant mortality, four children is enough for anyone to secure a genetic legacy. Robert, characteristically, did not phrase it that way.

'I need to give her a rest,' he told me with a wink, nodding in the direction of his wife. This on the day he referred to their bed as 'my workbench'.

It was not surprising to hear him talk this way. For most of his life, Robert could have been adequately described as a life-support system for a set of genitals. I have never known anyone more driven by carnality. To grow up in his shadow was to receive the message that a day without sex was a wasted one, his rampaging libido firing him through life with the momentum of a cannonball. But everything had its limits, not least the sleeping

Broken Biscuits

capacity of his three-bedroom home, so he headed off to the doctor to undergo what he believed would be a simple procedure.

Very soon afterwards, things started to go wrong. A complication or an infection, he was never clear with me about the root cause, but what matters is that Robert's testicles swelled to the size and colour of aubergines. At first, he made light of this, flashing them at us in the hope of eliciting a shriek of alarm. But then they became tender and painful. He began favouring baggy shorts, his gait stiff-legged as he waddled along to his GP for advice. He was prescribed painkillers but would also somehow source extra-strong ones from a less official source. Then there was the drinking, the antidepressants. To curb his alcohol intake, he took Antabuse, but even the vomiting it induced could not dissuade him. While I'll never be exactly sure why he took his own life, it seems there was a clear line from his operation to the overdose of pills that ultimately removed him from the world. And now, just like him and so many others on the forums, I was feeling changed and on the edge of something irreversible.

One of the main differences between Robert and me is that I have never been all that shy about discussing my feelings. While he saw speaking about his problems as a weakness, I recognised it as one of my few strengths. Robert had a lot of strengths, many more than I have, but

Broken Biscuits

his were mostly literal. If you wanted someone to throw a punch or demolish a wall, you turned to Robert. Vulnerability, though, was unnatural to him. The few times I saw him give into it, I also saw what it took from him. How it left him feeling reduced. But now I was living with the one thing I couldn't bear to open up about, scared that this thing was eating away at me and would keep going until I vanished entirely.

For my whole life, there hasn't been a single subject that I was ever afraid to discuss with my mother. I could pick up the phone and tell her anything, knowing I would never receive judgement, only love and advice. At the very least, she offered a release valve for the pressure my thoughts often caused in my head. But now I was experiencing something I could not talk about, an embarrassment so great I couldn't even discuss it with someone I knew would only respond with sympathy. She would not idly allow another of her boys to slip away from her, and to that end I'd promised after Robert's death to never keep a painful secret from her. With this one, though, I walled myself in. While I'd told her about the injury and the operation, I was not able to talk about the rest. It was strange to find myself unable to fully communicate for the first time, as if there was a limit to the reach of my voice. I was starting to feel like Robert might have felt. And worse, I was beginning to see the logic in the decision he'd made.

Broken Biscuits

Under one of the forum posts discussing suicide, someone had pasted a heavily saturated image of a California sunrise, overlaid with text:

Don't give up. Keep going. Have faith in yourself.

When everything's going okay with your life, inspirational quotes can easily come off as trite and meaningless horseshit. But when you're on the floor and all out of ideas, *live, laugh, love* language can read like the wisdom of the elders. And reading this one, I was surprised to feel a boost. An urge to keep going. So, hopeful that I might be reinvigorated by a baptism of fire, I gave dating one more try.

I was honest with the women I dated, explaining that I was in recovery from a circumcision, which wasn't the full, mortifying picture but offered enough of it that it set their expectations. I was not advertising myself as a man whose penis they should bet the farm on. So, I was surprised each time to be told that it didn't matter. Of course, I'm aware that women are painfully used to soothing male egos, suppressing their frustrations and deploying phrases like 'It's okay' and 'It doesn't matter'. Words so familiar to women it feels like they must be taught to recite them as part of sex ed. But it seemed that I'd matched with women who genuinely didn't care.

'You've got hands,' I was told, airily. 'You've got a mouth.' And once, the words preceded by a sigh of relief,

Broken Biscuits

'At least we can have a decent conversation without it having to end with a dick in my hands.'

It seemed to me that while men flounder, feeling inadequate about the lack of the twelve-inch cock and tantric endurance that they've become convinced every woman demands of them, no one, in fact, spends more time thinking about penises than the people who possess them. And proof of this seemed to arrive when one of my dates blossomed into a relationship.

But despite the accumulated wisdom of the people I dated, I found a way to fuck things up for myself, unable to get my head around the idea that my penis didn't really matter. However much my girlfriend might have told me she loved me, I found myself needy for reassurance. Always requiring more. I overcompensated with gifts and grand gestures, desperate to make up for what I felt was the missing piece of our relationship. But neediness is exhausting and the unsexiest thing of all, so when we finally broke up I blamed myself entirely. More accurately, I blamed my genitals, cursing them for destroying everything. And because no problem has ever been solved by shouting at a penis, I decided it was high time that I sought professional help.

At first, I turned to a specialist online service for erectile dysfunction, where I was asked to complete a multiple-choice 'sexology' survey that would go on to dictate the flavour of therapy I'd receive.

Broken Biscuits

How often are you stuck in your head during sex? I was asked.

I selected the option, *Almost always.*

How often do you worry about your erections in your daily life?

I selected the option, *Most of the time.*

After two dozen questions like this, I was finally offered the choice of online group therapy or a series of self-teaching modules. I decided on the latter. Not dissimilar to an online recipe, there were nine sections to complete, the idea being that, at the end, there was the very real possibility that I'd be rewarded with the kind of penis I'd had aged twenty.

In the first module, I was taught about the parasympathetic and sympathetic nervous systems, the latter of which controls the fight-or-flight response – a reflex that kicks in during times of peril and goes back to neanderthal times, when there was a realistic daily chance of being torn to pieces by a bear. Fight-or-flight increases your heart rate, sending your blood rushing to your muscles, and away from any cumbersome erection you might have had at the time of attack, allowing you the strength to run like hell. My problem, it seemed, was that my brain couldn't distinguish between the immediate threat of disembowelment and the anxiety I felt when presented with a naked, consenting woman.

Broken Biscuits

Next, I was asked to 'enter into a dialogue' with my inner critic, the voice that was devouring my confidence.

If the owner of this voice wore clothes, I was asked, *what do you think they'd wear? Where are they? Do they stand somewhere near you?*

I pictured my inner critic standing at the foot of my bed, a figure that was unambiguously Robert, a look of disappointment on his face. I closed my eyes and tried to think past this but found myself unexpectedly breathless, my heart pounding, signalling what felt like an incoming panic attack. My sympathetic nervous system kicked in and I snapped my laptop shut.

Deciding it was time I spoke to an actual therapist, I contacted an agency that specialised in 'intimacy issues' and was paired with a guy named Philip, who arranged a Zoom consultation that same week. When he appeared on my screen, his office decor new-age and Buddhism adjacent, I made a snap judgement. I usually find that sort of ornamentation to be a red flag, indicating the lair of a woo-woo bullshit artist. But when he introduced himself, his voice a warm, reassuring vocal fry, I immediately felt at ease and knew I'd come to the right person.

'Tell me everything,' he purred.

'Where should I start?'

'With the injury.'

I was used to that, at least: starting with the horror story. So, I described everything that had happened. The injury itself. The way I rushed to the shower to inspect the wound, watching the blood pour from me and circle the drain. 'Like that scene from *Psycho*,' I said, treating Philip as an audience I needed to entertain.

He didn't smile. Instead, he listened patiently to everything I told him, then he carried on listening, his quiet presence passively nudging me into talking about everything. I choked my way through all my problems. The fears, secrets, embarrassments and insecurities. Philip nodded gently through all of it, as if enjoying a playlist of smooth jams. Then finally, when I was done and he'd had time to think about it, he spoke.

'Okay, well you're clearly traumatised. From the injury, the operation, all of it. There's no pill for this. It's psychological. We have a lot of work to do.'

He was telling me what I instinctively already knew. Getting the confirmation from a professional, though – not from a forum or a prerecorded lecture but someone I could really talk to, was like receiving a gift. I felt as if I'd breathed in on the day of the injury and hadn't properly breathed out until I spoke to Philip. Despite the official confirmation that I had handed over control of my penis to my brain and, in doing so, had given it to my worst enemy, I didn't feel so bad. It wasn't the greatest. I'd have much preferred him to say, 'You know, I have just the thing,' then detail the easily obtainable, herbal medication that was 100 per cent guaranteed to take me back to that

Broken Biscuits

old, resonant clang. But Philip was offering solutions. There would be breathing exercises, techniques, deeper therapy; a long road, but importantly he offered the comfort that, finally, I was not alone in dealing with it. And in reaching this point, there was another conversation I needed to have.

'I'm in therapy,' I said, as my mother placed a fresh a pot of tea down beside the tin of biscuits. 'From my operation.'

I told her about the complications, the pain, how insane the whole thing had made me over the years and how perilous it had become. Like Philip, she listened quietly, waiting for me to finish speaking. To stop apologising for not telling her sooner and for failing to uphold the vow we'd made since Robert's death. Then, when I was done, she delivered a flood of warmth and care. No chastisement for keeping it to myself. She gave me everything I should have been brave enough to ask her for years ago. And also, something unexpected.

'You know, your dad had the same operation,' she said, 'when he was a boy.'

'Why didn't you tell me about that?'

'You didn't ask.'

I tried to imagine a universe where I would have thought to ask that question. Then I thought of my father upstairs, who'd recovered from the same procedure as me

Broken Biscuits

and went on to have children, support a dozen grandchildren and maintain a marriage to a burlesque dancer for almost fifty years. This emblem of a way forward, snoozing on his bed, his sweater littered with biscuit crumbs.

'Don't try to discuss it with him, though,' my mother warned, reading my mind. She plucked another penis from the tin and dunked it into her tea. 'Not everyone needs to talk about everything.'

Taken

I was scrolling through Facebook one evening, when I saw a status update from my friend, Nigel.

'Can anyone help me pick up a bike from Middleton Road way?'

Everyone knew what this message meant. We'd been following the story of Nigel's stolen bike for weeks. Someone had taken it one evening while he was drinking inside The Ostrich, a pub just a short cycle ride from his house. They'd cut the guttering that he'd chained it to and disappeared into the night, leaving Nigel shocked and bereft. As thefts go it was swift and professionally done, but the people who'd taken it had created a problem for themselves.

Nigel's bike was bright orange. The kind of radioactive citrus glow that soft drinks companies use to hammer home the idea that their product is teeth-rottingly juicier than any of the competition. It was Flymo orange. Hi-vis

Broken Biscuits

orange. There's a reason that Batman's costume is not tangerine, and we all know it without it needing to be explained to us. Whoever had stolen Nigel's bike would be conspicuous and easy to track down.

What they also probably didn't reckon on was how much Nigel adored his bike. Doted on it, kept it spotless and well maintained. There are members of the King's Guard who polish their boots with less assiduousness than Nigel applied to the chrome fixtures and whitewall tyres of his bicycle. So, when it was stolen, he demonstrated the same vengeful intensity that Liam Neeson displayed in the movie *Taken*, and headed out onto the streets to get it back.

We all thought he'd find it immediately. Even at night, Nigel's bike glowed like the element on an electric stove top. But he spent days looking for it, his eyes keenly calibrated to register flashes of orange. Double-taking at people in his peripheral vision eating Wotsits or drinking from cans of Fanta. When pounding the streets got him nowhere, he assumed his bike must be stashed somewhere ready to be sold, so took his search online. He trawled auction sites, obsessively refreshing the Bikes for Sale listings until, after a couple of days, it appeared, unmistakably his baby and priced at £150. He immediately contacted the seller and arranged to view it. But rather than pay the ransom, what he'd decided to do was steal it from the people who'd stolen it from him. And for that, he'd need help.

Taken

'I just want it back,' he added under his post. 'Nothing more than that.'

At first, there had been no response to his plea, and I got scared. Initially, by the idea that Nigel would go alone and get himself killed.

It's true that, just like Liam Neeson, Nigel has a very particular set of skills, but they're not necessarily tuned to combat. He's athletic but most notable for being a champion retro runner, which means he can run backwards incredibly fast. Almost as fast as he can run forwards. But I didn't have faith that, if things turned ugly, he could slam his legs into reverse and remove himself from the situation at a speed that exceeded the spring mechanism of a flick knife. Like I say, though, he has other skills. I have seen him twirl four Hula Hoops simultaneously. I know that his go-to karaoke song is 'Borderline' by Madonna, which he sings impressively and occasionally while standing on a table. But it would be wrong of me to suggest that he'd attract strong odds should he decide to step into a boxing ring. And all this led to my second fear, which was that if no one else stepped forward, I'd have to volunteer to go with him.

Up until I reached middle school, I'd been a brawler. I was never the strongest or tallest kid, but the one quality I did have in a fight was my inability to stay down. It didn't matter how often I was knocked to the ground or how much older or bigger someone was than me, I would immediately pop back up with the dumb resilience of a freshly struck Whac-a-Mole. I rarely lost a fight, winning by default when my opponents grew exhausted and disturbed by the number of times they'd had to thump a small boy who kept getting up for more, my face glazed with blood, snot and tears.

The secret to what I guess qualifies as my success was a credo instilled in me by my elder brother, Robert.

'Never stay down,' he told me. 'Even if you lose a fight, you don't have to be a loser.'

In 2024 this reads like a direct route to a CTE diagnosis, but for a big portion of the 1980s I considered it a code that I had to live by. This meant I spent that same period getting the shit kicked out of me then struggling to my feet, a pint-sized Terminator in short pants and a bloodstained Spider-Man T-shirt. It's an image that's horrifying to me now, but it made Robert proud of me, and back then there was nothing I wanted more.

This all started when I was about eight years old. Perhaps a little younger. I'd arrived home in tears one afternoon, my lips bloody and the diagonal imprint of a shoe across my forehead. Robert had been making his way downstairs when I stepped through the front door and the sight of me stopped him halfway.

'What the fucking hell happened to you?' he said.

Taken

'These big kids just started hitting me,' I said, heading to the freezer in search of a strawberry ice pop to hold against my face. 'I don't know why.'

Of course, I knew exactly why. My friends and I had sworn at a couple of teenagers as they'd passed the spot where we were playing, thinking we were a safe enough distance from them to get away with it. But they'd chased us, I'd fallen, and they'd seen their moment, kicking and stamping on me as if there was a time limit and a prize at the end.

Robert followed me into the kitchen, demanding to know more, so I told him who these boys were and what they'd done but neglected to include the 'why'. As I spoke, his expression shifted through intrigue, concern and anger before finally settling on the kind of cold, shark-eyed look that would be familiar to anyone who has seen Charles Bronson in the movie *Death Wish*. It turned out he knew these boys, and that they both lived on a street over on the next estate. Robert headed out of the door without another word.

When he returned half an hour later, I was lying on the sofa with a cold flannel on my forehead, watching cartoons, the ice pop eaten. He looked amped up and victorious.

'What happened?' I asked, sitting up.

'They won't touch you again,' he said, smiling softly as if recalling a treasured memory. Though I pressed him for

Broken Biscuits

details, he refused to elaborate but I guessed it involved the reason he kept rubbing his knuckles. In any case, he had something else on his mind.

'Come on,' he said, wrenching me up off the sofa by my arm and leading me out into the garden, where he uprooted the rotary washing line and leaned it up against the wall of the house. Then he stood in front of me in the new open space he'd created, his palms raised.

'Hit me,' he said.

I was immediately suspicious. Offers like this from Robert had previously always been a precursor to a dead arm, or worse. I wasn't really in the mood to be messed with. My head still pounding, my teeth feeling loose.

'I don't …' I managed, but he jiggled his raised palms and altered his stance, placing his left leg out behind him. Bracing himself.

'Go on. Hit me. Or I'll hit you.'

I sighed, then threw a reluctant punch. It made a noise against Robert's left palm like a dollop of mashed potato hitting a plate. He sighed.

'Come on,' he said. 'Harder than that.'

I threw another punch. It made a clapping noise as it connected.

'That's better,' he said, making a show of shaking his hand as if the impact had stung him. 'Again. And keep your arm straight.'

I threw another punch.

Taken

'No, I said *straight*. Don't fucking swing it, aim it. And don't tuck your thumb in. If you hit someone like that, you'll break it.' He grabbed my fist and wrapped my thumb around my curled knuckles, remoulding it into something fight-ready. 'Okay, again.'

There was something of the old-timey boxing coach about Robert. The way he stopped to light a cigarette, then kept it clamped between his lips as he chastised me for my form and technique. But I could tell he was enjoying it, his whole face lighting up whenever I did something just the way he'd asked. In those moments I saw what he saw when he looked at me. The miniature replica of himself that would soon head out into the battlefield of our estate. Over the course of that afternoon, he taught me to keep my face protected with my free hand when I threw a punch. To follow through with my elbow when I could. That if all else failed I shouldn't be shy about kicking someone so hard in the balls that I'd hear all of the air go out of their body when my foot connected. And crucially, I was taught to never stay down.

'*... you don't have to be a loser.*'

So, while I didn't set out to start fights, once I was in one I used everything he'd taught me. And though I often came home with bruises or split lips, a fight never ended with me lying on the ground.

'Did you win?' Robert would ask whenever I limped into the house looking breathless and tenderised.

Broken Biscuits

I'd respond with a smile, giving the answer I knew he wanted to hear. Either a confident 'Yes' or a chirpy, increasingly false-feeling 'Well, I didn't lose.'

Robert once confessed to me that fighting was his second favourite thing, placing just behind sex and before Ozzy Osbourne live in concert. Something about squaring up to another guy and brawling until he could no longer lift his arms made him feel alive in a way that few other things did.

'It's a fucking rush, isn't it?' he said to me one morning over breakfast, recalling a punch-up he'd had outside a pub the previous night. His eye a proud purple, a raw scuff on his cheek.

'*Yeah*!' I replied, my response so enthusiastic that I almost believed it myself. But while the winning part was fine, the actual fighting never excited me. It wasn't just that my punches never landed with the speaker-distorting crack I'd heard in Indiana Jones movies or that every part of fighting simply hurt. It was that, while I dearly wanted to get the buzz that Robert got from combat, it never arrived. I'm not sure where fighting ranked for me exactly, but it placed some distance below the time I'd been clearing out a loft and accidentally thrust my hand into a wasps' nest.

I was born six years after Robert, the first child of my mother's second marriage. While he would end his days considering my father to be his own and us as full blood

Taken

brothers, early on there was a disconnect. A sense within him that he didn't quite fit in with the new configuration of his family. His own biological father was largely out of the picture by the time I came along, and in those years, in that gap, an anger seemed to grow in him. I was obliviously born into the dynamics of all this, but this anger was evident in my very earliest memories, all of which feature Robert. Robert smashing toys. Robert kicking wing mirrors off cars. Robert hurling a half brick through a window and running away. And in all of these memories, I am adoring him. So excited and impressed by everything he did. I wanted nothing more than to become just like him. And from what I could see, the best way to go about that seemed to involve raising my fists and hoping that, in time, that rush would become as natural to me as it was for him. If achieving that cost me several hundred blows to the head, then I'd take them. And I kept it up, until I was forced to consider the costs.

On my first day of middle school, during afternoon break, a boy named Jason walked up to me on the playing fields and brought his face up close to mine, snarling in a way that made me think of a public information film I'd seen about rabies.

'Do you think you're hard?' he queried.

'What?' I said dopily, caught off guard.

'I said, do you think you're hard?'

Broken Biscuits

My new school was much bigger than my previous one, introducing me to a broader cast of kids from estates much tougher than mine. Jason was one of those kids. Noticeably bigger than the rest of my year, he'd made himself additionally notorious by arriving at school that day with a lunch box containing only a sugar sandwich. What concerned me in that moment though was his question.

'No, I ...'

This was as far as I got before his fist caught me hard in the side of the head. There was a brief period of darkness, as if someone had rebooted the sun. Then I fell to the grass, shocked by both the blow and a new sensation. While I attempted to get up, I found that I couldn't. There was a whistling fizz in my ears and the sense that, somewhere inside me, a gong was being sounded.

'That's what you get!' Jason shouted, then stormed off, leaving me on the ground confused and waiting for my legs to restart themselves.

The following day, he came to me and apologised, having mistaken me for someone else, but by then the damage was already done. He'd knocked me to the ground with a single, devastating punch and everyone in my new school had seen it. This led to a pattern, as other heavy-handed kids tried their luck with me and found victory to be surprisingly fun and easy. I had never been in fights like this before, never hit with such harmful intent, and I didn't like it. If this was the price of Robert's admiration and the path to becoming just like him, I'd need to check my figures again. This I did while horizontal, preferring to get hit once or twice instead of twenty, and hoping that Robert would never find out.

Every time I hit the ground, though, I felt like I was letting him down. Of course, this thought was never in the moment. Things like that don't occur to you when someone is pinning your arms down with their knees while alternately punching you in the face and pressing clods of dirt into your mouth. You're too concerned with the humiliation, or the possibility that you might suffocate. On the floor and profoundly down for the count, I experienced the unique form of shame that only comes from publicly acknowledging your own inferiority. The type that makes you want to cry, but you know that to do so would be the only thing that could possibly make the situation worse.

'Say it,' I'd be asked by boys who stood over me with balled fists, not satisfied with having knocked me off my feet and wanting something more. 'Tell me you'll stay down.'

'I'll stay down,' I'd say, losing like a loser. Repeating their order for good measure. 'I'll stay down.'

But during the long walks home on those days, thoughts of failing Robert would consume me. I'd creep back into the house hoping to avoid him, so I could spend the post-

Broken Biscuits

fight healing days trying to only present him with the least bruised side of my face. Not wanting to be pushed into fraudulently claiming that I could still remember what winning felt like.

You'd think that once I'd been easily defeated a few times my appeal as a punchbag would wear off, but what happened was that I became community property. Regularly confronted with the kinds of shoves and insults that would have previously seen me throwing punches. Instead, when I reeled around to confront whoever had slapped me across the back of the head in the lunch queue, I'd have my bluff called.

'What are you going to do about it?' I'd be asked.

Over time my answer would become a hard light dying in my eyes. A lowered head. A wordless, 'Nothing.'

'Yeah, I thought so ...'

This was a pattern that bled from middle school into secondary school, where the boys were bigger, and the punches grew even harder. I didn't feel that I could go to Robert for help with this situation, fearing what his reaction would be. Neither of us was ready for that kind of disappointment. But I had seen *Karate Kid* and knew that there was another solution for problems like mine. Our town didn't have a room to practise in – a dojo – but I'd seen posters for a kung fu class down at the community centre where my mother went for tap dancing lessons. So, I badgered my father to take me to one of their open days.

Taken

He didn't know why I wanted to go so badly, and I certainly wasn't going to tell him. How do you explain your urgent need to learn the one-inch punch before double History on Monday? But he was intrigued enough by my interest in something athletic to give in, so he drove me down to the class where we watched a demonstration by the students. Rows of variously sized kids held forceful stances and threw the kinds of swift, synchronised punches I'd only ever thrown in video games. I pictured myself in that line-up and liked it. Saw the unfuckwithable force I would become in the playground, the other pupils eyeing my hands warily as if they were holstered pistols at my side. On the drive home from the class, though, my father told me that I wouldn't be going.

'I looked at you standing there with your little belly and thought, *no, I don't think so.*'

While I'd been watching those other children and imagining the roundhouse kicks of my future, my father had been making a financial decision. He knew how lazy I was. Had been keeping note of my untouched cricket set and the tennis racket he'd bought me for Christmas and knew that sport wasn't for me. I would not be worth the investment of a uniform, the weekly tuition fee and, in the unlikely event that I stuck it out for long enough, the grading belts. I couldn't tell him that I was desperate. That it wasn't about sport but survival. So, I headed back to school, and resumed my position in the pecking order,

Broken Biscuits

avoiding fights whenever I could. When that became impossible, I learned to receive a punch then take to the ground as if it was a Slumberland mattress, where I remained, waiting it out until it was all over and hoping that these days would eventually pass.

In the summer of 1992, I walked out of secondary school for the final time, and I would make it through the quarter of a century that followed without ever getting into another fight. I was pretty happy with that streak and planned on keeping it going until I died a very old and unpunched man. Then there was Nigel, looking for someone to head into battle with him and finding only me. The one person, it seemed, who stood between him and a horrible death.

Fuck.

I watched the blank comments field under his Facebook post, waiting to see who would step in and help him. Knowing that it absolutely couldn't, shouldn't, be me. One minute. Three minutes. Five. Then I couldn't bear it anymore.

I'll go with you, I typed.

Fuck.

By the time Nigel was tapping out his response to me, his friend John had also thrown his hat in the ring. A taxi driver and, in his spare time, a white-collar boxer, John's day job involves regular confrontation and his hobby does, too. He was the perfect person to accompany Nigel,

Taken

and if I'd waited another minute I could have been a mere observer, watching the events unfold via Facebook notifications from the safety of my laptop. Instead, I was part of a posse.

Fuck. Fuck. Fuck.

But I couldn't back out at this point. And I was also coming to realise that, having publicly committed myself, I didn't actually want to. It seemed like something important that I had to do. For Nigel but also for me.

I headed to my bedroom to find some appropriate clothing for a confrontation, thinking as I did about the things people would say should this evening go badly for me.

'Did you hear Adam died?'
'No! What happened?'
'He stood up for a friend.'

This was the kind of clunky heroic fantasy I've used as a comforting mental retreat ever since childhood. Picturing myself saving an entire family from a burning building. Performing life-saving CPR. Stepping in to confront a gang of muggers surrounding a single elderly woman.

'What are you going to do about it?' one of them would ask me.

'Oh, you'll find out ...' I'd reply, cleaning house with my unholstered fists then walking away, not wanting to cause a fuss but leaving the woman wondering, *Who was that mysterious and humble hero?*

Broken Biscuits

I got dressed and checked myself out in my wardrobe mirror, having put on what I considered to be the toughest item of clothing I owned. A black hoodie bearing the slogan of a local pro-wrestling company: HARD HITTING, HEART STOPPING. Crucially, it was baggy and made the truth of my body a secret, posing the question, *is he muscular or just fat?* No one would know unless they hit me, and I had to pray that wouldn't happen. In tonight's fantasy I would be playing the role of 'man with quiet potential for violence', and if I inhabited it well enough, we might all get out of this without anyone getting hurt.

When I arrived at Nigel's house, there was a nervous, giddy energy about him and as we paced up and down on the street outside, waiting for John to arrive, he turned to me.

'Are you ready?' he asked.

'Yeah!' I replied. *Absolutely not*, I thought. *But I'm doing it anyway.*

John pulled up in his cab and Nigel hugged his wife, then slipped into the passenger seat.

'Take care of him,' she said.

'We will,' I said, climbing into the back seat and closing the door, wondering as we set off how I'd take care of myself.

Nigel and John chatted excitably up front, while I sat behind them in a state of suppressed hysteria. Something

Taken

I disguised with bonhomie. Chipping in with the conversation. Making jokes. Not wanting to let on how much I wanted Nigel to announce that he'd changed his mind and was calling the whole thing off.

We pulled up outside a three-storey 1970s block of flats on a street lined with identical buildings. It was the bike we saw first, resting against the wall beside the entrance, its paintwork as prominent as cocktail-bar neon. Then we saw the thief, haloed by street lighting. He was young, in his twenties, but the addition of the bike made him appear as if he'd come fresh from his paper round. So, let's call him Babyface. He displayed a flicker of confusion as the three of us climbed out of the cab, but this was quickly replaced with a salesman's smile as he wheeled the bike towards us.

He had another guy with him, about my size, who eyed me, silent and expressionless, from within a jacket so puffy and voluminous it could have been concealing a machete or a microwave oven. There was a tension in his presence, as if they'd expected something to happen. eBay Power Sellers didn't act like this. I found myself holding my arms in a way that made me appear bigger, puffing myself up like a cat under threat. Mentally practising the faded advice Robert had given me.

Punch straight.
Use elbow.
Kick balls.

Broken Biscuits

Nigel took hold of the bike, offering it admiring looks and wheeling it back and forth as if trying it out for the first time, a rush of obvious excitement in the way he gripped the handlebars. *Stay Calm*, I thought, hoping he'd pick up on this telepathically. We were so close to the moment when everything could change. When it could all go horribly wrong.

'What do you think?' Babyface asked.

'Yeah, I like it,' Nigel said, to himself, to all of us. 'I think I'll take it.' Then he wheeled the bike over towards the cab and John opened up the boot, getting ready to load it in.

'Woah! What are you doing?' Babyface said, grabbing hold of the saddle.

'You stole my bike,' Nigel said, his voice trembling but still defiant. This was his moment. 'I'm taking it back.'

There were denials then, assertions, voices raised in volume and octaves. I hoped that I wouldn't have to join in with this, knowing that my words would squawk like I was taking another horrific trip through puberty. Blowing my cover.

Intrigued by the disturbance, faces began appearing at the balconies of the block, looking down at us. The guy in the voluminous jacket looked at me. I looked back at him. Everyone seemed to be looking, waiting for something to happen. My legs felt suddenly uncertain.

The guy in the voluminous jacket stepped towards me.

Taken

I stepped towards him.
He stepped back.
I stepped back, too.

It was like a cross between the hokey cokey and a timid slow dance at a school disco. But it was also a semaphore, each of us sending an unspoken message.

We are both scared. This is not worth it. Let's do nothing and hope that no one notices.

'Hey!' Babyface shouted, and I turned to see John calmly taking hold of the bike and loading it into the back of the cab. Then he started the engine and Babyface aimed his fingers at Nigel.

'Man,' he said, marching down the street towards another building. 'I'm gonna come back and light you up.'

I understood this to mean one thing; that he was going to get a gun and shoot us. Up on the first-floor balcony, a woman was looking down and talking on her phone.

'Yeah, these guys have turned up,' she said. 'Get down here.'

I didn't have many reference points for assembled gangs, so I can't lie and tell you that my first thought was of anything but *West Side Story.* Of the mob that would soon begin flooding from the other blocks and filling the streets, snapping their fingers in two-four time as they advanced on us. I looked around me for sudden movements, doors flying open, the army of figures who would surely soon round the corner and choreograph us to death.

Broken Biscuits

'Okay, go,' Nigel said, and we bundled into the cab. Pulling away, I looked out of the rear windscreen at the shrinking figures now standing in the road, thinking of the bullets that would soon shatter the glass and introduce themselves to my skull. Wincing in preparation, waiting for my world to go black as the contents of my head flooded the immaculately valeted interior of John's cab. I breathed in, not exhaling until we turned the corner and connected with the main road leading to Nigel's house. Then there was chatter, more bonhomie. Questions.

'What does "light you up" mean?' Nigel asked.

'I think it means "shoot you",' I said.

'Oh,' he said, then performed a flitting double-take. 'Oh, wow.'

There was a realisation in him then of the possibility that we could have all just died in the name of an orange bicycle. Still, when we pulled up outside his home, he was jubilant, the captain of a winning sports team. His bike glowing like a trophy as he wheeled it into his house with a cheer. His wife greeted us at the door, grateful to see that we were all back safe.

'Thank you for looking after him,' she said.

'No problem,' I said, accustomed to telling lies by this point.

At home later, lying in bed, I read about all this on Facebook. The tense miniature drama I'd been a part of replayed in the comments, which were all about congratulations and relief. I wanted to be thrilled by this, my reportedly valiant place at the heart of an adventure. Instead, I felt like I'd grabbed hold of a snake that I'd been avoiding for twenty-five years and only narrowly avoided being bitten by it. All for the sake of something that I thought had long ago been beaten out of me. A commitment to an idea that had only ever done me harm.

I put my phone down and switched off my bedside lamp, wanting to sleep. But closing my eyes, I could only think of Robert. Of how I'd have retold this evening to him. The breathless way I'd overplay my part in things, rebadging my fearful actions as sensibly wary. Still desperate to impress him after all these years. To hear his response.

'It's a fucking rush, isn't it?'

And as I wrapped my duvet around me, not planning on getting up again for a very long time, I replied quietly but firmly to the silent and uncomprehending darkness.

'No.'

An Inside Job

I was standing in a fine dining restaurant in Hull's vibrant Fruit Market district, taking photos while I waited to be called through into the kitchen. Nothing like the Hull I remembered from the 90s, the décor was a mix of chic and hipster. Exposed brickwork and original timber, polished fixtures gleaming under atmospheric lighting that made the air appear as if it had been lightly infused with fine gold. And at the heart of this building – a huge, vibrant noise braying from the kitchen – was my younger brother Ben.

'Here,' he said, beckoning me into the kitchen and lifting a bucket-sized container of olive oil to my face. 'Smell that. It's been marinating for days.'

The oil was swimming with bulbous, bruise-coloured cloves of Italian garlic and threads of fresh rosemary, plucked from the herb-filled flower boxes that line the restaurant's rooftop terrace. The mixture smelled sweet and pungent and my immediate reaction to it was a primal attraction, drawn to its contents.

'God, that's incredible,' I said, unsure whether I wanted to taste it or lower myself into a bathtub of it.

He set down a huge tray of proved dough onto a stainless-steel worktop with a heavy clang, the contents shuddering like a freshly spanked belly. His hands disappeared into the container and came out bearing two fistfuls of infused oil, which he slapped onto the dough, slathering its surface and working in the oil.

'It's my famous focaccia,' he said. 'People travel for miles just to try it. It's the first thing I was taught when I was inside.'

In 2013, Ben was sentenced to five years in prison. A period of time he often refers to like this: casually, as if it was no big deal. An unfortunate commute, where he hit a very long series of red lights. These are the moments when I most starkly feel the difference between us. If I'd been sent to jail and somehow survived, I know I would *never* take my story lightly; never miss an opportunity to impress on people how brave I'd been while inside. There would be, I can assure you, books. Ben, on the other hand, simply looked at his situation, accepted it, then got to work on making the most of an opportunity.

* * *

An Inside Job

I'd never wanted a younger brother. The whole idea was inconvenient to me, because, before Ben came along, I was ruling things in our home. The first child of my mother's second marriage, my father's firstborn and his parents' first grandchild, my birth was loaded with significance. I was treated like a precious gift. An idea, I'm told, that I cottoned onto early.

I was born two months before my parents' wedding, which was not uncontroversial in 1976. But that didn't really matter, because this event became all about me. I howled throughout, turning the ceremony from a celebration of my parents' love into one that could only focus on the result of it. This screaming beetroot at the centre of every photo while those around me struggled to maintain smiles, privately cursing me for not being born with an off switch. My mother would not hold this against me, though, and when later that year I had a brief brush with infant mortality she learned to treasure me even more. Knowing how close she'd come to losing her perfect little cherub and only making my behaviour worse.

One thing my mother couldn't see, but others could, was that I was an objectively ugly infant, cursed with the sort of unsettling features you just shouldn't see on a baby. I had a big, mannish head, a puff of downy chicken-feather hair and an inability to breathe through my nose, which left me slack-jawed and dribbling like a leaking tap. Still, my mother looked at me with nothing but heart

Broken Biscuits

eyes, compelled to fill photo albums and capture my beauty for future generations to enjoy. ME smiling in the bath; ME giggling in my baby bouncer; ME naked on a fur rug, grinning like a cheesecake model. Always happy, because why wouldn't I be? I had it all. Love, attention, my buttocks delicately cushioned by downy sheepskin. It seemed that the world had been made for me and me alone.

Never one to be selfish, my mother entered me into Bonnie Baby competitions at church fêtes and county shows. God, she believed, had spared me for a divine purpose: to share my good looks with the world. To that end, she dressed me up in ruffs and bootees, did her best to cowlick my hair and presented me alongside other, genuinely appealing children, which only served to make me look like a family pet dressed up for Halloween. Had she placed me on the prize marrow table, I might have stood a chance of achieving a ribbon. Instead, I fared badly. My mother was always baffled by these results, but rather than explain they had decided the winner should be a baby that actually looked like a baby, the judges placated her with kind comments about my outfit or my lovely smile. Rightly recognising that a woman who would enter a baby like me into a beauty competition was capable of anything.

Still, at home I remained a pin-up and, quickly learning that the world belongs to the beautiful, I established

An Inside Job

myself as the family despot. Show me a room and I'd thrust myself into the middle of it. Allow the focus to slip from me and I'd snatch it back, removing my clothing and yelling for the attention that I felt was my birthright. My elder siblings bristled at this, but they had little choice but to resent me and daydream about a world where my parents left me outside an orphanage and drove away.

Then, in 1980, not long after my fourth birthday, my mother announced that she was pregnant. There would be a new baby of the family. I responded as anyone who was panicked about losing their job might and tried to reason with her. I thought that pregnancy might be something she could reverse somehow, a purchase she could return. My family likes to remind me that during the months leading up to Ben's birth I padded around on all fours, making gaga noises and yelling 'I can still be the baby!' But I couldn't hold back the inevitable and, that December, startled by the news that John Lennon had been shot, my mother went into labour and gave birth to Ben the following day.

From day one he was almost supernaturally beautiful and, while she never said it, I know that seeing him caused the scales to fall from her eyes and she began to doubt my future as a matinee idol. Most babies are born looking like they've been knocked out in the eighth round of a heavyweight title fight, but Ben popped out as if he'd arrived to audition as the baby on a fabric softener label, all tumbling

Broken Biscuits

amber curls and pinchable cheeks. Out in public, people looked into his pram and regarded him with curiosity, likely asking themselves, *Is that baby wearing make-up?* before turning to me and wondering how genetics could be such a cruel lottery. It was clear to everyone, me included, that there was a new cherub in town.

'It's like John Lennon died to make room for Ben,' our neighbour Irene had said, looking down at him dozing in his cot.

These days I know this is just the kind of line that people trot out when someone dies around the time of a birth, but back then I took it at face value, evidence that I could justifiably resent Ben. I mean, who wouldn't hate the boy who had murdered everybody's favourite Beatle? Not my parents, apparently, who proudly gave him the middle name Lennon. This they felt marked him for greatness. And given that Ben had managed to kill the most famous man in the world before he was even born, they were maybe on to something.

While in the decades that followed much of what I learned about John Lennon would make me wonder why anyone waited so long to shoot him, in 1980 it felt like someone had murdered an angel. That Christmas, The Two Ronnies shared the TV with footage of John and Yoko in the White Room at Tittenhurst Park. 'Imagine' shared the radio waves with 'Merry Xmas Everybody'. And I shared attention with Ben, who shifted the focus of

An Inside Job

Christmas from me to him. This was something I wasn't willing to tolerate.

'John Lennon's dead,' I'd tell guests when they'd arrive to drop off Christmas presents and a little something extra for the new arrival. 'He had to make room for Ben.'

I thought of this act as a simple equation: people's love for John Lennon + associating his death with Ben = everyone hates Ben and remembers to adore me again. If I could poison the well of his public affection, I could regain my position. But anyone else would surely have seen my behaviour for what it was, the desperate vengeance of deposed royalty.

Ben would grow up to behave exactly like a child who had got away with murder and from the moment he could ball up his fists and punch me in the crotch we were at war. If it could be said that we had one thing in common back then, it was our intense aversion to one another, and no day went without a skirmish. His angelic features were the perfect mask, concealing a devious, conniving mind that delighted in luring me into hitting him, only to play the wronged and confused innocent when my parents arrived on the scene having heard his cries.

'I don't know what happened,' he'd sob, pointing at me. 'Adam just started attacking me for no reason.' Then from the wings, out of sight of our parents, he would watch me being punished, smiling as he silently mouthed, 'Shithead.'

Broken Biscuits

When we weren't setting each other up or beating one another with sticks, we excelled at adversarial schadenfreude. Each of us saw the other's failures as personal victories. When I tripped on a cattle grid and broke my nose, I swear the sight of it actually got him high. Likewise, the memory of the time when a wasp stung him on the head and he ran panicked into a lamppost became my regular happy place. Each night we drifted off to sleep in our bunk beds with new bruises and a fresh list of simmering injustices waiting to be avenged. Our final words to one another always a series of dozily fizzling curses.

'Goodnight, you wanker,' he'd say, kicking the underside of my mattress from his bottom bunk.

'Goodnight, you little shit,' I'd reply, hissing down at him.

'Bastard ...'

'Prick ...'

'Arsehole ...'

'Dickhead ...'

It wasn't until I left town that we drifted into a kind of armistice, forged by the simple act of not having to deal with one another anymore. Only hearing updates of each other's lives via our mother. In this way I learned of his many doomed, get-rich-quick schemes. That he was working as a doorman in a strip club in Ibiza. That he'd overstayed his visa in Thailand and needed to pay a fine

An Inside Job

before they'd let him leave the country. And eventually, that he'd been sent to prison.

My mother hadn't wanted to tell me about this at first, hoping that he'd somehow avoid a custodial sentence and that she could keep the whole thing quiet. So, while he'd been arrested in January 2013, she didn't tell me about it until six months later, when he'd actually been sent down and she'd have to find an explanation for the empty chair at the table during Christmas dinner.

'He got caught with a taser,' she explained. 'Just a little one. But it's treated like a firearm.'

'Fucking hell!' I said. 'How long has he got?'

'Five years.'

I could hear how sick those two words made her feel. The nausea they carried as she spoke them. They made me feel sick, too, but perhaps for different reasons to hers. There are few things I fear more than going to prison, to be trapped in a box with society's most violent and terrifying people. Sharing meals and showers with men who are calibrated to recognise fear and easy targets and might decide to brutalise you simply for daring to look their way. I know without it needing to be tested that a single night behind bars would reduce me to tears and worse, the pressure of the situation crushing me under its heel. I once woke from a nightmare about being sent to jail and my cellmate holding me down, attempting to remove my eye after lights out. The sweaty sense of fear had remained

Broken Biscuits

with me long after I'd woken, my arms flapping in terror. So, the idea that Ben would be inside a prison for years, for five birthdays, that chair empty for five Christmases, was a horror movie that I couldn't get out of my head.

'He'll only do half of that,' she added, trying to inject a sense of hope into things. 'Thirty months, as long as he's good.'

I thought of how difficult being good is when you're inside. How prisoners get pulled into all sorts of things. Find themselves owing debts that they're forced under threat of violence to pay off. To involve themselves in prison politics by long-term or powerful criminals. My ideas of prison were almost exclusively informed by scenes from TV dramas and movies. *The Shawshank Redemption. Sons of Anarchy. Breaking Bad. The Wire.* I thought of beatings and shanks. The movie *Scum*, snooker balls in a sock and shouts of, 'I'm the daddy now!' A horrific scene in a prison drama that a work colleague had once described to me – involving a hurled mixture of boiling water and sugar – that had made certain I would never watch that show. But it put the thought in my head, and now Ben was inside I knew I would think of it every day until he got out.

Thirty months. How strange that time period sounded, but comforting in its own way. It was shorter than the contract on my iPhone. Thinking of it in this way made it digestible. The time would fly by and, before I knew it, I'd

An Inside Job

be due an upgrade and a rehabilitated little brother. It also reminded me of the way that parents discuss their toddlers. Their early years talked about in months, during which they would be expected to take huge developmental leaps. But Ben would be making no leaps at all, not anymore, because he was trapped. His way of life, any plans he might have had for his future, were irrevocably changed. It was more likely he would go backwards. And not back to the beautiful boy whose life was once overflowing with possibilities. Instead, he would reverse into a new version of himself, where all opportunities for anything good would be gone. He would be pushed into a life of darkness and desperation because that's all the world could offer him now.

While she never said so, I knew that part of the reason my mother had not told me about this sooner was because she'd guessed how judgemental I'd have been. And her instincts would have been correct. Hearing the news ignited the part of me that had always been so frustrated with Ben. Resentful of the way that he seemed to have had so many opportunities handed to him, but just couldn't get it together. Never holding down a job for long, flitting from one fanciful plan to another. Regularly leaving home to start a new life in a different part of the country, only to return a couple of months later with a new rack of debts he'd need help with, but it was okay, because he had another plan brewing that would turn

Broken Biscuits

things around. 'Just wait, you'll see.' This was a show we had all seen before and seemed to be on permanent repeat.

So, when my mother told me this news there was an instinctive flash of meanness in me. I had been judgemental, but also so angry with him. For putting our parents through all this, but also for what I considered to be his behaviour finally catching up with him.

'*Well, his luck ran out at last,*' I wanted to say. '*He finally landed in a hole you couldn't dig him out of.*'

This is a part of me I don't like very much. But what I liked even less, the real storm in my head, were the thoughts that followed and overwhelmed those initial mean ones. The panicked, fearful thing that I couldn't say to my mother. Could barely say even if I'd wanted to.

I can't lose another brother.

But because he was in prison, this felt like a certainty. One way or another, Ben was done for.

* * *

When I'd first arrived at Ben's restaurant, he was prepping for the day's service and singing along to the music of Hot Chocolate, his bassy voice blasting through the sharp clatter of kitchen noise.

I'd not heard Ben sing since he'd practised 'The Holly and the Ivy' for a primary school Christmas concert in the mid-80s. When we'd last lived together, during the late 90s, he was exclusively listening to happy hardcore and

An Inside Job

Gabber, his music taste so intense and unlovable that it gave me palpitations. So, it was a surprise to hear him, an ex-con now, full-throated and harmonising with Erroll Brown as disco soul played from the Google speaker in the corner.

'Give me a minute,' he said as he spotted me in the doorway. 'I'm just setting up.'

'Take your time,' I said, holding up my hands. 'There's no rush.'

I was in his restaurant that evening to write about him. About how he'd reached this point in life and what he'd overcome to get there. But also about the two of us, and our relationship. So, while I waited to talk to him, I stood back and watched him work, this man I was bonded to by birth but with whom I had spent so little of my adult life. Learning about him as if we'd only just been introduced.

As Hot Chocolate gave way to Lionel Ritchie, I watched as his hands demonstrated years of deft muscle memory, switching between tasks with ease. The 3D chess of running a kitchen: chopping, slicing, turning to monitor sauces then almost dancing across the kitchen to grab a griddle pan and flip its contents with a well-practised jerk. Preparing his famous focaccia. Seeing him work, this controlled and organised side of him so alien to me, I was reminded of the first time I gave my friend Zoë a lift in my car.

Zoë has known me for my entire life, and always as a klutz. To her I have only ever presented as a slightly hopeless figure, baffled by anything involving technology and coordination. So seeing me behind a wheel, confidently shifting gears and chatting easily while negotiating heavy traffic, was a discombobulating experience for her.

'I'm sorry,' she said. 'But this is so weird. It's like watching a dog riding a horse.'

And this is exactly how I felt watching Ben. He was always, to my mind at least, a calamity. So, to see him take control of things in this way gave me a sense of tear-inducing pride, as if his achievements were somehow my own. But I know this is all him, and that makes me feel even prouder. Because I know that to get to this point he had to climb out of a hole I would have buried myself trying to escape from.

'You have to let it rest,' Ben said, calling me over so he could talk me through his process as he prepared a steak for himself before opening time. The fuel he'd need to keep him going for the busy hours ahead. 'It keeps cooking after you take it off the heat. It's like when you burn yourself and run your hand under cold water. If you don't, you'll start to cook. It's the same with a steak. Let it rest.'

There was a clank of the pan then, a flick of his wrist that was both forceful and dainty, a process involving melted butter. He stood back to admire his work.

'Now *that* is perfect,' he said, smiling at the steak in the satisfied, paternal way he does every time he engages with his food. 'You can't get any better than that.'

An Inside Job

Ben is no longer beautiful, but is particularly boyish in the manner that all the men in my family are in our own ways. None of us, though, maintains this quality quite like Ben. Everyone in the family holds an image of him in our heads, and in it he is no older than nineteen. In reality, he is forty-three years old, bearded and as greying and lined as I am. But he will always be the baby of the family. A part of him still gripped by a sense of chaos that has billowed around him like a Pig-Pen dirt cloud since the moment he could crawl. So, it's wild to see him in his element, at the heart of something so complex, so time sensitive, so fucking hard and exhausting, and discover that he is not just coping but thriving.

While at university, I worked for one summer as a porter in a hotel kitchen, chopping vegetables and washing greasy pans. I came close to walking out several times, always fucking up, dropping things, raising the ire of the head chef. Crying in the toilets because the sous chef asked, 'Who fucked up the carrots?' and I'd had to admit it was me. I'd hated every second of my time in a kitchen and couldn't believe that anyone could work in a place like that with a song in their heart, let alone their mouth. But there was Ben in front of me, on more than one level, singing.

'You go and sit down, and I'll bring your food through,' he said. 'Then we can have a chat.'

The restaurant was still a while away from opening, so I had the run of the place. I chose a table not too far from

Broken Biscuits

the kitchen so I could still hear him work. Catch snatches of chat between him and the other staff. About the business, notes of gossip, advice on seasoning. A tray clanged, a pan clonked. His voice boomed the lyrics to a Fine Young Cannibals hit.

It was very easy for me to hate the boy he was, but it's even easier to love the man he has become. This gregarious air horn that I have come to enjoy the presence of at weddings and funerals, which is where we most often see each other these days. Watching Ben work a room is something else, buying drinks and spreading joy. Poking fun at himself, flirting with aunts, making sordid in-jokes with people he has only just met. This sort of thing has always been easy for Ben, and it made him popular. He has never struggled to gain friends, many of whom he's held close for decades. People who wouldn't let a little thing like prison come between them. His Facebook is full of photos of him in clubs and on beaches, posing with huge groups of his mates, something I could never replicate. I can count my close male friends on the hand of Homer Simpson. Ben would need more arms than Vishnu.

Watching him working in his kitchen, I can see why he chose this profession. It allows him to be the same person at work as he is at play. The only difference is that, with this work, there is order to that play. He is commanding everything, and nothing can be allowed to go wrong. It's

An Inside Job

obviously difficult, but listening to the sounds of him spilling from the kitchen it's impossible not to think of that old saying, variously attributed to Confucius, Mark Twain and LinkedIn: *'Choose a job you love, and you will never have to work a day in your life.'*

'My mate just made ten grand on crypto ...' I could hear him saying, flicking back and forth between social and business duties. 'Google, play "Close to Me" by The Cure ... Can you get me more red onions? Yeah, so if you go on YouTube and follow this guy: Captain Crypto, he's called ...'

This was the easy-life Ben sneaking through into the tough and hard-working version. Making itself known in a job I'm certain he would still do tomorrow even if he won the Euromillions.

After twenty minutes or so, he came out of the kitchen and set a plate of food in front of me.

'Salmon fillet on a bed of petit pois served with leek and horseradish dauphinoise.'

He delivered these words in the same booming East Yorkshire accent I was familiar with from growing up. The voice that would fill my teenage bedroom as he barged in to say, 'I hate you, you fucking wanker!' While I still carry the largely southern accent I arrived in East Yorkshire with, Ben was eleven when we moved north, and he assimilated the local accent within about forty-five minutes of our arrival. Some people would be hard pressed to believe that we grew up in the same country, let alone the same house.

'Wow,' I said, looking down at my plate. 'This looks amazing.'

'It is,' he said, as I photographed the food and tapped out a quick note about it on my phone. 'D A U P H I ...' he began, spelling out the dish for me then describing it to me in detail.

'I've had it before,' I said, digging my fork into it and trying a mouthful.

'Not like this, you haven't,' he said with a wink. But there was something almost coy about him as he watched me taste that first bite. He's confident in his abilities but it clearly means a lot to prove himself to me, to any member of our family who comes to eat in his restaurant. To have us be impressed by something he can do that the rest of us can't. This skill he learned under extreme duress. Suffering a pressure that would have crushed me but formed him into a diamond.

The food was incredible, as I knew it would be: strong flavours, well-seasoned dishes, eloquently balanced. Eating Ben's food is to know him in a new way; to know him properly.

I thought of one of the few non-combative images I hold of us together as children, sitting on the sofa and watching TV as we ate cereal. We have both always been driven by food, the two of us ravenously greedy. One

An Inside Job

third of a six-person household, we knew that what we didn't eat would be gone – and quickly. Digested by four other eager stomachs. So, we demolished the weekly shop, cramming ourselves with snacks. Clamouring for sugar-caked cereals. It was the only time we were silent in each other's company. Ben with a box of Sugar Puffs on his lap, his fist repeatedly crawling into it and gathering another handful to palm into his mouth. Me, beside him, dunking a spoon into a mixing bowl filled to the brim with supermarket brand Coco Pops. The contented and happy silence of eating.

I try to think about things like this more and more these days. The qualities that unite us, rather than the ones that have separated us. They are more important. Especially since our brother Robert died. His was a sudden, unexpected death that made me consider my remaining loved ones in a way that brought them into high definition. Making me painfully aware that I only have them for so long. They could blink out of existence before I am ready. Of course, the truth is that we are never ready, but you must make the most of those people while they're around, and make yourself available to them, too.

The people I have cried the hardest for at funerals are the ones I didn't value enough, didn't spend enough time with. I wasn't devastated by the death of my maternal grandmother, Kitty, not because I didn't care, but because

Broken Biscuits

I'd always loved her with my whole heart. I never spent a second in her company without making the most of it. To be around her and not adore her was simply impossible. I drank fully from her existence and, while I still miss her, the love I had for her is still with me. I didn't let her go to waste. I realised I had come close to doing that with Ben, so pledged to make a concerted effort to appreciate him.

Naturally, that is a bit much to be on the receiving end of. The person whose voice you heard each night calling you a 'fucking piece of shit son-of-a-bitch fucker' before you drifted off to sleep reappearing in your life. Telling people about how proud of you he is and clearly wanting to say 'I love you, man' but not quite finding the words. Wanting to write about you. Neither of us quite knew what to do with that kind of affection. So, Ben responded in his own way, reciprocating this new challenge of love the best way he could.

'Sage and onion patty with pea purée, triple-cooked chips, curry ketchup and a malt-vinegar gel,' he said, standing beside my table as a waiter slid a plate in front of me.

He watched me take a bite.

'Fucking hell,' I said, stunned. Sitting back in my chair and looking up at him. 'That is amazing. How do you *do* that?'

He smiled and headed to the kitchen, telling me he'd be back in five minutes. When he returned, he was carrying

An Inside Job

a crème brûlée. He placed it in front of me and sat in the chair opposite, groaning slightly from the effort of stopping.

'Okay,' he said, watching as I cracked the caramelised surface and deposited a heaped spoonful of dessert into my mouth. Enjoying the look of delight on my face. 'Ask me whatever you want.'

'Are you sure you're okay talking about all this?'

'Definitely,' he said. 'I want people to know.'

I looked down at my list of questions and decided to ask him the one I had thought of more often than any other.

'Were you scared when they sent you down?'

I was thinking of something our sister Becky told me. She'd been there, in court, supporting him on the day he went before the judge. When the sentence was announced, Ben had looked suddenly pale and sick. 'It was unbearable,' Becky told me. 'I was so scared for him.'

'I was a *bit* scared,' Ben replied. 'But honestly, I was more annoyed.'

The charges had been for more than just a taser, he explained. He'd also been growing and selling cannabis. But not in a quantity that would have led to a custodial sentence. Small fry, easy money. The last get-rich-quick scheme he would try.

'I wasn't *completely* innocent,' he said. 'I had weed, growing equipment, but it was small amounts. Without the taser I would've got a year's suspended sentence.'

Broken Biscuits

The taser was seen by Ben as a novelty item. Designed to look like a mobile phone. For a while you could buy the same model on Amazon, he said. That its charge was mild, a zapper rather than anything the police might deploy. He'd bought it from a market stall during his trip to Thailand.

'The stupid thing is, I didn't even want it. This woman made me. Persistent, you know? I brought it back through customs, so thought it was fine. But the police found it when they raided me and put two and two together.'

'What, that you were using it to protect your stash?'

'Yeah, it suited this story. That I was "protecting my crop". In the end I pleaded guilty to production of cannabis, possession of an offensive weapon and possession of a disguised firearm. Because it looked like a phone it was "disguised", which is a Section 6 charge. It's seen as more vindictive.' Listing these charges for me, I could see how bothered he was by the picture they painted of him. 'I haven't actually harmed anyone, I'm not violent. Everyone knows that.'

Just like me, Ben uses his hands a lot when he talks. As he explained his day in court, I could smell the lingering scent of rosemary and garlic oil on his darting, illustrative hands. But while my hand movements are a flamboyant, elaborate semaphore, Ben's are solid gestures of clear direction, occasionally used for acting.

An Inside Job

'The judge says "Five years, Ben Farrer. Take him down." They put the cuffs on and took me away ...' Ben held his upturned arms towards me, balled his fists and bonked his wrists together as if shackled. 'Clink!'

He was initially sent to HMP Hull, an imposing, three-tier Victorian structure that I used to see twice a day while taking the bus to college. I'd watch visitors arriving and leaving, often with small kids who skipped along, oblivious about the monstrousness of this castle-like building they were visiting. The adults beside them always droop-shouldered and burdened. Each time I passed this building I twitched with anxiety.

'It was daunting,' Ben said of the moment he was taken behind its walls. In the end he only spent three weeks there, having his induction while it was decided where he'd be transferred to. Stuck in a grim holding pattern. 'I was eventually sent to HMP Wolds. Disneywolds, they used to call it. It was pretty cushy, I suppose. But not when I got there.'

I asked him what it was like. Trying to be tactful, not wanting to stir up anything too traumatic. But I was morbidly curious about what he'd had to contend with and how he'd coped.

'There are people you instinctively know not to mess with,' he said, his hands dancing again. 'You have to bite your tongue with certain things. But I know how to play people like that. I know to not push people too far.'

Broken Biscuits

Ben spent seven years working security at strip and lap-dancing clubs in Ibiza. He bumped up against criminality daily and learned how to deal with it, developing a set of soft skills that allowed him to navigate that world. Everyone's friend, no one's rat.

'So, you took your people skills from the clubs and applied them to prison?' I asked.

'Kind of, yeah. If I saw something kicking off, I knew what to do. I didn't panic. You distance yourself.' He looked over at the diners who were starting to fill the restaurant, sending a darting glance over to the kitchen and his pending responsibility. He checked the time, made sure we were still good to talk then continued. 'I remember this guy walking right by me with a blade, going to stab someone. So, I made sure I wasn't paying attention. The wings are camera'd up. The guy got caught. No one died. There were things like that all the time. But I never got in that kind of situation,' he said, taking another look across the restaurant. 'You don't borrow anything; you don't get in debt. If you don't bother anyone, you get no problems.'

Instead of getting involved in prison politics, Ben had made the most of things, throwing himself into the educational opportunities and studying for an IT diploma. The busy work of making the most of a bad situation. Of not making enemies and of building up trust. Using the grease of his natural charm, he somehow

An Inside Job

ended up teaching an IT class. Helping prisoners work through their sentence plans.

'Some of these are dangerous criminals who've killed people,' he said. 'But they have these long plans, these things they have to tick off so things can get better for them. Someone has to help, so I did it.'

This did nothing to hurt Ben's own sentence plan, which was to work through his own targets until he reached Category D status. This would mean that he could be transferred to an open prison. Ben achieved his targets pretty quickly, and was soon offered a place at North Sea Camp in Lincolnshire.

'I didn't want to go because I'd heard it was full of rapists and paedophiles, but I was told if I didn't go then I'd lose my chance at an open prison. So, I went and, *behold* –' he threw his arms wide '– full of sex offenders.'

Despite myself, it was hard not to laugh at his use of 'behold'.

'I went to be an IT teacher there, but you can also do thirty days of community work, so I was hoping to get out in the world. But it was hard to get work from North Sea Camp because, you know,' he shrugged. 'No one wanted to employ anyone from the sex offender place.'

Unhappy with Ben's plight, our mother became a letter-writing machine, appealing to prison authorities until he was transferred to another open prison called Kirklevington Grange in Teesside, where he used his good behaviour to get a job in the office. From there he wrote CVs for other prisoners and drove them to their day-release jobs, getting a preview of what the free air would taste like. One of the prisoners he was transporting worked as a pot washer in the kitchen of a chef named Matty Roath. When that prisoner was due for a release, Ben saw an opportunity to spend more time outside prison property, so asked for and was given his job.

'I showed interest,' Ben said. 'Matty taught me how to make that bread you saw. Stocks. Desserts. And the fundamentals of classic French cooking. He didn't have to do any of this. I worked for him for a year while I was in Kirklevington. Six days a week.' He gestured to the restaurant, tables filling with excited, anticipatory diners. 'He changed my life.'

When he completed his thirty months, Ben moved back in with my parents and would immediately be offered chances to work in kitchens at pubs and restaurants in East Yorkshire, until Roath invited him to work in his kitchen at a country-house hotel in the town of Yarm. Ben headed off there, renting a log cabin in a thirty-acre forest on the grounds.

'Ten pounds a week, I paid. I walked to work in five minutes. It was brilliant. I paid attention, I learned. It was a three-rosette place. I was working with chefs from Michelin-starred restaurants. In eighteen months, I went from basically a pot washer to junior sous chef.'

An Inside Job

I told him I'd heard that restaurant kitchens were full of ex-offenders. That a chef once told me, 'Kitchen staff are basically pirates.'

Ben laughed hard at this.

'We *are* all pirates. We've all done some stuff. There's this chef down the road, we call him Sketch, because he's done some sketchy stuff. He's a beast, he's the best chef in this city. We've all got some kind of background. Everyone who goes to a restaurant has eaten something by an ex-offender. By a fucking pirate.'

You can see why this kind of work appeals to ex-cons. Kitchen workers are a special breed. People with the kind of stamina that comes from a wild life. Who thrive on the pace that most people can't handle. Working in a kitchen had crushed me because I didn't have the dynamism or itchiness of presence that the job needed. This constant requirement to chop, peel, stir and scrub. The right ex-prisoner will burn their way through a teetering stack of greasy washing up and beg for more. And if they're looking for a chance to prove themselves, for a way out, they will do whatever you want. Ben was one of those people.

'I thought, *I'm never going back*. No way. There are guys I was in with who are on their sixth sentence now. If your sentence is more than four years, you're told that you're basically done for. That your sentence will never be fully spent. It traps you in a life of crime.' He sat forward in his chair and looked across at me. 'Fuck that, you know? I'm not having that.'

Ben moved from restaurant to restaurant, building up his skills and reputation, working long shifts that killed his back and his knees but loving the results of that work. Loving the work itself.

'There are loads of shit chefs out there,' he said. 'Gastronomic gunslingers. Wallop jockeys, I call them. Crap food. There's no love. I do it right.'

Ben eventually ended up at a waterfront restaurant in Hull and impressing the owner, who also owns the restaurant where Ben works as head chef.

'He closed this place down for a while during lockdown. When he reopened it, he told me he was giving it to me. I was happy, you know, "Yeah, cool," I said, but he said "I don't think you understand. I'm *giving* you this place. I trust you. I have faith in you. You control it all."'

The thought of this choked me up, my eyes suddenly glassy. I cry easily. Ben does not. Something that likely served him well in prison. So, I composed myself, aiming for Ben's steady emotional level.

'If you think about yourself when you were inside,' I asked him. 'Could you ever have imagined a time when someone would put this kind of faith in you?'

'No, never,' he replied firmly. 'He's had hundreds of chefs work for him. He's never done this with anyone else.'

An Inside Job

I got to enjoy a moment in which Ben visibly stopped to consider the enormity of that act of faith. Seeming to understand that there was a reason people in the industry were willing to do so much to help him, and that was because they trusted him. There was a satisfied glow about him then, which lasted until he suddenly jumped to his feet as if something had just bitten him on the backside.

'Shit,' he said. 'I need to get the bread out of the oven.'

He strode purposefully across the restaurant floor and disappeared into the kitchen, heading back to tend to his famous focaccia. People had travelled for miles.

I paid my bill, thanked the other staff and made to leave. Ben wanted to say goodbye properly and grab a quick cigarette while he let his steaks rest. He assembled a roll-up, and we stepped out onto Humber Street. I cooed about how pretty the area looked in the evening, the other bars and restaurants across from his ablaze with activity. I took a few photos while Ben watched me, draining his cigarette.

'Okay then,' I said, thinking of my drive back to Manchester. Of writing up everything we'd talked about. 'I'd better be off.'

We hugged goodbye, and I realised as his arms closed around me that we'd only ever done this once before, just after Robert's funeral. I also realised that the cigarette in

Broken Biscuits

his hand was burning me. So, I pulled away and took a good look at him, standing there in his chef's whites. He took a drag from his cigarette, the smoke drifting up towards the shimmering bulbs above us, threaded between the buildings.

'Let me take your photo,' I said, impressed by how the lighting made him look. He posed in the centre of the street, shoulders back and chest out, smiling softly, the cigarette still smoking in the hand at his side. Later I would send this photo to him, he would immediately forward it to our mother and set it as his WhatsApp profile image.

'Okay,' he said, a little awkward in that final moment of farewell. At this new kind of affection we had shown for one another. 'I need to get back to my steaks.'

'Yeah,' I said. 'See ya.'

'See ya.'

He crushed his cigarette into an ashtray and opened the door of the restaurant. I wanted to call him back as he ducked inside, needing to explain that I was so proud of him I could cry. That I was sorry for not placing the kind of faith in him that others had, for the things I'd sometimes thought of him. How often I'd wished I could unthink them. Most of all, though, I wanted to tell him that I loved him and that I was so glad he was born.

But I said none of those things. I just let him get back to work. Because we've never been those kind of brothers, and we're not going to start now.

Bonnie
Black Hare

When I first began reading stories about my life in front of audiences, there was one tale I returned to over and over. It always got a good reaction and I am nothing if not receptive to praise. Over time, I started to learn what gets a response from a crowd. In the way comedians often do during the early stages of their stand-up careers, I was still working out the dynamics of storytelling and realised that I could skate by on shock material until I really got the hang of things. So, I often chose this particular story as my go-to. It starts with something sordid and attention-grabbing that happened when I was twenty. A tale from the distant past featuring a version of myself that I was happy to play around with. And, because it was true, I could easily inhabit the narrative and keep the audience with me, ultimately achieving the laughs and applause that I came to need like oxygen.

Broken Biscuits

The story began like this.

Clare lowered herself off the sofa with a thud and knelt in front of me. Twisting her fists into the carpet. Breathing deep and slow.

'If you just say the word,' she said, placing a hand on my knee, 'I'll have that dick out of those pants and in my mouth so fast it'll make your head spin.'

It wasn't so much her words I disliked, as the way she said them. Forcefully, through clenched teeth. Pitched to be sexy but reminding me of my parents having a suppressed argument in another room. I thought of the younger me, who had often fantasised about offers like this. Never dreaming that they could be made to sound so much like a threat. So much like a mugging.

I attempted to cross my legs, but Clare blocked me, feeding her hand along my inner thigh. My buttocks flinched with the force of an angrily slammed door. I backed away and wanted to keep moving back. Through the sofa, through the wall, apologetically into next door's living room. But because that wasn't an option, I considered my immediate future. Saw myself giving in through pressure and politeness, suffering whatever she had planned. I pictured her gnashing teeth. Her hand yanking on my penis as if it were the pull cord of a stubborn outboard motor. The morning after.

Bonnie Black Hare

'I'd love to,' I said, feigning disappointment. 'Honestly. But you know I can't.'

'Fine,' she said, her voice turning suddenly cold and distant. Then she pushed herself to her feet and headed into the kitchen to find a knife.

It's not the worst start to a story. To be honest, I don't hate it even now. But I can see what I was doing. The slamming buttocks. The stubborn pull cord. I was hunting for crude laughs and getting them, largely because my audiences were often drunk. Then there was that dark turn with the knife. It engaged the room while I rolled things back and recounted the events that had led to that point.

It was my housemate Jay who brought Clare into our home that night. He'd come fresh from a student club night, a pound a pint and shots for fifty pence. Jay was big on a bargain, so had loaded himself up. It was in that club that he'd bumped into Clare, and, full of the affection that always possessed him when he'd had a drink, he invited her back to his place. Our place.

I was in the living room watching TV when they stumbled through the front door, Clare holding Jay upright. He slumped drunkenly against the banister and introduced her to me, his words sing-song and slurred, as if a hinge on his jaw had come loose.

'Hiya!' she said, offering me a smile and a cutesy wave. Then she settled herself down on the stairs and began unzipping her black PVC thigh boots. Everything she wore was black. Her dress. Her bodice. All of it standing in contrast to her hair, which was peroxide roasted to the colour of a Hollywood smile.

She hadn't needed to introduce herself. I knew Clare by sight and reputation. Everyone did. She'd once tried to pick up my friend Geoff in the student bar, leaning into his ear to whisper something to him.

'You know,' she said, 'I actually prefer … small penises.'

Lines like that just stick, particularly with Geoff, who'd made the mistake of telling us, his dear friends. The words had a repeatable quality, and we'd often reference them, like a sitcom catchphrase. So, when Clare appeared in my house it was like finding myself in the presence of a celebrity. Her words so familiar to me I half expected her to say them as a conversational opener. A band playing the hits.

I headed into the hallway and Jay began recounting the evening that had led to their arrival in our house. The vodka shots that had taken control of his legs, the moment he met Clare on the dance floor, the competitive way the two of them had downed more shots at the bar followed by the stumbling journey home. But somewhere towards the end of this retelling his voice started to give up, along with the rest of him.

Bonnie Black Hare

'Y'know what?' he yawned. 'I need some sleep. I'm going to bed.'

As he crawled up the stairs, Clare shot him a dark look of disdain. One that wasn't alleviated by the heavy spattering sound of Jay throwing up that evening's bargains in the bathroom. Whatever plans she'd had for him were ruined. But Clare knew how to adapt to a situation, and quickly altered her focus. She looked across at me, her features softened back to a smile, and I realised that Jay had been confined to the past. It was clear that I was her new point of interest. I wasn't all that accustomed to female attention at the time, but I knew enough to recognise that something was off about this. She'd decided someone was going to give her some attention that night and that person was going to be me. I retreated into the kitchen, realising as she slunk after me that I'd cornered myself.

'Erm ... do you want a coffee?' I asked.

'That'd be nice,' she said, making a show of messing with her hair while I fussed with the kettle. 'I've just had it done,' she said, fingering her curls, letting them drop over her Kohl-rimmed eyes. 'You like?'

'It's nice,' I said, and I meant it. These tumbling, platinum ringlets that framed her round face. The porcelain skin. The slashes of cochineal-red on her lips. She was pretty by anyone's standards, but there was still something about her eyes that I didn't like. Large and unblinking, like a Blythe doll. I wasn't sure if she was drunk or high, but when I looked at her something made the back of my head itch.

I turned to reach for the sugar and she saw her moment, moving close to me and breaking into a song. A lilting folk tune called 'The Bonnie Black Hare', about a hunter meeting a willing maiden in the woods.

'Lock your legs around me and dig in with your heels/ For the closer we get, oh, the better it feels …'

On stage, I always made a meal of this part of the story, singing her lines lasciviously. But when it was actually happening and I was on the other end of her performance, I made myself small. Blushing, embarrassed by the intensity of her focus.

'It's an old song about a girl,' she told me, 'having *sex*.' This last word come out of her mouth with a whispered sizzle, and she tried to hold me in a significant gaze. I broke it, pretending to be searching for a spoon.

'Every generation thinks they invented sex,' she continued airily. 'But people have been at it for hundreds of years.'

'Thousands,' I replied, banking on the fact that there is nothing less attractive than a pedant. 'Tens of thousands.'

'You know what I mean, silly,' she said, laughing and swatting me playfully on the arm. She shifted a heap of dirty crockery out of the way and arched her back against

Bonnie Black Hare

the worktop, looking intently across at me. 'I meant, *fucking. Blow jobs. Anal.* That sort of thing.'

She used these words as if they were new to her. Naughty and dangerous. Like a child saying 'bum' for the first time and waiting for the reaction.

'Don't you ever just want to get … dirty?' she said, a raw silk in her voice. Breathy. But too much. As if she'd flipped to a setting on her throat labelled 'Heavy-handed seduction'.

She went on to detail a laundry list of sexual interests that made me blush so intensely the heat felt like it was bleaching my hair. This was a graphic part of the story that I really played for laughs when I talked about it in front of an audience. Discussing the acts she'd mentioned. Ones that I'd only ever heard about in jokes or seen illustrated in bathroom stalls and couldn't quite believe anyone actually did. But Clare had made it clear that she did them all the time and, what's more, she wanted to do them with me.

'Look,' she said, as I handed her a mug of coffee. 'Shall we go somewhere more comfortable?'

'I'm fine in here,' I said, holding onto my own mug for emotional support. Stifling my need to talk with sips of scalding coffee.

But Clare was a guest in my home, so when she told me her feet hurt and she needed to sit down, I found myself showing her into the living room. She sat down on the

Broken Biscuits

sofa and patted the space beside her. I lowered myself onto it and she slid up close to me. Our thighs touched.

'This is cosy,' she said, snuggling in. And it was. But in the way a coffin might be. Or a pillow placed firmly over your face. She leaned in to kiss me and I jerked away. A reaction that would've upset me, but Clare just smiled, seeming to believe it was all part of the game.

'Don't you have a boyfriend?' I asked.

I was pretty sure that she did. I'd seen her around campus a few times, linking the arm of a guy whose face wore the desperate, helpless expression of someone who knew he could be free if only he could remember his safe word.

'Yeah,' she said. 'But we have an open relationship.'

'Does he know that?'

She laughed lightly.

'Of course. We're both free to see other people.'

I thought of her boyfriend shackled naked somewhere, waiting for her to come home. As free as his choke chain would allow.

'I can't,' I said, finally playing my ace. The card I'd been holding off from using until I was absolutely sure, despite everything, that I'd not misread the situation. 'I've got a girlfriend.'

This wasn't true, but I didn't think the truth mattered at that moment. All that mattered to me was that I put an end to this.

Bonnie Black Hare

Clare responded with a smile, then eased herself down onto the carpet and knelt between my legs.

'If you just say the word ...'

Which brings us back to the knife. At the time, I was grateful for the fact that she'd left the room, quietly hoping that my rejection had been too much for her. That she was pulling on her boots and getting ready to leave. Instead, I heard a commotion in the kitchen and headed in there to find her standing in front of an open drawer, pressing a blade into her forearm.

'Oh God!' I yelled, my panicked hands flapping like a seal demanding a fish. 'What are you doing?'

'Cutting myself!' she said.

But she wasn't. Not really. She was using the butter knife, one so blunt I'd had trouble using it to cut through actual butter. But the drawer had left her with few options. A spatula. A wooden spoon. The rolling pin that came with the house. She was making the best of what she'd found.

'Please,' I said gently, edging toward her. Wincing as she pressed the blade into her skin. Blunt as it was, welts were appearing in its wake and the sight made me queasy. 'Stop that.'

'Are you going to sleep with me?'

'You know I can't.'

'Fine,' she said and recommenced sawing.

'Look,' I said, regretting the words even as I spoke

Broken Biscuits

them. 'Just put down the knife and come back into the living room. Please?'

She placed it on the sideboard and I took her hand, leading her back to the sofa. Unsure of what I would do from that point but glad we were away from the knife.

'What is it?' she asked me. 'Am I ugly? Do you not fancy me?'

I wanted to tell her that she scared me.

'It's not that,' I said. 'You're not ugly.'

'You hate me.'

'No, I don't.'

'Then why won't you sleep with me?'

She got up and ran back into the kitchen then, howling. Back to the butter knife.

The next few hours followed this routine. Her advances. My rejections. Her dry-eyed sobs. The knife. Three a.m. Four a.m. Five a.m. When the soft light of day arrived, exhaustion had weakened my resolve. I just wanted it over with and was ready to do whatever she wanted as long as all this stopped. And then, somehow, we were at the open front door, the chill morning air flooding in. Clare slipped past me, hobbling on her heels as she stepped onto the gravel path. She began to walk away then stopped and turned back to me, issuing a promise.

'You'll fuck me one day,' she said, a determined pulse in her words. 'You'll fuck me. You will.'

Bonnie Black Hare

I probably told this story at different spoken-word shows about five times, always getting the general response that I'd been hoping for. But after one performance in Manchester, a woman took my arm as I was leaving the stage and asked to speak to me. I was worried that I had crossed a line. Been too crude or used an obviously troubled young woman for story fodder, but what they were concerned about was assault.

'The whole time you were talking,' she said, 'I was thinking: *Imagine if a woman was telling that story about a man?* I wanted to say I'm sorry that happened to you.'

I'd thanked her but waved off her concern, saying that Clare likely had problems she was working out and that she'd just worked them out with me. It was no big deal. Just a weird thing that happened.

'Yeah, I don't know,' the woman replied, shaking her head. 'I don't think you should make excuses for her. Like I say, you wouldn't be doing that if she was a man. People wouldn't be laughing.'

This bothered me, an idea that would sizzle away inside me during the days that followed. But when I picked up a couple more slots at literary events and needed reliable material, I turned to this story again. I told it at events in Sheffield and Lancaster and each time a woman came up to me afterwards and offered me their sympathies. Told me to reconsider things with the genders reversed.

Broken Biscuits

It was no surprise to me that women would interpret the story like that, just as it was unsurprising that the men in the audience never asked me to rethink it in this way. Women are acutely aware of assault in a way men aren't. They have to be. It's happened to at least one in four of them. Women are wary, fearful and fucking sick of this stuff. They see it everywhere, and they're more sensitive to examples of it than I was. So, I stopped telling this story entirely, uncomfortable about the whole thing. I didn't want to upset anyone, to stir up anyone's bad memories. I'd also never thought too deeply about how Clare had behaved and now that I was being asked to, my funny story didn't seem so funny anymore. That it was about a time when I'd narrowly avoided being pressured into something I hadn't wanted.

Not long after I made the decision to stop telling that story, I met up with my friend, Anna, for a walk. As we threaded our way along a hilly desire path banked by brambles, we got talking about the responses the story had started to receive from women.

'Do *you* think it was assault?' I asked her. 'Like, which bits of it were the assault?'

Anna had seen me perform this story three times. On each occasion she laughed at the parts I'd hoped people would laugh at, gasped where I'd hoped people would gasp. Like me, she had interpreted what happened that night as having an entertaining shape, ripe for a spirited

Bonnie Black Hare

retelling. But placed on the spot and forced to reframe it, to flip the genders, she admitted she had problems with what went down.

'You made it pretty clear you weren't interested, and she was still pushing,' Anna said, having chewed it over. 'If that was me and a man was doing that, I'd start to feel scared pretty quickly. Especially that thing with the knife.'

We got talking about coercion then, pressure, how worried it made us for our daughters who were growing older and would be heading out into the adult world before we knew it. Likely confronting situations with people who might try to talk them into something they didn't feel comfortable with.

'I mean, I've been coerced into doing things …' Anna said, opening her mouth to go further before lapsing into silence. Her usual confidence and brightness suddenly absent.

She looked away from me then, out across a view that took in at least three towns. Toy-sized cars threading their way along the roads. I felt angry, about what must have happened to my friend to shut her down like that, but also about the place her memory had taken her back to. Whatever she'd gone through, I got the sense she was still blaming herself for it. Not entirely, but a little, which was too much. Because where the assignment of blame falls doesn't always feel so clear cut. Something happens to you that you didn't like, you feel bad or confused about

Broken Biscuits

it and find yourself turning the responsibility inwards. Taking the blame, feeling you must have encouraged it somehow. Either because someone explicitly tried to make you feel that way, or because there was no other way for you to feel but bad. So, you carry it with you, a part of yourself that gnaws at you whenever you're reminded of it. Blame is so much easier to self-assign, especially if you're vulnerable and conflict averse. And, because vulnerable was what Anna and I were being, and it had been preying on my mind, I decided to tell her about Donna.

Donna was a friend of a friend. We'd met in the pub a couple of months after that night with Clare. The two of us got chatting and found we had things in common. Music, films, our sense of humour. We joked around, had a few drinks and she asked me back to her place for coffee. So, I went, thinking quietly about the implied connotations of 'coffee' but never presuming. Not confident enough in myself to ever presume.

We sat on her sofa for a while, cradling coffees and talking, then naturally fell into kissing. It was nice, something relaxed and innocent about it. Just two people talking and kissing. In time it took what I guess was the next logical step and she moved to feed her hand down the front of my jeans. I stopped her, getting an overwhelming sense that I didn't want this. I don't know where it was coming from exactly, aware that this was the

Bonnie Black Hare

sort of thing I should want and hope for. But I didn't want it. I wanted to call the whole thing off and go home to bed. Hopeful of sleep.

'I think I'd better leave,' I said, getting to my feet and making an excuse about having work in the morning. Needing to be in early for a job I didn't really have.

'I'm sorry,' she said, reaching out and grabbing my hand. 'Just stay a bit longer, please? We can just talk.'

I felt bad then, so I sat back down. We somehow smoothed over what had happened before and fell back into talking again. After a while, she leaned in for another kiss and I kissed her back. I don't know why. Out of politeness, maybe? Because it wasn't awful, because I'd been drinking, because I didn't want her to feel bad and we'd made an agreement about how far things would go. Then her hands were on my jeans again, unbuttoning them. I brushed her away and told her again that I didn't want that. Then I went one further and told her that I didn't like sex. Again, this wasn't true, but I wanted whatever was happening to stop and that seemed like a pretty nuclear way of going about it. She told me that she understood, but she was lonely, had recently broken up with someone and just wanted to be close to somebody. To touch me. So, I let her. I know shouldn't have, but I did. After a while she went down on me, and I let that happen too. I closed my eyes and I guess she saw this as an opportunity. It was a fast move, far quicker than anything I could have expected. As sudden as a sucker punch, it came in a series of rapid movements. She was on me, straddling me, pushing me inside her, apologising as she did.

'I'm sorry,' she said, placing the tips of her fingers on my lips, on my chin. Smothering my protests. 'I have to.'

I told her again that I didn't want this and tried to wriggle out from under her, but I also didn't want to push her. To be physical. Because what would that make me?

'Please,' she said, her hand moving down onto my chest, pushing me back onto the sofa. I let out a deflating breath. Then I just allowed it to happen.

When it was over, when she'd got what she wanted, she thanked me. 'It's okay,' I said, then I left and walked home, wondering why things like this kept happening to me.

I'd often hear people say, 'For men, all sex is good sex.' But I had learned that wasn't the case. There had been no pleasure for me in what happened. None of the glow that a consensual act would have carried. That comes from two people wanting each other. Instead, there was a hollow, sick feeling. The uncanny sensation of believing you've been pickpocketed that makes you pat your clothes for your wallet.

'Fuck,' Anna said, when I finished telling her about Donna, a look of surprise at the way this story had tumbled out of me. 'Okay ... Oh, wow. Fuck.'

Bonnie Black Hare

'Was that assault?' I asked her. 'Really, I've never been sure.'

'Oh, it fucking was. You said no.'

'But I let it happen. How different was it to what happened with Clare, really?'

'Well, it wasn't fucking funny for a start. How did it make you feel?'

'Oh, horrible,' I said, uncomfortable about the words I was about to say. 'But honestly, I felt kind of flattered.'

For most of my life up until that point, no one had been interested in me sexually, in any way. I'd only had one serious relationship and it had ended miserably. So to suddenly find myself desired, pleaded for, thanked for the use of my body, I had never felt so wanted. It was the same with Clare. When she was gone, out of the door, her attention had felt like a huge compliment. An endorsement of my attractiveness and worth.

'But it wasn't about you,' Anna said. 'It was about wanting something and taking it. You shouldn't be flattered that someone took something from you.'

'I know,' I said. 'I know.'

But I still felt that way. I always told myself that what happened was my fault, accepting the part I played in it. That, yes, Donna had taken something from me, but I'd also given it to her, albeit in slow unwilling stages. I had gone home with her, I had let something happen and while I didn't want what happened next, I eventually

Broken Biscuits

came, so where was the crime? So, I took what I decided was a compliment and tried not to think too hard about what happened. Aware of it only occasionally when something would remind me. It was a tiny stone in my shoe that would occasionally irritate me then shift to a position that I couldn't feel anymore. Wearing away to something so small it felt like it had gone away completely. Then I was made to think about that night with Clare in a new way and what happened with Donna grew from that little, almost invisible stone into a bulky, heavy rock. Unavoidably dragged with me wherever I went.

Wanting to get this straight in my mind and to know how common this sort of thing was, I'd looked up coercive assault statistics and found a report in *The Lancet*. It said that one in ten women had stated they'd been forced into sex against their will. In terms of the first time they'd had sex, that stat rose to one in two. Coercion, it seemed, was a very popular tactic. Persistence, wearing down, it gets results. But with assaults against men, that number was much smaller. Closer to one in a hundred, and often it is other men who were committing that assault. But not exclusively. The report confirmed what I knew to be true, that women can pressure men into sex, too, and I had to think about myself in new terms. As part of a statistic.

The problem was, I didn't think I qualified to be any part of those figures. That by even thinking of myself in those terms I would have belittled and trivialised them. I

Bonnie Black Hare

wasn't a survivor or a victim. Victims, I believed, do not feel flattered. What I had was one strange story and another that made me feel gross. And as uncomfortable as I was about both of them, they'd left me feeling wanted and I hadn't known quite what to do with that. Could something that was wrong have made me feel that way?

'I suppose part of the difference when it happens to men is fear,' Anna said. 'It doesn't sound like you were ever afraid.'

'No, I wasn't,' I replied. 'Well, I was but it was different. I was scared Clare would hurt herself. And a bit of Donna and what might have happened if I protested too much.'

What I meant by this was that I was scared I'd be accused of something if I didn't give in to her. That she would cry wolf. So, letting it happen seemed easier, and it turned out to be the right decision. Nothing more ever came of it. So no, I was not afraid. At least not in the way Anna was talking about.

Women spend so much of their lives in fear of assault. Afraid of men. Trying not to go out alone, certainly not in the dark. To never wear both earbuds at once. Walking with keys held in their fists as they head home, or a pen handy as a makeshift weapon. Not taking shortcuts that might leave them vulnerable to attack. Trying not to wear anything that might be treated as an invitation for a man to approach them. It's the reason my daughter always calls me when she's walking alone and catching the bus or the tram. Me staying on the line with her makes her feel protected.

I was never made to feel afraid by women. I have complete freedom to walk in the park wearing noise-cancelling headphones and tight jeans. Even when Clare had been holding a knife, I wasn't scared, at least not for me. I felt pressured, worn down and, in the case of Donna, tricked, but never scared. When I think about her now, on top of me, I feel the opposite of arousal. Like something at the base of my spine is withdrawing. A snake, a worm, something slimy that crawls out of me. Making me shudder.

Clare and Donna will both be well into their forties now. They may have done something like this again and they may not have. But what I feel pretty certain about is that they likely don't dwell on it or think they did anything wrong, not really. That it was nothing serious. Donna knew she was transgressing, had admitted it to me several times even as she was doing it. But I hadn't made a fuss about it, and I'm sure she'd taken comfort from that. Soothed herself with the same ideas I did. That I went home with her. That I came. And like they say: all sex is good sex.

What I never talked about on stage was that a year or so after I'd finished university and left town, I got a phone call. I was living in a flat in Salford with a girlfriend at the

Bonnie Black Hare

time, and she was the one who answered the phone.

'It's some woman,' my girlfriend said, handing me the receiver. 'She said you'll know who it is.'

'Hello?' I said.

'Hello to you, too,' a voice replied.

'Sorry, who is this?'

'You know, silly.'

The connection was pretty bad, but the way she said 'silly' confirmed to me that it could only be Clare.

'Oh,' I said, as if we were old friends. 'How are you doing? It's been a while.'

After that night in my house, I actually saw a fair bit of Clare. It seemed that I was bumping into her everywhere. In the pub, in the row behind me in the cinema, unaccountably on my street or outside my house, with a frequency that exceeded my neighbours. But just passing, she'd say. In the area. My friends had teased me that I had a stalker and, again, while it was a bit strange, I was flattered by the attention. I had thought leaving town would be the last of it. Now here I was again, cornered but by long distance. Not sure how to bring an end to things.

Clare told me that she knew I'd moved to Manchester and was planning on visiting the city the following week, so was hoping we could catch up. Reconnect.

You'll fuck me one day. You will.

I managed to convince her that I would be out of the city, adding unnecessarily that I was sorry about it.

Broken Biscuits

'It's a shame,' I said. 'Maybe next time.'

'*Definitely* next time,' she replied.

We said our goodbyes and just as I was about to hang up, I thought to ask her something.

'Wait, how did you get my number?'

'Oh,' she said, 'Jay gave it to me.'

As I put the phone down, I found that I couldn't stop giggling at this. At what felt like a joke that I'd heard once before.

'Why are you laughing?' my girlfriend asked. 'What did she say?'

I wanted to explain to her, but I couldn't. Not to anyone. Not until years later, when I was on a stage and had found a reason to talk about it, along with the words. So, I gave her the only response I could manage at the time. An answer that would eventually turn out to be the truth.

'Honestly, I don't know,' I said, wiping my eyes. Taking a composing breath. Looking back to the phone. 'It's really not that funny.'

This is Your Brain On Drugs

Though he was thirty-seven when he died, I'm aware we could have lost my brother Robert at so many points in time. At any age. It could have been when he was fifteen and smuggled a live bullet out of army cadets then conspired to ignite it under a railway bridge on his way home. Or one of the many times during his teens when he'd dangled himself from the walkway above the busy A143 out of town. There was the day that he'd purposefully rewired all the plugs in his school's science block, explosively shorting the electrics in the building. The street brawl that cost him half a front tooth and the one that ended with his head being smashed through a pub window. All that before we even get to the motorcycle accident that ripped his shoulder from its socket or the multiple occasions when he somehow fell from roofs. Blessed with more lives than a litter of kittens, Robert would survive two suicide attempts

Broken Biscuits

before finally succeeding during the icy Spring of 2008. But the first time I was aware that we could have lost him was in our living room one evening when I was eight years old and listening to a police officer explain that he had been moments away from driving over Robert's head.

'He's lucky I spotted him,' the officer said. 'I saw him wobbling about on the pavement then he fell right into the road. He went down like a tree.'

I should have been fast asleep when all this was happening, but I was woken that night by a firm and steady knocking at our front door, which was situated directly below my bedroom window. The knocking was followed by a general commotion downstairs. Murmured speech, groans, a mysterious soft scuffling sound. I recognised my mother's concerned voice but the others were male and unknown. This was all too intriguing to keep a child like me in bed. So, I slipped out of my room to peer down the stairs, where two police officers were helping Robert into the hallway.

Robert's head was lolling loosely, slack-jawed. His legs offered him all the support of overcooked spaghetti, his limp feet paint-brushing the cork flooring in the hall as the officers guided him into the living room. They were followed by the bustling figure of my mother and, shortly thereafter, me as I edged down the stairs to get a closer look.

This is Your Brain On Drugs

'I don't know how much he had to drink,' the second officer said, 'but it was too much. God knows what else he's taken.'

Robert can't have been much older than fourteen at the time. This might seem like an early age to arrive home paralytic, but it made complete sense to me. Robert had barrelled through life impatiently, wanting to gobble up every experience that adulthood could offer, despite only being on the fringes of it. He started smoking aged eight, had lost his virginity before he was out of middle school and now, having landed in his teens, had become the kind of heavy drinker I was familiar with from TV shows and cartoons. The staggering, sozzle-voiced booze hound added to scenes for comic effect. But there was nothing funny about Robert that night. The sight of him was both scary and compelling.

I picked my way downstairs then slipped into the living room just as my mother was placing our washing-up bowl beside Robert's head. She turned to glare at me, annoyed that I was out of bed and witnessing this. It was a brief, flashing look that somehow delivered both a lecture and the sting of a smacked leg. I was in trouble and would hear more about this later. But she clearly didn't feel she could shout at me while the police were present. And besides, she had more pressing concerns. So, I hopped onto the sofa and looked down at Robert, lying motionless on his front, his face turned my way and his eyes

Broken Biscuits

pinwheeling. Maybe he could see me, maybe he couldn't, but I shuddered under his possible gaze. The tassels on his leather jacket were splayed around his arms, his long, dark hair lank and sprawling. He looked like a man-sized crow that had crash landed onto our living room carpet.

'When I got out to check on him, his head was right under the wheel,' the first officer said, a note of excitable shock in his voice. He raised his hand, holding his thumb and forefinger a few millimetres apart. 'I was *that* close to running over it.'

I drew my knees up to my chin, arms wrapped around my shins, and watched as Robert raised his head to vomit a clear, yellowish fluid into the washing up bowl. I thought about the wheel of the police car flattening that head like rolled dough. Those drunken eyes popping out. His brains expelled down the street like toothpaste from an aggressively squeezed tube. In that moment, I decided that as God was my witness I would never touch drugs or a drop of alcohol for as long as I lived. But as I looked at Robert lying there, I also thought something else. Something so at odds with the image he was presenting.

God, he is so cool.

As if he could sense this thought, the first officer turned to look at me.

'Let this be a warning to you,' he said, deploying the flat, personality-free tone they must teach in police college. 'Now, off to bed.'

This is Your Brain On Drugs

I darted from the room and rattled up the stairs. Fearful that he'd arrest me if I didn't. I got back into bed and listened to the officers leave. But it was a long time before I got off to sleep, worried that Robert might not survive the night.

So, I was surprised the next morning when I came downstairs to find him standing at the stove, heating a pan of baked beans and listening to the radio.

'Morning, dickhead,' he said, adding a glug of Worcestershire sauce to the pan. 'Make me a cup of tea.'

It was baffling to see him like this, recovered and buoyant, having appeared to have been dying only hours earlier. I obediently filled the kettle and flipped the switch.

'Did you hear about last night?' he asked, an impish grin spreading. 'Police almost ran over my head.'

Even then, Robert was dealing in the currency of battle scars and intense experiences. Almost dying was an adventure, and he would seemingly become hooked on it until the end of his days. I dropped a tea bag into a mug and listened to him talk about the previous night while the kettle rumbled, unable to shake two seesawing, contradictory thoughts.

Let that be a warning to you.
God, he is so cool.

* * *

Broken Biscuits

Robert and I were in our back garden firing at cans with his air rifle, when he stopped to light a cigarette. I watched him as he did this, the gun no longer interesting to me, shifting my focus to the small ceremony of smoking. The way he tamped the pack before selecting a cigarette. The uncharacteristically delicate way he cupped his hand around his mouth as if, rather than lighting the cigarette, he was whispering it a secret. The barely audible sizzle as he took the first drag. Every stage of the process fascinating to me.

'Want one?' he asked, registering my interest and extending the pack.

I was fourteen at the time, and he'd just switched to a brand named Death, which came in a jet-black package bearing a skull and crossbones, as if he'd taken to carrying around a pocket-sized pirate flag. The pack bore the warning, *Death is a responsible way to market a legally available consumer product which kills people when used exactly as intended*. It was a purchase that stated, *I am risking my life and LOVING it!* These days, this sort of thing would initiate sighs, the look-at-me choice of the edgelord. But heading into the newly minted 1990s it seemed as exciting and dangerous to me as if Robert had taken up the hobby of placing a part-loaded revolver into his mouth and clicking the trigger.

The part of me that dearly wanted to be just like him daydreamed about my response to his offer. I saw myself

This is Your Brain On Drugs

replying with a casual 'Sure' as I confidently took the pack from his outstretched hand, lit a cigarette and began blowing immaculate smoke rings.

'You,' I imagined him saying, 'are the coolest little brother anyone could have.' Then we'd head to the pub together, to talk about girls and fighting and when I'd buy my first motorbike. Brothers so close people might say we were twins.

But the fantasy ended there, colliding with the inescapable reality of the person I actually was.

'No, thank you,' I told him, waving away the pack. 'It's a gateway drug.'

This response surprised both of us and I flinched as the words left me, waiting for the sharp punch in the arm that I usually got when I said something Robert could perceive as backchat. Instead, he laughed. A whip-cracking sound that came from somewhere deep inside him.

'You funny little fucker,' he said. 'Where did you come from?'

The answer, of course, was him. I was the creature he had created. This little prude, born out of a life observing his behaviour. I know he'd had dreams of seeing me grow into a replica of him. And the truth was, I wanted that, too. But there is the person you want to be and the person you are, and after a certain point very little can be done about that.

When I was younger, I'd been bold and fearless, an embryonic Robert, showing every sign that I'd follow in his footsteps. But this part of me had been replaced over time with a timidity that saw me both fascinated by and fearful of the way he lived. The beginning of my transformation traceable back to that policeman's knock in the middle of the night.

Robert's reckless behaviour should have had the opposite effect on me. He drank, smoked, took drugs, and was rewarded for this with a large circle of friends, a rich and varied existence and a revolving cast of girlfriends who regularly marched past my bedroom and into his. There seemed to be a clear connection between the things he consumed and the life he lived, and he made it look good. But by the time I reached the age where I could make decisions about drugs and alcohol, I had grown far too careful. And not only that, I was also worried that I wouldn't be able to live up to the standard that Robert had established. So, I made resistance a considered choice and become a judgemental, teenage finger-wagger. A personality that I could drape over my fears and unfulfillable desires.

So much of making this work involved convincing myself. I could have had a parade of girlfriends if I'd wanted, but I was not willing to fry my brain for them. My parents weren't going to be presented with the sight of me being dragged home by the authorities, oh no. Because I knew right from wrong. Experiences like that, I decided, were unconscionable, and they all burst through the gateway of that introductory cigarette.

This is Your Brain On Drugs

I'd picked up on ideas like this at primary school, where each day I would pass the anti-smoking posters pinned beside the main entrance. These featured Superman battling a raspy-voiced, tobacco-advocating supervillain named Nick O'Teen, who wore a stovepipe hat designed to a resemble a filtered cigarette, and crept around in the shadows offering tobacco to children.

'I've got something to help you grow up fast!' he'd say, offering a hapless child one of the 'deadly tubes' he gripped in his nicotine-yellowed gloves until Superman, the ultimate prude, intervened, hoisting Nick by his collar and bellowing 'NEVER SAY YES TO A CIGARETTE!' before hurling him into the sky.

Robert had grown up fast and what had that got him? Years of joyous debauchery, yes, but there was all that other stuff, too. The reckless behaviour, the fistfights, the collapsing in the street, and God knows what was happening to his lungs. So, even if Robert was offering me a cigarette, *especially* if Robert was offering me a cigarette, I would politely refuse. Knowing exactly where it could all end for me.

Growing up in the 70s and 80s, anti-drug and alcohol propaganda was everywhere. All of it reassuring material for the aspiring killjoy. I absorbed the government-funded ads warning against the dangers of pills and intravenous narcotics. The glossy American teen dramas that addressed drugs in special episodes, where beloved characters went

Broken Biscuits

off the rails and into the dark heart of addiction then on to recovery, over the course of twenty-six minutes and an ad break. Closer to home, there were drug storylines on the school drama series *Grange Hill*, where I winced at the sight of Danny Kendall's overdosed body being found dead in a stolen car. Saw Zammo's heroin addiction and subsequent criminal behaviour. The cast of the show recording a pop song for the *Just Say No* anti-drugs campaign, and being invited to the White House to meet Nancy Reagan.

For a lot of kids, a message from the Reagan administration explaining that they disapproved of drugs was only ever going to be perceived as an endorsement of a good time. The danger of it becoming part of the lure. But other kids weren't also contending with my mother, who recognised Robert's influence over me and grew concerned about which way the wind was blowing. Regularly hitting me with her own homespun public ervice announcements.

'I read a story in the paper about a boy who tried LSD and thought he was a superhero,' she told me. 'Jumped out of a window. Splat. The ambulance had to take his body away … in buckets.'

It was never my instinct to question stories like this. I didn't think to ask, 'How did anyone know what this kid thought if he was dead?' or to challenge the idea of the buckets. Instead, I pictured a boy who looked just like me,

This is Your Brain On Drugs

leaping from the window of a tower block, his arms held straight out in front of him as he collided with the concrete below. And just as I didn't question this example, I didn't challenge any of the ones that followed it either.

'I read about a boy who smoked marijuana and forgot his own name.'

'I heard about a boy who took ecstasy and danced until he died. It's true!'

For every drug and substance, my mother was able to offer me a tragic cautionary tale. Heroin, amphetamines, glue sniffing, all of it had the possibility to transform me into the subject of an alarmist tabloid headline, my smiling school photo juxtaposed against a picture of my grimly discovered corpse. I took everything she said at face value and made my decision. I would just say no.

But in the same way that the loudest right-wing moralist railing against deviancy will inevitably be caught exiting a brothel with a wad of cocaine residue welded to their septum, I was the prude who longed to transgress. I dearly wanted to try drugs. I wanted to know what was on the other side of this wall I'd built in front of myself. And wherever I looked, it seemed like there was something showing me what I was missing out on. Inevitably, most of what I saw came from Robert.

Once during my teens, he arrived in my room with a stack of underground American comic books he'd been given by one of the guys who sold him weed.

Broken Biscuits

'Here,' he said, dumping them on my bed, 'I think you'll like these.'

They were a window into drug-fuelled counterculture, featuring strips by Robert Crumb, Gilbert Shelton and S. Clay Wilson, where sex and drug use was rampant and thrilling for me to read about. Many of these comics were devoted to *The Fabulous Furry Freak Brothers*, a trio of hippies who spent their days either getting stoned or conspiring to. I marvelled at the technicolour light shows that went off in their heads when they dropped acid or took a bong hit and I wanted to experience that, too. But I had feasted from the all-you-can-eat buffet of worst-case scenarios for too long, so I regretfully filed the Freak Brothers away as I would any other comic book: as a fantasy. Just as I would never kick a car into the sky like The Hulk or fire energy blasts from my hands like Captain Atom, I would also not be snorting dope then hovering off the ground like Freewheelin' Franklin, a firework display of colours and SPROING ZONK POW sound effects exploding in my brain. The risks were too great.

I quickly learned that when you decide to say no to something, people will make it their mission to change your mind. Whether it's religion, politics or green olives, if you explain that you are not interested in a certain thing, some folks will refuse to take no for an answer. Robert would continue to offer me cigarettes as if he were campaigning for Big Tobacco. Friends tried to break me

This is Your Brain On Drugs

down with cans of pilfered lager or bottles of brandy from their parents' sideboard. My cousin, Michael, tried to trick me into drinking cider during a family party by decanting it into a Coke can. But I would not budge, turning down these offers with such puritan determination that Robert began calling me 'Vicar'.

When it came to drugs, though, I was only ever approached at secondary school. Through my work in art class, I attracted the attention of a dealer in my year named Carl. Though his eyes were as heavy-lidded and bloodshot as a St Bernard's, he'd been able to see enough of my art to recognise a potential customer. Whenever my course work was done, I'd kill time at the end of lessons by filling large sheets of paper with freeform images of crosshatched, Crumb-inspired grotesques, each of them connected by meandering noodles of pipework and tanks of bubbling liquid. Rip-offs of the kind of psychedelic images I'd seen in the comics Robert had given me.

'You should have some of this, then see what you come up with,' Carl said, leaning over to look at my artwork and rolling a tarry chunk of hash between his fingers. 'I'd love to see what you'd draw. Your doors of perception would be perpetually open.'

This was such a bizarre thing to hear, especially from Carl, who was always out of it. In classes, he was at best monosyllabic. Either nodding off at his desk or giggling at how he never knew the answer to any of the questions

Broken Biscuits

our teacher might ask him and thinking it the funniest thing. But what I was drawing had activated him, making him parrot lines that he could have only heard from other stoners who had met someone who had met someone who had read Aldous Huxley. Or, more likely, owned an album by The Doors.

In any case, Carl was presenting me with a scenario I had seen on TV countless times before and knew well. Scenes where ominous music plays while a grinning dealer homes in on an innocent patsy.

'Try this,' they'd say. 'The first one's free.'

Cut to that patsy a few months later, all colour drained from his face as he expires in a garret, a needle dangling from a ropey, well-used vein in his arm.

'No, thank you,' I told Carl, as if I were in recovery and proud of my six-month chip from AA. 'I'm sober.'

This was as big a pose as if I'd started smoking Death cigarettes, but with that pose came safety. While I desperately wanted to live in the moment, the place I actually lived was the future. In the 'one day' and the 'what if'. A place where actions had devastating consequences. So, I decided it was much wiser for me to abstain and be thought of as a dweeb. The alternative being the fall and the road and my eyes looking up in a daze for the very last time as a wheel headed towards my helpless skull.

* * *

This is Your Brain On Drugs

While I was able to avoid succumbing to everything else, Robert finally led me to alcohol on my eighteenth birthday. I capitulated because it was now legal and morally correct, but also because he had been excited for this day, organising a pub crawl in our old hometown in Suffolk. Its long, single high street offered a pub every few yards and a crawl could easily involve twenty bars, all of which I had heard legends about. A murder in The Bell. The rumour that a fifteen-year-old boy had once tried to buy a drink in The Plough, only to be thrown through the window like a quarrelsome wrangler in a western. I steeled myself, knowing this was a rite of passage. I had to do this for Robert. Convincing myself that's what it was about.

'What do you think?' he asked, watching me sip from my first pint and eager to find out what I thought about the taste of adulthood.

'It's lovely,' I said, wincing as if fresh from having just licked the carpet.

'You'll learn to love it,' he said, tearing open a pack of pork scratchings and setting them on the table between us. 'Get it down you. There's more to come.'

I doubted that I'd grow to enjoy it. Whatever he'd ordered smelt and tasted to me like something that had been tipped out of a rain-soaked boot. But an hour later, my second pint gone and a third on the way, I was in a pub toilet, swaying in front of the mirror and studying my reflection. I poked my numb hands into my face, finding it doughy and unreal. But I also felt light and confident and happy. I loved the feeling of drunkenness, just as I'd always known and feared I would, and I was ready for more.

I awoke the next morning on the living-room floor of Robert's flat, my body draped across his sofa cushions. My mouth felt as if I'd spent the preceding hours sucking on a hair dryer and I had a headache so oppressive I was worried I'd fractured my skull. Robert was in the adjoining kitchen, cooking bacon, and, in that moment, I had never wanted anything more. But the smell of it also made me want to throw up, so I did that, racing to the bathroom just in time to reach the toilet bowl.

'Yeah, you did that last night, too,' Robert said when I staggered back to the living room, having gulped thirstily from the cold tap.

An image of myself slumped beside the bathroom radiator resurfaced then disappeared behind dense fog. I realised then that I didn't have many memories of the previous night, so Robert filled in more of the blanks for me. He explained that after the ninth pub we returned to his flat and I'd stumbled inside, thrown up in the bathroom then announced that I was tired and collapsed onto his living room floor as if I'd been shot. What saved me from injury was Robert's quick reflexes, tossing the sofa cushions into my path in time to break my fall. But before

This is Your Brain On Drugs

that, he told me, I had been a happy drunk. Chatty, confident and fun to be around. The unbuttoned version of me that he'd always hoped was in there trying to get out. Apparently, I had things to say and a lot of them. I'd made people laugh. These were the kinds of compliments I wasn't used to hearing about myself, especially from Robert, and I was hungry for them.

'I remember a woman,' I said, a moment in one pub suddenly coming back to me through the fog. 'She touched my hand and said hello, but I didn't know who she was.'

He laughed. 'That was Karen,' he said, spearing a rasher of bacon with a fork and dumping it onto a slice of buttered white bread. 'She was chatting you up.'

'Oh, I didn't realise.'

'Fucking hell, mate. We need to get you drunk again. We need to get you laid.'

I sat back down on the floor, and he placed a mug of strong tea and a bacon sandwich onto the coffee table next to me. I looked at them with sickness and longing. While it felt as if I might never recover from my hangover, it seemed like I was now a part of the world I'd always been keeping at bay. And I wanted more of it, now aware that while alcohol came with its dangers, it also came with a different version of me. This confident, bold Adam. He sounded like the preferable version of me, and I wanted to meet him again.

Broken Biscuits

'So, I was funny?' I asked, needing confirmation of something that always mattered to me. The thought that I could make people laugh. 'Really?'

'Yeah,' Robert said, squirting tomato sauce into his own sandwich. 'I can't wait to see what you're like when you're stoned.'

I spent the months that followed chasing the fun version of me to the bottom of pint glasses, but in my eagerness I'd often end up drinking too fast and skip the confident stage completely. Progressing straight to the drunken mess and the zombifying hangover. The version of me that Robert had met on my eighteenth birthday had rarely shown its face again. So, I folded back into my shy and reticent ways, spending hours brooding in my room and haunting our house like a maudlin character from a Victorian novel until my mother finally had enough.

'You're going on a date,' she told me.

'What?'

'Do you remember me telling you about Tracy?'

Tracy was the daughter of a woman my mother worked with. She was cute, I was often told, and about my age. Had a head of red curls and dressed in tie-dyes and the kind of floppy hats girls wore on episodes of *My So-Called Life*. 'She's just your type,' my mother would say, and when I didn't take the hint, she went ahead and arranged a date for us.

This is Your Brain On Drugs

'Oh God,' I said, mortified. 'Why did you do that?'
'Because you need it.'
'I'm not going.'
'You bloody well are.'

No one wants their first date to be set up by a parent, but once I got used to the idea I couldn't deny that I was hopeful of the possibilities. So, I dressed to impress, arriving at Tracy's house wearing my leather jacket, black jeans and my prescription sunglasses, my body enthusiastically coated in a film of Lynx Java.

'Hello,' Tracy said, smiling as she opened the door to me. 'You look very cool.'

This was a line that had previously only ever been directed at me by my mother, and then only with a note of protective pity. So, to hear it coming from someone I wasn't related to, and with apparent sincerity, was intoxicating. It grew more so when she led me along the hall of her single-storey home and into her room, then invited me to sit on her bed.

We hung out for a while making cautious small talk. Feeling each other out and getting on. It didn't seem stilted or awkward. I made a mental note to both thank and apologise to my mother.

'Do you want a drink?' Tracy asked. 'And some toast?'

I said yes to both and while she was in the kitchen I took the time to properly admire her bedroom. The whole

Broken Biscuits

place had a muted bohemian vibe, aided by the pleasant scent of something heady mixed with patchouli. The curtains were drawn and through them the fierce glare of the sun was filtered into the kind of muted lighting that makes everything and everyone look better. Above her bed she had a ceiling fan, the type I'd only ever seen in American films. I was looking up at it when Tracy returned, handing me a plate of buttered toast and a can of bitter. She sat down beside me. A little closer than she had before. I took a gentle sip from the can. We talked some more, chewed toast and drank. Everything seemed to be heading to a positive place.

'Do you get high?' she asked.

'Yeah,' I said, my principles suddenly standing for nothing when presented with the offer of drugs from a woman I wanted to impress. Not caring if it was a gateway drug or if I'd be dead within the fortnight. I'd take whatever she wanted me to. 'I get high all the time.'

'Cool,' she said with a smile, turning to retrieve a small tin from her beside drawer. I watched as she opened it up, withdrew the contents then began thoughtfully constructing a joint, crumbling a chunk of resin across its length. She lit it, took a drag and passed it to me. I took it from her hand with what I believed was easy confidence, hoping that the petticoat of my puritanism wasn't showing. Alcohol had made me personable and confident, and I was curious about the effect that drugs would have on

This is Your Brain On Drugs

me. Now finally here one was, full of unknown potential, smoke curling from its tip.

I placed the joint in my mouth, aware as I did so that I had no idea how to smoke. I'd not thought that far ahead. But I'd seen enough people doing it, had studied Robert's cigarette use as if I were a nature documentarian. How hard could it be? I took a long drag, holding the smoke deep inside me, hot and smothering, then passed the joint back to her. Following the etiquette I'd seen on TV. Not bogarting it.

At some point I'd have to breathe out, I knew, but I wasn't sure how. As a plume? A ring? A nasal snort? In the end the choice was taken away as the smoke left me with a spluttering cough, heading upwards where it was smashed to cotton-ball pieces by the spinning fan. I felt immediately woozy. Whatever it was, something was happening to me.

'Are you okay?' Tracy asked, her brow wrinkling.

'Yeah,' I said.

'You don't look okay.'

'I'm fine, honestly.'

'Okay, lay down,' she said, ignoring my reply and turning to her stereo. She pressed play on an album by Pink Floyd. 'Just go with the music.'

I lay back on her bed and looked up at the ceiling fan. The churning of the blades made me feel queasy, so I closed my eyes, trying to connect with the music and not

Broken Biscuits

think about how much I hated Pink Floyd. I felt as if I was passing out on a rollercoaster, and maybe this meant something exciting was about to happen. I pictured myself in a Freak Brothers strip and readied myself for the SPROING ZONK POW of it all. For the nausea to pass and my fun, stoned personality to finally greet the world.

'Breathe,' Tracy said slowly. 'Just breathe.'

I inhaled deeply, but when I exhaled I felt something rise in me. Something unstoppable. If it was another personality, I wasn't sure I was going to like it.

From the right angle it might have looked impressive, the way the vomit rose upwards and out of me. Reaching such a surprising height that it's possible I broke a world record. But if a Guinness official had been present and taking notes, they'd have retreated behind their clipboard at the moment when that vomit connected with the ceiling fan. There was a gentle spattering sound then, as the blades began whipping flecks of regurgitated toast and bitter around the room, coming to land who knows where. Tracy squealed, covering her head with her hands as she raced to switch off the fan. I looked around me in horror. What hadn't connected with the fan had painted a good quarter of Tracy's duvet. I opened my mouth to apologise and threw up again, covering the three quarters of her bed that I'd missed the first time around.

'Can I ...' I managed through clamped lips, 'use the toilet?'

This is Your Brain On Drugs

Tracy's expression suggested that she would very much like it if I did, and quickly directed me down the hall. I darted inside the bathroom, locking the door behind me and kneeling in front of the toilet so I could get down to serious work of retching. In time, when I was empty and the dry heaves had passed, I laid down on the floor and rolled my forehead back and forth across the cold tiled flooring. The one comfort I could draw from all this. It crossed my mind to drown myself in the toilet bowl or perhaps bash my own brains out on those cool, hard tiles. But instead, I rinsed out my mouth, unlocked the door and sheepishly returned to Tracy's room. She had stripped the bed, the duvet cover bundled up in her hands like a hobo's bindle. Air freshener had been sprayed liberally around the room, killing that heady scent and replacing it with a mix of forest pine and puke.

'I'm sorry,' I said.

'I think it might be best if you went home,' she said.

I agreed, apologising once more as she guided me to the door.

'It's fine. See you soon,' she said as I waved goodbye, but what I heard was, '*I can't wait to never do this again.*'

I couldn't blame her at all. I couldn't wait either.

In 2019, my then girlfriend and I took a ferry trip to Amsterdam to celebrate my forty-third birthday. It was unseasonably warm and by the time we arrived in the city it felt positively Mediterranean. We made the most of this weather, spending the day sitting outside bars, drinking lager from chilled glasses and smoking cigarettes on the picturesque banks of the canal. People with catwalk bodies cycled elegantly past us on the tow path. We could only imagine what it must be like to be so fit and healthy. To have such great posture. I took in all this beauty and made a decision.

'I want to get stoned.'

It was through this girlfriend, just a few months earlier, that, at the age of forty-two, I had finally smoked my first cigarette. We were sitting outside a pub in Salford, enjoying a drink, when she lit up. She'd squinted curiously at me through her exhaled smoke, registering my interest in what she was doing.

'Do you want a cig?' she asked, gesturing to the pack on the table between us.

'Yes please, but ...' I took a pause before confessing, 'I don't know how.'

She'd known when we met that I wasn't a smoker, but not that I'd never done it. Most people my age had at least tried, and the amused look of surprise on her face made me blush with embarrassment. But now I'd admitted this to her, I needed to commit to the next step.

'Can you show me?' I asked.

'Okay,' she said, smirking softly, clearly finding this a ridiculous thing to be explaining to a middle-aged man.

This is Your Brain On Drugs

Surely learning to smoke was – like puberty or phasing out jeans from your wardrobe – just a stage we all went through at some point. I sensed the fact that I hadn't managed this sooner came off to her like a defect. A discovery as unattractive as learning that I still slept with my childhood teddy bear. Still, she decided to be gentle with me, carefully talking me through the steps while I closely followed instruction, the class swot keen to earn top marks. 'Well, first you put it in your mouth and light it,' she said, instructing me on how to inhale a little smoke, hold it in my mouth, then slowly draw it into my lungs. 'Now exhale. There you go. You're smoking.'

'That was easy,' I said, removing the cigarette from my mouth and regarding the glowing tip. 'I like it.'

'Congratulations,' she said flatly. 'I'm happy for you.'

She was being flippant, but it was a celebratory moment. For me, nothing had ever stopped smoking from looking cool. Not Superman. Not the images on cigarette packs showing laryngeal stomas or the kind of teeth I was only used to seeing in zombie movies. Not even the discovery during his autopsy that Robert's lifetime of smoking had done so much damage to his body that, had he survived suicide, it would surely have killed him. Despite my decades of protest, nothing had diffused the appeal and dangerousness of cigarettes. So, the gateway having finally been opened and my girlfriend and I now

Broken Biscuits

in the city synonymous with getting high, I finally felt safe to do it. It was time to become a Freak Brother.

Since that day at Tracy's house, I hadn't smoked another joint. Not really. Over the years I'd been handed them at parties and placed them in my mouth, feeling the need to fit in. But I was always wary, only taking small performative drags then quickly puffing the smoke away from me before it could do any damage. I faked giddiness and hoped that everyone else was too out of it to notice. But we were in Amsterdam now, and things were different. It was permissible. And more than that, it felt like it was something I needed to do.

At the time of our trip, I was beginning to sense that the relationship between my girlfriend and me was on shaky ground. I wasn't sure what it was exactly, but it seemed that a distance was growing between us. A coldness. Before we got together, she'd been in relationships with guys who were much more exciting than I considered myself to be. Musicians, comedians, actors, people I knew by reputation as having lived lives of excess, and I worried that I didn't measure up well against them. But here was a chance to show her that I could do things that were unexpected. That I could throw caution to the wind by embracing something that seemed so ordinary in this city and, honestly, to most people over the age of fifteen. But it was extraordinary to me, and at that point it seemed essential. Neither of us had met stoned Adam before, and

This is Your Brain On Drugs

maybe he would be the one to fix what was going wrong between us.

We had about an hour left before we had to catch our coach back to the ferry, so we hurried off to find somewhere to buy a joint, deciding on the first place we encountered. A little shop by the canal with ice-white walls and shelving, like a cross between a pharmacy and a fun-sized Apple store. A sales assistant swooped in to greet us, giving us an elevator-eyed assessment then offering us his recommendation, feeding a perfectly formed joint from a lacquered box.

'It's strong but not too strong,' he said. 'Just take it easy. Are you going to be okay with that?'

'Absolutely,' I said.

There was a moment when he looked at me as if I was the kind of person who walked into Indian restaurants and boldly requested their hottest curry. But this passed quickly, and he took my payment, directing us to the nearest dimly lit café where we could settle down and enjoy smoking it. The clock ticking, we headed to the café, took a seat and my girlfriend lit the joint, taking a hungry drag before passing it to me. I mimicked her technique, pulling on it hard and realising far too late how little suction it had actually required.

'I don't feel good,' I said. 'Oh shit, I don't feel good at all.'

'Okay,' my girlfriend said calmly, taking my hand and looking into my eyes. 'You're having a whitey. Go to the

Broken Biscuits

toilets and have a sit down. Throw up if you need to. Just breathe. You'll be all right.'

I headed to the bathroom, splashed water on my face then looked in the mirror, studying myself. I looked pale and sick, as if I had a norovirus. I gulped water from the tap and took small, composing breaths until I started to feel capable again. Then I headed back to the bar, where my girlfriend was crushing the remains of the joint into an ashtray.

'Are you going to be all right?' she asked.

'Yeah,' I said, 'I'm cool.'

'You're really not,' she said, smiling as she linked her arm into mine and led us out onto the street, where we began wobbling our way to the coach, each of us fucked up in different ways. Her, nicely toasted and amused by everything she saw; me, trying to hold it together, my head swimming and my feet unsteady as if I were trying them out for the first time.

We climbed onto the coach and settled into our seats. As soon as it pulled away, though, I knew that I was in trouble. I tried to focus on the scenery, but it was a blur. A paint smear of hurtling colour. I closed my eyes and saw sickly lights swirling. My forehead got clammy. There was no SPROING. No ZONK. No POW. Just a queasily spinning bad time, growing worse by the second.

'Give me that, quick!' I said, frantically directing my girlfriend to the small polythene litter bag hanging on the

This is Your Brain On Drugs

corner of our seat. She handed it to me in stoned slow motion and I immediately threw up into it. From the back of the coach a group of men cheered.

'Do you need another bag?' my girlfriend asked. I made a horrible noise that she rightly interpreted as a yes. By the time we reached the ferry port, I had filled several more bags, each of them sheepishly sourced by my girlfriend, who had made her way down the coach to request them from other passengers.

'I'm sorry,' I said to her each time she handed me one. Then I'd puke to a soundtrack of back-seat cheers while she sat beside me, her buzz now killed, trying not to say anything mean. Apparently figuring that being me was its own punishment.

Back on the ferry, we made our way to our cabin, and I crashed out on my bunk. My girlfriend headed out to grab some food and do something more interesting than watch me pass out between apologies in a room that stank of vomit.

'One drag,' she said, shaking her head before she slipped out of the door. Unable to believe the state I was in. 'I can't believe it just took one fucking drag.'

We eventually reconvened in the bar, where a TV set to mute was showing the *Eurovision Song Contest*. My girlfriend handed me a bratwurst and I sat in a bucket chair, taking small bites of meat and riding out my nausea while the screen broadcast a kaleidoscope of lights and twirling

Broken Biscuits

bodies. I imagined the music that might be playing and tried to go with it. During the Spanish entry, I looked over at my girlfriend to find she was looking at me. Not lovingly, not sympathetically, but embarrassed to be in my company. We didn't wait up to see who won the contest, choosing instead to return to our cabin and sleep. The sooner we did that, the sooner it would be morning and we'd be back in England, where she could be free of me.

The next day we ate breakfast in silence then headed upstairs to smoke cigarettes on the deck, the two of us staring down into the dark and churning North Sea.

'I'm sorry,' I said.

'You need to stop saying sorry,' she said. 'It's not a problem, but it will be if you keep apologising.'

'I'm s— Okay.'

She walked away then and stood at the bow of the ship, looking out across the water as Hull shifted into view through the mist. I wondered if she'd placed this distance between us to remove what must have been the overwhelming temptation to shove me overboard. It might have been the best for both of us if she had. Instead, not long after, she broke up with me. In time I was able to recognise this trip as the lighting of the fuse that had detonated everything. Whatever remaining affection had been holding us together before we went away had been erased by my weak constitution and a half-dozen sloshing bin bags.

This is Your Brain On Drugs

A couple of weeks after the break-up, I headed out for consolatory drinks with my friend, Anna. As we sat in a bar, me staring mournfully into a double whisky, she nailed the problem at the heart of my newly dead relationship.

'It was embarrassing watching you together, to be honest,' she said, recalling an evening we'd all spent in the pub a few months earlier. 'Seeing you in the beer garden, trying to smoke, I knew what you were doing. It was like watching someone at school trying to hang out with the bad girls.'

'I know,' I said, trying to smile through the painful truth of this. 'I get it.'

I could have done with this conversation years ago. Decades ago. Before the embarrassments. Before the wheels started rolling over me. But it was a long time before I had the kinds of friends who would call me out and set me straight. Years before I had an Anna. I was just happy she was here now. Grateful she got to me before one of those wheels finally reached my head.

'At some point you need to accept what you're not,' she said, pausing to drain the whiskey from her own glass. 'And honey, you're not one of the bad girls.'

I opened my mouth to say something, but decided against it. Watching as she raised her hand and gestured to the barman that she wanted to order another round.

Exposures

It's odd to realise that you have reached an age where the job you once did is almost obsolete. Odder still to consider that, in your lifetime, that job had previously been associated with the white heat of technology. But during the late 90s and through into the early noughties, I ran a high-street photo lab, operating what was then the most sophisticated machinery of its kind. So, obsolete it is.

Back then it seemed like there would never be a time when there wasn't a place for that job. Every town had a photo lab; some of them several. But these days, when my daughter Effie asks me about my time working in one, I feel as if I'm recalling an era when I manned a spinning Jenny and looked forward to dying of scrofula at the age of forty-two. In those moments, I feel dusty. Profoundly aware of myself as a technological relic to be filed alongside Betamax video and the power adaptor for an Atari Lynx.

Broken Biscuits

The visual onslaught we're presented with today is so much greater than anything I could have envisioned during my lab years. More images were captured between 2021 and 2023 than were taken in the entire history of photography that preceded it. Each day, 3.2 billion images are uploaded to the internet. If you viewed every one of those images for a single second it would take you 101 years. It's likely that these statistics don't even surprise you. Chances are that within your grasp is the technology to take a photo of your armpit, and within seconds make sure that everyone on the planet has had the opportunity to see it. The one thing you'd be unlikely to consider is the act of heading to a lab to get that photo printed. Not least because the world where that was possible no longer really exists.

During my five years working in a lab, my daily routine was largely unchanged. Each morning I'd arrive at the store around 7 a.m. and meet up with Rodney, the store security guard. We'd roll up the shutters, he'd turn off the alarm system and I'd flip the light switch, my eyes following the crackling wave of tube lighting as it rolled across the ceiling and illuminated the shop floor.

Our store was located on a tennis-court-sized patch of city centre retail floorspace, a flagship location for a company that had stores nationwide and was expanding daily. If it had a lens, there was a good chance we sold it. We stocked SLRs, compact cameras, Polaroids, handy-

Exposures

cams, spy cameras and telescopes, selling them in astounding numbers and beating all the competition for price. Up at the back of the store, in the pro equipment section, we sold zoom lenses the length of prosthetic legs, which cost about the same as a mid-range hatchback and allowed paparazzi photographers to sit a quarter of a mile away from a soap actor and take pin-sharp photos of their latest breakdown. And on a shelf behind the main counter, there was a tiny section of cameras labelled 'Digital', which would indicate the future that would one day bring the whole swollen enterprise crashing down.

All I cared about in those days, though, was my photo lab: £250,000 of Fuji printing and processing power, which sat in the centre of the shop floor surrounded by plexiglass walls, allowing customers to peer into the lab and see me work. They'd press their faces against it and regard me with fascination, as if I were an unusually dextrous orangutan behind the glass of an ape house.

'I want people to see where the magic happens,' said Paul, our area manager, on the morning the store opened. 'Imagine I'm Joe Customer. I come into the shop and say "Wow! This is so cool. Look at this lab." Everything Joe Customer sees, he should say "Wow!" I want them to leave this shop just thinking *Wow!*' He paused to give me a serious look, placing his hand on my shoulder. 'Adam, can you be that wow?'

Broken Biscuits

I told him I could, and wondered how Paul managed to look at himself in the mirror each day. I want to say it must have been agony for him, but my guess is that he did it easily and that he practised lines like this as he monitored his reflection, altering his levels of sincerity and emphasis each time. 'Can *you* ... be *that* wow?'

While Rodney performed his morning rounds of the building, I'd slip behind the counter of the lab and hit more switches. An illuminated panel on the side of the negative processor, others on the printing machine and the lab computer. There were bleeps, fluttering LEDs, a hum as the machines calibrated and the developing fluid warmed to the correct temperature. I put on my lab coat, loaded a reel of photo paper onto the machine, then got to work.

Okay, I thought despite my best instincts as I grabbed a handful of films from a rack beside the processor. *Be that wow.*

I worked without really thinking, my muscle memory so well programmed to load film canisters into the machines that I could have done it drunk. The only time I really thought about my work was when I was bracing myself for what I'd see coming out of the other end of the printer. Because that job peeled the lid back on the world, showing me lives and behaviours I'd have never considered or encountered otherwise. Before curated online personas, the perfect Golden Hour selfie and Instagram vs

Exposures

reality, there was me, sifting through snapshots of your life before even you saw them. Quality checking, colour correcting, adjusting the exposure and brightness. Making them as perfect as they could be before I placed them in your eager hands, the envelope as warm as a fresh loaf of bread.

What my customers never seemed to consider, though, was the person who processed those photos. Who'd sat with their head down over countless hours, analysing millions of exposures that captured births, weddings, funerals, giddy highs and crushing lows, the most private of moments. I was the uninvited guest to them all. A guest who, often against all my best interests, remembered everything.

Exposure No. 38,862

'It's that guy again,' Jenny said.

'Which guy?' I asked.

Jenny was a member of my counter staff, who dealt with a lot of men who could have been considered 'that guy'. Angry guys, smelly guys, drunken guys. But the way she approached me, holding an order envelope at arm's length as if it were a sopping wet nappy, told me everything I needed to know.

'Oh,' I said. '*That* guy.'

This was a customer who liked to photograph himself masturbating. Not our most extreme regular, but still,

Broken Biscuits

unpleasant. Whether he just liked capturing the act on film or got a kick out of handing the canister over to the twenty-two-year-old woman working the counter, I'll never know. But the way he always smiled at Jenny when he handed over his film gave her the creeps. So, she took his money, dumped his envelope in the order box then headed out the back to wash her hands.

'Never turn work away,' Paul had told me. 'If you don't like what you see, set the machine on auto and don't look at it. Remember that we're here to make a profit, not a moral judgement.'

I was expected to make a legal one, though. The company could be prosecuted and fined for producing obscene content, and there were many things we couldn't print. Next to my machine, in one of the few areas not visible to customers, there was 'The No List', a laminated sheet detailing everything the law prohibited us from printing. And it was the first two items on this list that caused me the most problems.

1. Images of erections.
2. Images of sexual penetration.

My problem was that people loved to have sex and photograph it, and that photos featuring items 1 and 2 on the list amounted to a decent percentage of the lab's profits. So, we were taught to turn a blind eye. As long as everyone looked to be consenting to what was happening, we were given carte blanche to process it and try not to think about the consequences. When I processed a film showing a naked woman defecating onto a guy's forehead, I showed the photos to Carol, our store manager, who asserted that this didn't contravene our guidelines.

'I mean, nothing is *penetrating* anything,' she said, her nose wrinkling as she handed me back the photos. 'The opposite really. And honestly, I wouldn't call that sex. Just take their money and try not to get into conversation.'

What was important to Carol, and therefore should be to me, was that these people always wanted their photos fast, and paid a premium for it. 'One-hour service, please,' was so often code for erotic content that we could have gone ahead and changed the sign above the till. Some of these customers were calm and confident, handing over their films as if they contained innocent snapshots from a two-week walking holiday in Provence. Or, like 'that guy', made a game of it. Others gave themselves away by blushing. Or if they were a couple, giggling about a shared secret that would very soon become my secret, too. Most often, though, these customers made an exaggerated show of innocence and distracting jollity, all smiles and small talk. It was a display that said 'nothing to see here' as they slid a film across the counter, containing images of them lying naked on the floor of a hotel room, their genitals being methodically crushed by a woman in stiletto heels.

So, we were encouraged to welcome these customers and to never show any indication that we'd seen what

Broken Biscuits

we'd seen. In time, I would come to suspect we'd gained a reputation as a safe place for this sort of thing. We grew to be on friendly terms with many of the sex workers who operated out of a brothel three streets away and dropped off the disposable cameras they'd used during the previous night's shift. Then there was the wealthy, local wholesaler who liked to take photos of his wife while she lay on their kitchen island performing erotic displays with increasingly sized fruits and vegetables. And the elderly couple who loved each other very much and each week would drop off a film that demonstrated exactly how much. The list seemed endless, and I was happy for their custom.

If we beat our sales targets by a certain percentage, the company awarded the team a cash bonus to spend on something for the staff. One month we made so much money on the lab from disregarding the list of restrictions that we received that bonus. I used it to buy a PlayStation 2 for the staff room and every time I walked back there and found members of the sales staff playing Tekken on their coffee break I'd get a real sense of achievement.

'You've got to feel proud,' Jenny said, patting me on the back. 'All that happiness entirely paid for in dicks.'

Exposure No. 120, 901

'Oh God,' Mr Landry said as he sat down in the waiting area beside the lab, his eyes flooding with tears. 'What am I going to do?'

Exposures

While I've only been to a dozen or so weddings in real life, I must have attended a thousand through the lab. Most of the photos I dealt with were taken by guests, but quite often they were the work of professionals. People who had charged the bride and groom, say, £1,000 to capture one of the most important days of their life, then got the images printed by someone like me for £20. This was my introduction into the world of small, high-profit business. Most people wouldn't know enough about photographic printing to realise this was happening. They wouldn't pick up on anything unless the photographer really messed up, which happened more often than anyone would like. Those once-in-a-lifetime pictures very often emerged blurred, poorly composed, badly lit or featured group shots of guests seemingly captured in the moment of having swallowed a bee.

In these situations, I would do what I could, unwilling to penalise the married couple for not realising they'd been ripped off. After all, people don't really get married often enough to develop a nose for these things. But some photos were beyond saving, and when this happened I could only console the photographer when they arrived to collect their work, their faces turning a sickly green as they leafed through the images and gradually realised they had ruined someone's life. And quite often, just like Mr Landry, they would sit down and cry.

Broken Biscuits

'Is there anything you can do?' he asked, offering me a pleading look. 'Please?'

'Not unless they're willing to get married again,' Jenny said.

Mr Landry's expression darkened at this comment, then became suddenly hopeful. He pulled out his mobile phone and dialled a number, Jenny and I listening in as he apologised to the bride for 'a technical fault' and offered to restage the photos.

'It's really no problem,' he said. 'I'll do it free of charge.'

At this, Mr Landry sharply moved the phone away from his ear. The screams from its speaker broadcasting across the store and lingering with me long after he left.

Exposure No. 389,421

The first time I saw a dead body, it wasn't on the news or at an open-casket funeral, but by chance, in a half-dozen images at the end of a series of photos from a resort holiday. There were smiling kids splashing in the sea, a mum and dad raising cocktails alongside a handsome and clearly uncomfortable waiter then, all of a sudden, Grandma. While it was the first time I'd seen a corpse, I knew with complete certainty that she was dead rather than just sleeping. Her jaw loose and sinking back towards her neck, the bloodless pallor of her skin. All the wind so clearly out of her sails.

Exposures

I would soon discover that this was not a one-off. In fact, I'd average at least one of these photos a month. Mostly, they featured elderly people laid out on their deathbeds. Occasionally their families were huddled around them, all smiles for the last ever group photo with Grandma or Grandpa. Propped up on a pillow, the body took pride of place at the centre of the frame, its slack, lifeless features and open mouth like a haunted expression drawn on sackcloth. I'd try to think of the motivations behind capturing these images, picturing relatives flicking through photo albums in years to come.

'Aww, do you remember this?' I imagined them saying. 'It's Grandma just before rigor mortis set in.'

There was nothing on the restrictions list that suggested I was not allowed to print photos like this. So, I did my job. One set of images showed a corpse lying in the cold store of a slaughterhouse awaiting a funeral, while the business of butchering goats carried on in the background. Another revealed the immaculately tailored body of a woman lying in an open casket, her skin shiny and unreal, like an expensive doll presented in a lacquered display case. But more often than not, it was these deathbed photos. This final moment of life having just slipped away, captured for purposes beyond my understanding.

Jenny came over to me while I was sifting through one set of these photos, the contents causing me to balk.

'What's up?' she asked.

Broken Biscuits

I showed her a series of images of a man lying in bed on white sheets, his skin gradually turning purplish grey as the photos progressed. Each new shot showing a different set of sobbing adults and confused toddlers paying their respects to his decaying body. Then finally, there were images of the empty bed, showing the yellowish imprint his corpse had left on the mattress.

'God,' I said, telling Jenny about the second-hand bed I'd bought when I first moved to Manchester. 'Do you reckon someone died on it?'

'Oh, definitely,' she said. 'Give me Saturday off or I'm telling everyone you slept with a dead body.'

Exposure No. 769,922

The early days of our store's Photoshop services were thought of in magical terms, where the impossible was now possible. And in truth, we could do amazing things. Make your old, faded photographs look like they were taken only yesterday? No problem. Delete your piece-of-shit ex-husband from the group shots at your grandma's ninetieth birthday party? With pleasure. Give me five minutes. The problems only came when people expected miracles.

'Do you see a problem with this?' one guy asked, angrily slapping a photo down onto the counter. He'd come in the previous day to request that we remove an unsightly-looking bin from an image of four people

Exposures

posing on the banks of a river. And we'd done that, pretty seamlessly, I'd thought. You'd have never known it had been there. Yet here he was at the counter, his face turning the colour of a Royal Gala apple and showing through the thinning hair covering his scalp.

'It looks okay to me,' Jenny said, scrutinising it.

'Really?' the guy said, incredulous, 'There's nothing *wrong* at all? You can't see anything that might be ... *missing?*'

'No.'

'Then, where,' he said, forcefully tapping the photo with his finger as if he were also sending his complaint in Morse code, 'is the dog?'

'There wasn't a dog in the photo,' I said.

He tapped the image again, at the newly empty place, and replied through clenched and furious teeth.

'It was behind *the bin.*'

Exposure No. 1020,324

When the news came in that a plane had hit the Twin Towers, I had been taking a long bathroom break. I returned to the shop floor to find the rest of the staff listening to an emergency news broadcast on the radio.

'A plane's crashed into the World Trade Center!' Jenny told me.

'Oh God,' I said, then timidly, stupidly asked, 'What's the World Trade Center?'

Broken Biscuits

She sighed then explained them to me, and I realised that of course I knew them well from countless movies and TV shows. I'd never had cause to think of them as anything more than just another couple of buildings on the New York skyline. But just as we all did in the days and weeks that followed 9/11, I would soon become intimately familiar with the towers. With the oddly cinematic horror of it all and the panicked narrative about what the attacks meant. War, certainly. And in the meantime, speculation. This was something global and terrifying, but the lab brought it all back down to the individual level I was used to dealing with. Customers returning from trips to New York and arriving at my counter with stories. Needing me to stop for them and pay attention.

'I was at the top of the first tower just last week,' one woman said, dropping off her film a few days after the attack.

I was taken aback by this, shocked by her close shave with death. So, I offered her the sympathy that would have come naturally to anyone in that moment. Later that day, a guy came in with his own story.

'I can't believe I was up there three days before it happened,' he said, clearly going through something as he paid for 8x6 prints with an extra set.

The following day another customer arrived with a similar tale. And another. Everyone was reckoning with this event and seeming to want in on it. To place

Exposures

themselves in the narrative of this rare, incalculable occurrence so that they could experience its residual glow. Feel the terrifying whoosh of a near miss and let other people know how close it had been for them. Over and over, I heard a familiar refrain: 'It could have been me.'

It was my colleague Pam who seemed to have had the closest shave. She'd been in New York at the time of the attacks and photographed the towers from across Hudson Bay, smoke billowing from each in the minutes before they fell.

'I was on my way to the tower,' she said, filling out her request to have the images printed in sepia tone. 'I should have been on top that day.'

We shuddered in unison. It really could have been her.

About a fortnight after the attacks, a woman appeared at the counter with a photo of herself posing at the top of one of the towers, the breathtaking expanse of New York City laid out behind her.

'Can you blow this up to A2 size?' she said. 'It was taken on September the tenth. I want it hanging in our lounge to remind me of how lucky I am to be here.'

I agreed with her that she was incredibly lucky, and at this she picked up the photo again, regarding it as if it was new to her.

'It's strange to think that it's gone but I'm still here. Like there's a part of me floating up there.' She gave this

Broken Biscuits

a moment's thought and brought her hand up to her chest. 'I *am* lucky, aren't I?'

At this she placed the photo back onto the counter and I noticed the timecode burned into the corner of the image: 10/9/1999.

'So lucky,' I said, as I took the payment from her trembling hand.

Exposure No. 1,671,089

People deal with loss in all kinds of ways, and I quickly learned to make no judgements. It was rare that a week went by without me hearing the story of a bereavement then dealing with the photos that had been chosen to capture a life lost. These might be a treasured moment memorialised on a canvas print or a portrait blown up to poster size so it could be mounted on an easel at a gangland funeral. Whatever someone needed to get them through, we'd do what we could. Offering the kind of counselling we'd never been trained in. Over time I grew to be pretty unflappable, but some customers' stories remained with me much longer than others.

The young couple who arrived at my counter in the winter of 2001 were both thin and exhausted looking, as if it had been weeks since they'd last experienced food or the comfort of sleep. The man did all the talking, putting on a show of affability as he laid an envelope on the counter and asked if I could touch up an image in

Exposures

Photoshop then enlarge it so they could mount it in a frame.

I opened the envelope and withdrew a photo of a stillborn little girl lying in a Moses basket, her miniature body swamped by a lacy newborn-sized dress. Her eyes closed as if napping.

'If you can just clean her up,' the man said, his hand gesturing to the bruised-looking areas at the top of his daughter's head. At the miniature pinch of her nose. Her lilac skin. 'And y'know …' he struggled to find adequate words then went with the basics, '… fix her?' His partner remained behind him as he spoke, looking at the floor and picking at her nails, seeming to punish them, as if they were responsible for all of this. While I was filling out their order form, the man broke away from me to study the selection of photo frames on a stand and the woman trailed sleepily after him.

'These are nice, aren't they?' he said brightly, pointing to some large, elaborate gold designs and taking one down from the shelf. 'If we had that in the living room, d'you think?'

The woman nodded briskly. It could have been acceptance or a nervous tick. I wasn't sure. But it was clear that she just wanted this over with.

'Yeah,' he said, holding the frame out in front of him and admiring it, apparently picturing the doctored photo of his daughter mounted behind the glass. 'Shall we have

Broken Biscuits

that one?' he said. Not to her then, but to himself. Not expecting an answer or getting one. 'Yeah, I think we'll have that one.' He was talking for talking's sake. Filling the space left by his partner's nauseous silence and my awkward, respectful one.

I was giving them time and distance. I didn't rush them. I understood that something tragic and complex was happening to them. So, I stayed behind the counter, leaving them to it and waiting for them to need me again. While I was doing this, Carol moved behind the counter and sidled up to me. Placing her mouth close to my ear.

'Remember,' she whispered. 'It's three for two on frames.'

Exposure No. 2,301,296

'I don't want it,' Mrs Clowes said as I handed her a free film, tossing it back onto the counter then dismissively brushing it towards me with the back of her hand. 'Give me a Kodak.'

All our customers automatically received a free replacement film for each one they dropped off for processing, meaning that, in theory, they need never buy another again. The problem was that this film was our own brand, and for some people that was not good enough.

'I'm sorry,' I said, 'but Kodak isn't part of the offer.'

'Okay,' she said, sighing heavily. 'Then I'll pay the difference.'

Exposures

I explained the well-worn company line that it was on the system as a free film so there was no difference to pay. Effectively it had no value.

'But you're *selling* them,' she said, pointing at a display stand beside the counter. Hundreds of these films beneath a sign clearly stating the price. 'You're selling them right here for ninety-nine pence! They're worth ninety-nine pence. Give me ninety-nine pence off a Kodak. Now.'

I knew Mrs Clowes well, but only as a problem I'd so far avoided. She was tall and wiry, her salt-and-pepper hair pulled back into a tight, face-straining ponytail. The sight of her marching up to customer services to raise a complaint had long been familiar to me, her arms bracing the counter as she stared down whichever poor member of staff encountered her that day. And now it seemed it was finally my turn. She stared at me through round wire-framed spectacles, which magnified her eyes to glaring accusatory baubles while I tried to explain to her that this wasn't how the deal worked.

'Okay, then give me ninety-nine pence and I'll use it to buy a Kodak.'

'That's not ...' I stumbled, trying to formulate a reply. 'I don't ... The thing is ...'

Mrs Clowes smiled at me then, pouncing on this moment and repeating my words back at me in a dopey, stuttering voice.

Broken Biscuits

'"The thing is ... Duh, duh, duh ..." What is the thing? Is this too complicated for you to understand?'

We'd started to draw a crowd. A queue was building up behind her. Curious shoppers peered over from the other counters to see what was going on. Other staff hovered nearby, enjoying the show.

'Look,' I said, trying to keep my tone steady, 'the ones on the stand are for sale and the ones you get as part of the deal are free.'

'What? What does that even mean?' she said, throwing her arms up and turning to the audience she'd attracted. Like she was attempting to start a revolution. 'They can't be both. Either they're free or they're not.'

I didn't know what to say, painted into a corner where I'd somehow have to explain the concept of Schrödinger's film. So, I blamed the computer.

'See,' I showed her, typing in the code for her photos, where it showed a value of zero.

'Right,' she said decisively, apparently resigned to the idea that she was getting nowhere, 'Okay. Right. Fine', She snatched the film from the counter. 'So, this is mine?' she asked, eyeballing me. Gripping it in her fist.

'Yes.'

'And I can do anything I want with it?'

'Yes,' I said, sensing that the sun had not yet set on our confrontation. 'It's yours.'

Exposures

'So, I could just jump up and down on it? Is that what you want?'

Before I could say that I didn't want that at all, she marched to the middle of the store where everyone could see her, placed the film on the ground and began angrily stomping it flat.

'This,' she managed between stamps and grunts, 'is what ... you ... wanted.'

Not knowing what else to do, I gestured for the next customer to come forward and, as I did, felt an object whizz past my head, followed by a spittoon clang as it struck the printer behind me. I looked down to see the film canister on the floor of the lab, now mangled into a disc. When I looked up, Mrs Clowes was staring at me and smiling.

'There,' she said, hunched over slightly. Frozen in the act of having thrown something. 'Have *that* for free!'

She stormed out into the street and the next customer looked down at the flattened film on the floor.

'Aww,' he said mournfully. 'I could have had that.'

Exposure No. 2,981,591

'Do you want to see a photo of a ghost?' Mr Pellegrini asked, opening his wallet.

He was maybe in his late seventies, well dressed and with a strong resonant Italian accent. I dealt with a lot of older customers, many of them regulars. They'd appear at

Broken Biscuits

the counter to discuss a piece of potential work, but what they really wanted was the conversation. There was Mr Philips, who came in two or three times a week to discuss slide projectors and just catch up, always offering me an Uncle Joe's Mint Ball as if in trade for this additional service I was offering. Mr Akhtar who was so grateful for the time our staff spent with him that he'd once carried a box of gulab jamun 4,000 miles from Pakistan simply so he could present it to us as a thank you. And then there were guys like Mr Pellegrini, who just wanted to share stories.

He slipped his fingers into the space behind his driver's licence and removed a small, weathered photograph, beckoning me close to look at it. It showed a living room captured sometime in the mid-70s. While the photo was faded, the furnishings and wallpaper still throbbed with vivid, bold orange-and-brown patterns. Running vertically down the centre of this image was a white, fuzzy-edged band.

'See,' he said, tapping this band. 'There she is.'

'Wow,' I said, knowing instantly what this ghost was. I saw similar images all the time, where items had come to rest on or in front of the lens. They might be specks of dust or blobs of rain but people with excitable imaginations would often mistake them for spirits or UFOs. In this case, the ghost was obvious to me as a camera strap that had fallen across the lens and been blasted with a flash. Out of focus and distorted, it vaguely resembled a figure. Enough of one for Mr Pellegrini to assume its gender.

'I took it about thirty years ago,' he said, 'Ever since, anyone who has crossed me has met with a sticky end.'

While I didn't believe his photo had captured anything paranormal, there was no harm in him holding on to that belief. A part of me was wary of correcting him and invoking the wrath of the spirit that defended him. But mostly, I wanted more details.

'How sticky an end, exactly?' I wanted to ask, but I knew I would get this answer from him in a few days. All I had to do was wait.

Exposure No. 3,023,912

Tom wasn't my lab assistant for long. One of a huge list of part-time hires from the abundance of photography students living in the city, I had never expected him to stick around for more than a few months. Not just because he was a student, but because he was confident in a way I wasn't used to seeing, especially in our store. It always felt like he was destined for something better.

'I'm only here for the staff discount,' he told me, and I couldn't hold it against him. Honestly, it was tough to hold anything against Tom.

He was good looking, witty, and harmlessly flirtatious with most people he met. Seeing him serving customers was like watching an aspiring political candidate make

Broken Biscuits

nice with voters in the run-up to polling day. While a few members of the sales team had charm, none of them had what Tom had. So, we were disappointed when he suddenly announced that he was leaving.

What drove him to this was the 2003 Iraq war. Within days of the conflict beginning, he announced that he'd be leaving to become a human shield in Baghdad and start work on a photographic record of what was happening over there. While it was a quick decision, he took it seriously. He bought language guides and stacks of books about the Middle East, spending his breaks in the staff room, diligently reading up on what he'd be heading into as if prepping for a test.

'You're gonna get killed, son,' Rodney said bluntly, as he flipped the switch on the kettle.

'Probably,' Tom replied, grinning. 'But if I do, I promise I'll come back and haunt you.'

The danger aside, he seemed confident it was the right decision, certain that he would just go over there, do some good work and take some incredible photos. Believing wholeheartedly in the unmatched power of photographic journalism. He talked admiringly of Robert Capa and Kevin Carter, photographers who'd both captured powerful images of war-torn countries. I pointed out that both of these men had died young.

'Yeah, but you know who they are, don't you?' he said, that charming smile spreading.

Exposures

We carried on in this gallows way; Tom blasé about the risks, each of us making jokes about bullet wounds or the limbs he would lose.

On his last day at the store, I was chopping negatives and feeding them into plastic sleeves when his face suddenly appeared at the Plexiglass screen. I jumped at the sight of him, and he laughed.

'I'll be back with photos,' he said. 'Don't fuck them up.'

I shooed him away with a dismissive waft of my hand.

'Oh, go and get shot,' I said.

He laughed and fired pistol fingers at me, then disappeared into the warehouse to grab his jacket before walking out of the store for the final time.

After he left, I'd get updates on his adventures from Vicky, one of the sales team who was following his blog. She told me that he'd arrived in Iraq but had quickly been moved on and was now in Rafah on the Gaza strip, employed as an aid worker as part of a group called the International Solidarity Movement.

Because none of us ever really believed anything would happen to Tom, we weren't afraid for him. We thought he'd evaded danger by being pulled from Iraq. It would be my then wife who broke the news to me that Tom had been shot. She worked for a news organisation and saw the photos coming in on the wire.

'You won't want to see these,' she said, but I pressed her.

Broken Biscuits

'It's fine. Show me.'

I believed that I had seen so much during my day job that I could take whatever was coming, thinking, *How bad could they be?* But I wasn't prepared for the images of Tom being lifted from the ground, his eyes both glazed and shocked. His blood-soaked head being cradled while people around him screamed. His body being carried through the streets of Gaza, an unbroken column of blood pouring from a hole in the back of his head and hitting the dusty ground. There was our dark humour, bad jokes about death, and there was this, the reality of it. This thing I could never quite imagine happening to him. And while he'd talked about it often, I don't believe he thought it could happen to him either. His confidence had convinced the rest of us that he was immune to what could happen to someone out there. An attitude that was big enough to protect him and spread to everyone who knew him.

The story goes that he'd spotted a group of children playing in an exposed spot, bullets being fired around them by IDF snipers. While some of these children ran for cover, others froze in panic, so Tom rushed over to help them. He successfully moved one child out of the line of fire but when he returned to help another he was shot through the head.

He would be taken to hospital and transported to London, where he would spend the following nine months

Exposures

in a coma. During that time, we'd get updates on his progress. A lot of this news was hopeful. We'd hear that, despite the severe damage to his brain, there was a chance of survival. Of some kind of recovery. So, it took us all by surprise when we learned that he'd died. Convinced by his room-altering self-belief that he'd somehow shrug it off and wake up with a smile and a joke, keen to hear about everything he'd missed out on while he'd been away.

Exposure No. 4,012,983

Rodney came from a part of Manchester where being a 6ft 4in security guard had its advantages and disadvantages. It was a region where disputes were settled quickly and violently, the aftermath involving ambulance crews but rarely the police.

'I nailed his hand to the fence,' he told me once during a coffee break, discussing a row he'd had with a neighbour, 'then I went off to find something else to hit him with.'

Rodney was full of stories like this. Long, diverting ones that all seemed to work to the same format. They might start with 'So, there was me and Bobby Atkins, right ...' And end after two or three harrowing minutes with, '... blood *everywhere*.'

He pronounced a double t as 'ck', an affectation that could be cute coming from a toddler but was unnerving when it came from the mouth that claimed to have once bitten off someone's ear.

Broken Biscuits

'So, I bockled the cunt, then drove him to hospickal to get his stitches.'

'Oh my God,' I'd say, when he'd finish one of his stories. 'That's ... awful.'

He'd rub at his fight-flattened knuckles.

'That's life.'

By the time I met Rodney he'd already had a career working the doors of clubs across the northwest, and as muscle for protection rackets masquerading as private security companies. But he was trying to settle down and become legitimate. Looking for a life that involved less drama. The on-the-level security job in our store was a step towards that.

'I'd become a prize on my estate, you know,' he told me, changing his shirt in the staffroom and revealing a torso bearing an ordinance survey map of variously sized scars. 'People would start on me in the pub, and I'd have to fight them. My missus just wanted to go out for a quiet drink, so eventually I just had to let someone beat me. I stayed down, took a kicking and that was it. I'd lost my shine and people left me alone.'

Because of this, I'd grown used to Rodney as a benign figure. Someone who spoke of former glories, like a gone-to-seed boxer. So, it was a surprise to hear a cry of 'SHOPLIFTER!' and see him racing across the shop floor, his long legs quickly outpacing the short, slightly built guy who'd just grabbed a camera from a display and made a run for the exit.

The guy had just rounded the doors and reached the street, when Rodney caught hold of his collar, lifting him off his feet and bringing him down hard, his head slamming into the ram bars protecting the store's display window. Blood exploded from the guy's nose. Rodney pinned him onto the pavement.

'Let me go!' the guy shouted, blood cascading down his face and into his mouth. 'I've got AIDS!'

'Yeah, yeah,' Rodney said, knowing every trick in the book, 'so have I, mate.'

Rodney dragged the guy back into the store and into the staffroom, where he told him to sit down.

'Keep him here,' he told me, and the two of us sat in silence waiting for Rodney to return. I handed the guy a wad of tissue paper for his nose. When Rodney came back, I was relieved to learn that he'd gone to phone the police and not to find something to hit the guy with.

Exposure No. 4,362,722

Tony had worked for the company for as long as anyone could remember. The silhouette of his stout physique and bald head were more redolent of the company than its official logo. He'd held onto his job through six general elections, two recessions and a management buyout, but if you asked him about his time with the company, he had

Broken Biscuits

no problems with telling you that he'd hated every second of it.

'If I had choice,' he told me, 'I'd be out of here like a shot. And I wouldn't look back either.'

For most of his life Tony had lived with his mother, his loyalty to her such that he felt he could never leave her side. When he was in his forties the two of them had taken out a mortgage on a flat together. Though he despised his job, the company offered him the security of a steady wage and fulfilled his need to support his mother.

'I've actually been proposed to a couple of times,' he once told me in the staffroom when we got talking about relationships. He snapped a biscuit in two and dunked one half into a mug of milky tea. 'But I had my mum to look after, so that was that.'

When his mother died, the mortgage payments had all fallen on him and upon reaching his mid-sixties he found that he couldn't afford to retire, so he carried on working. There was only a couple of years of the mortgage left to pay when he was diagnosed with cancer. He received chemotherapy, had surgery to remove a large part of his hip, and as soon as he was mobile again, he was back in work, hobbling across the vast shop floor with the aid of a walking stick. Clearly in pain but having no other choice but to carry on.

'I fucking hate it here,' he told me, the last time we spoke. 'I just hope they don't carry me out of here in a box.'

Exposures

Not long after this conversation, Tony died, the cancer having returned with a vengeance. His younger brother was his only surviving relative, so the job of arranging the funeral had fallen on him. They weren't all that close, so he interpreted Tony's years of service as a reflection of his love for the company. To that end, he honoured this by making sure that Tony was buried in the clothing he'd worn for most of his adult life: his staff uniform.

'Oh, my God,' I said when Jenny told me about this, 'I think that might be the most depressing thing I've ever heard.'

'It's the worst, isn't it?' she said, 'Up there in Heaven with his little badge on. Just wearing it for eternity. Can you imagine?'

Then we both fell silent, imagining it.

Exposure No. 4,900,212

Some members of staff stuck to the company line, never questioning the decisions or wisdom of head office. Our team leader, Ali, was one of those people. Although our wages were low and store profits were high, you could always rely on guys like him to advocate for the company and push through any initiative that could squeeze a little more juice from the lemon.

'So, they got a university to work out the maximum time it should take to serve a customer on the lab,' he said, smiling as he explained our new working practice, effective immediately. 'You should be able to take their order, fill out the docket and take their payment within fifteen seconds.'

These figures extrapolated, he explained, meant that we could serve four customers per minute, 240 an hour. The average photo order costing £5.99, this meant a turnover of £23.96 every minute, £1437.60 every hour, and £11,500.80 every working day. Across the week that was over £80,000. 'And that's not even factoring in multiple films and larger sizes. Think of the bonuses!'

All I could think about was the capability of my printer, which could only produce around 2,000 photos per hour. The formula would require many times that capacity along with an unbroken stream of customers, not to mention exhausted staff who never took breaks to eat, drink or visit the bathroom to burst into tears. I scraped an F in my GCSE Maths but even I could see the flaws in these calculations.

'Wow,' I said. 'That seems ... impossible. Which university worked this out?'

'Just a university,' Ali said dismissively, picking up a pen as a customer approached the counter, 'and it's very possible. Time me.' He readied himself, his pen poised above an order envelope, determined to prove me wrong. 'How can I help you, sir?'

I stared at my watch while Ali hustled the guy through his order, took his payment and handed him the receipt.

Exposures

'Okay,' he said, turning to me. 'How long?'

'Fifty-eight seconds.'

'That can't be right. Time me again.'

I did this for him as each new customer arrived at the counter. One minute, twenty-three seconds. Two minutes, forty-five seconds. The best he managed was fifty-one seconds and that was because the customer was in a hurry and already had his cash in his hand. Some people didn't make up their mind about what they wanted until they reached the counter. They umm'd and ahh'd. Asked for recommendations, wanted to chat or ask about cameras. Where the calculation fell down was that it somehow hadn't factored in humans and the way they are.

'I don't think it's going to be possible,' I said, regarding Ali's flustered demeanour. His flushed cheeks. He slapped the pen into my hand.

'Your job,' he said as he walked out of the lab, 'is to make it possible.'

Exposure No. 5,233,021

'You're like that guy in that film,' the customer said with a smile. 'You know the one.'

I did know the one. It was mentioned to me three or four times a day at that point and on each occasion I reacted as if it was the very first time I'd heard it.

One Hour Photo is a Robin Williams movie about a photo lab operator with no friends or loved ones, who

Broken Biscuits

becomes dangerously obsessed with the family he's printing photos for. I wondered if this was what the guy saw when he looked at me. A pathetic drudge. A lonely man on the brink. I hoped he'd not seen the film but had just registered the title. Perhaps also the stills of Williams dressed up in the same white lab attire as mine and staring into a sheet of negatives. Either way, if this is what he thought when he looked at me, what so many customers saw, then I needed another gig.

And really, I was ready to leave, because the job had started to affect me. Arriving at work each day I'd feel as if I was stepping into a closing fist. The pressure to achieve targets leaving me anxious and tired. I developed a spasming eye twitch that began at the start of my shift and persisted long after I lay down in bed at night.

I was also aware that, outside of the lab, my perception of the world had tilted. I would begin to see celebrities everywhere. They might be peering at the meal deals in the supermarket or ordering a coffee from Costa and I'd rack my brains trying to remember their names. *What have they been in?* I'd think, struggling to place which movie or TV show I recognised them from. *They're definitely someone.* But that someone, I would eventually realise, wasn't famous. I hadn't seen them on TV or in glossy magazines but at work, in photos that captured every detail of their lives. In the lab, *everyone* was a celebrity, and I had all the gossip.

Exposures

I could tell you all about the veteran glamour photographer, a faded peacock of a man who was cheating on his partner and had once sagely told me, 'Never argue with a Russian woman, especially if she's naked.' The executive from a local accountancy firm whom I'd seen smiling as she squatted over the roof of a Porsche and released a long stream of piss across the windscreen. The man who'd had sex with several items of furniture in his home and whose behaviour I thought of every time I moved into a new house. I had seen and knew too much, and it was making me crazy. The cost of the job was great, the money was bad and if I didn't want to end up like Tony I needed to get out.

I applied for and scored a job in a university library, where I learned to slow down. Didn't have to think about my every action being monitored and timed. And in the long breaks between tasks, I'd share stories with my new colleagues about my time in the lab. The more I talked, the more I was able to register the way those years had changed me. The things I'd seen and experienced acting like a strong, steady wind that gradually weathered me into a new shape.

What I also learned was that I'd left just in time. A lack of attention paid to digital technology and internet retail would ultimately sink the company not long after I quit. One morning the staff would arrive at the store to learn that it'd had gone into receivership, and everyone was

Broken Biscuits

being fired. People had digital cameras, less of a need for printing. Overnight the demand for a lab on every high street suddenly seemed as pressing as a chain of penny farthing-repair shops. Shelving books in the library, I felt as if I'd disembarked the *Titanic* during its stopover in Ireland.

After the store closed its doors, the site quickly reopened as a Tesco, a company my daughter would eventually work for. I knew it would be tough for her. That the hours would feel long and it would bring her into contact with some wild and challenging people. And that after work her feet would throb impossibly from the moment she sat down. But I always looked forward to picking her up after her shifts. I'd pull up outside, she'd open my car door and throw herself into the passenger seat, exhausted but animatedly talking as she put on her seatbelt. Desperate to unload a shift's worth of stories.

'God,' she would begin, 'there was this one guy …' and I'd pull out of the car park, listening as she rolled out a story that would alarm and fascinate. Offering tales about a job that was peeling back the lid of the world.

A Picture of Health

My family were holiday-camp people. Each year we'd book a week in a chalet at a Butlin's or a Pontin's and arrive ready to squeeze every second of joy from the place. See every show. Enter every competition. When I first started going on these holidays, I was young enough for my parents to leave me in the crèche while they slipped away for cocktails at the Beachcomber bar, and from that point on the camps became an annual tradition. As central a part of our family calendar as birthdays and Christmas. When the summer holidays began, I would ache for the moment when we'd arrive, so we could drag our bags from our overloaded car and bundle in through the primary-coloured chalet door to pick out our rooms. On the drive home at the end of that week I would be exhausted, satisfied and already fantasising about the next year. But by the time I reached the age of thirteen, my enthusiasm for these holidays was starting to wane,

Broken Biscuits

teenage self-consciousness impacting on my willingness to be seen competitively disco-dancing or riding on the back of a donkey. The rest of my family, though, was still all in. My father rolled up his trousers for the Knobbly Knees competition, my mother won Worst Singer in the World and my little brother Ben competed in a male fitness contest named A Picture of Health.

For this competition, entrants were ordered to remove their shirts, line up in the middle of the camp ballroom and flex their muscles to pop music while a man in a brightly coloured blazer inspected their physiques. He'd then rank them based on audience approval and pick a winner. These days this kind of thing could earn its own three-part documentary series on Netflix, but back in the late 80s it was entertainment, and we were all complicit. So, I cheered hard for Ben, who came a grumpy second in the under eleven's category. Then the man in the blazer announced that there were no entrants for the over eleven's division and that he was looking for any healthy boys who might be interested in entering. No one stepped forward and, sensing an opportunity, my mother leaned into my ear.

'Take your shirt off and get up there,' she whispered. 'You'll get a trophy.'

'What?' I replied, shocked that she thought I'd even consider it.

In 1989, I was still a few years away from the lean body I'd have at sixteen, cursed at the time with a torso

A Picture of Health

that looked as if it had been carelessly constructed from wads of uncooked dough. It was a physique reflective of my diet, and I was *not* a healthy boy. But my mother didn't care about that. She knew the measure of my abilities and that taking part in a competition where I was the sole entrant was likely going to be her only chance of ever seeing me win something. I may have looked like the before image on a Charles Atlas bodybuilding ad, but I'd have a Picture of Health trophy and nobody would have been able to take that away from me. The only problem was that I didn't want it.

'Go on!' my mother said.

'No!'

'Go on,' she insisted, talking through her teeth now. 'Take your shirt off. Nobody cares.'

'I care!' I said, picturing myself getting up there then being heckled by the audience, who'd loudly suggest bra sizes or recommend that I buy a girdle. But my mother was driven, her words seeming to come from somewhere deep and serious.

'Take. Your. Shirt. Off.'

My mother had seen me lose at a lot of things. She'd watched me let in a dozen goals during my one game as keeper for my primary-school football team, come a panting eighth in the potato-and-spoon race on sports day, and now she was watching me fail in a tournament of one. I wanted to be a winner for her – but not like this.

Broken Biscuits

Alone and topless under a mirror ball. The thought of it, of being made to stand up there on my own and attempt to demonstrate evidence of my biceps to the strains of 'So Macho' lit something inside me. I felt an angry pressure building and the words left me before I knew what I was saying.

'Can you just … *piss off*!'

I'd never had cause to defy my mother before. I'd certainly never sworn at her. But now I'd done both and there would be, I was sure, consequences. I felt a sickly, boiling sensation in my stomach as she looked at me, her expression impossible to read. But I'd taken a stand and braced myself for the fallout, aware that this was a defining moment.

I don't know what set her off exactly, whether it was my words or the defiant expression on my face, but it was a long time before she stopped laughing.

'Okay, tiger,' she said finally, composing herself and wiping the tears from her eyes. 'Okay.'

While I hadn't wanted the embarrassment of this contest, the fact was I would have loved to have got up there and shown off my toned and incredible body. To stand in front of an applauding audience and be admired, initiating impressed whoops as I made my pecs dance a cha-cha-cha before accepting my trophy then proudly handing it to my mother. My win, finally, for her. But I didn't have a body like that, even though for as long as I

A Picture of Health

could remember I'd wanted one. To be muscular. And not just that, I wanted to look superheroic.

Growing up in the 80s, it was hard to avoid the sight of a sculpted male body. On TV, in movies, even the toys I played with, wherever I looked I'd be presented with the image of what the ideal man should look like. Every action figure I owned looked as if it was dosed up on growth hormones and training for the East German Olympic team. And this had not been lost on my father, who had had been raised in an era where toy soldiers kept their shirts on, and the muscularity of matinée idols played second fiddle to decent tailoring and a well-appointed side parting. Charm always took precedence over the body beautiful. So, finding me playing in the living room one afternoon, a dozen jacked-up action figures littering the carpet around me, he was fascinated. He picked up a He-Man figure, turning it in his hands and scrutinising its obscenely muscled physique.

'How could he even scratch his nose?' he said, marvelling at the cumbersome beachball shaped biceps and bloated pectorals that seemed to him such a hindrance. 'How could he bend his arm?'

Like most of the figures in the He-Man range, it was created from the same muscular mould. Broad-backed and as unsustainably built as a Mr Universe finalist, it was decked out in furry underpants and matching boots.

Broken Biscuits

But that body shape burned an idea into my brain at a developmental stage: *this* is what a man is supposed to look like. A He-Man, but a man, nonetheless. Everyone on He-Man's planet of Eternia was built this way. Man at Arms, Fisto, even Skeletor, each had torsos bejewelled with smooth, perma-flexed muscles. Competing alongside them in a Picture of Health competition even Arnold Schwarzenegger would have felt insecure. But what looked so absurd to my father looked like perfection to me.

While I wanted a body that impressive and powerful, no one around me looked like my action figures because these were physiques drawn from fiction. An impossible achievement, I believed. But then I skipped from *He-Man* cartoons to watching American pro wrestling and discovered that there were people out there who looked exactly like the contents of my toy box. The Ultimate Warrior, Ravishing Rick Rude, Lex Luger, each of them rippling with veins and inflated limbs. Had I squeezed one of their watermelon-sized biceps, I'd have expected it to be as firm and resistant to pressure as if they'd trundled off the Mattel production line. It was through wrestling that I learned about triceps, deltoids, lats, pectorals and quads. I'd sit on the sofa watching these guys throw each other around and perform feats of strength and agility, while I dunked two-finger Kit Kats into Coca-Cola and wondered how I'd go about achieving a body like that.

A Picture of Health

When I wasn't watching them on TV or reading about them in comic books, I was drawing pictures of my favourite wrestlers and superheroes on the reams of fax paper my father liberated from work. Designing my own dream body, brought to life through diligent hours of shading and cross-hatching. A physique carved from 2H pencil. And while I drew, I'd think about the information on the backs of my WWF trading cards, which showed the physical statistics of each featured wrestler.

- Height: 6ft 10in
- Weight: 328lbs
- Biceps: 24in
- Chest: 60in

I had no real idea what these numbers meant in practical terms. All I knew was that, when compared with the photo of the behemoth shown on the front of the card, they equated to something gargantuan. But when it came to putting in the work to gain a body like that for myself, I didn't see the point. It felt that, just like a four-octave singing voice or green eyes, a huge, magnificent body was largely a matter of genetics and there wasn't much I could do to change that. As hard as I tried, I was never going to be as tall and mighty as Razor Ramon or The Undertaker, so why bother?

Broken Biscuits

Besides, when I started watching wrestling, I was still in primary school, a time when there was nothing embarrassing about having an ordinary or even pudgy body. Unless you were skinny or chubby enough to gain negative attention or words of concern, no one commented on anyone else's physique. For the most part, we were all pretty doughy and unbothered by it. Back then, my friend Zoë and I would sit on the edge of our local swimming pool, hunch forward and count the rolls of flab that gathered around our bellies.

'I got four!' she'd say, with a note of victory.

'I think …' I'd say, grunting competitively as I attempted to scrunch up more of my flesh, 'I've got … five.'

There was no loss of status or shame in not having a great physique, because no better was expected of us. A gym body was something only possible in an imagined future and then it was only really something the stars of Hollywood and WWF programming had to worry about. So, Zoë and I performed what now seem like acts of body positivity, squidging and enjoying our soft, pliable fat, and delighting in it. It was only later, when other boys started to develop at a rate faster than me and began resembling men, that I would pay attention to the deficiencies of my own body.

In the changing room, getting ready for PE, it was tough not to notice the physical progress of the other boys in my class. Those with bodies that seemed to have

A Picture of Health

sprung into sudden, chiselled shape simply from lazily tapping a football around while smoking. I would marvel at the easy muscularity of their bodies and wonder why I didn't look like that. Then I'd bend forward to tie my shoelaces and feel my fat rolls gathering, sweet wrappers crinkling in my pockets.

Instead of admitting that I might be part of the problem, that I could do better, I decided that my lack of a great body was down to my lack of physical gifts. Some kids in my class possessed these gifts, and others didn't. That's just how it was. This attitude was supported by my secondary school PE teacher, Mr Cox, who wrote in my school report, 'Adam does not like PE, and he is not good at it.'

Some would have taken this as a blow, but what I saw was freedom. Mr Cox knew I was a lost cause, so didn't waste his time on me. Instead, he gave me the gift of his disdain.

'Look,' he said, 'if you just help carry the equipment to the playing fields and put it away after class, you can do whatever you like. There's no point in making you go through this.'

So, he let me read during lessons. I'd sit on the crate that contained the cricket gear, leafing through the pages of an Agatha Christie and occasionally looking up to see the other boys running around and stumbling in the mud. I did not like PE, I was not good at it, and I was absolutely fine with that. By lifting and carrying I was getting my

Broken Biscuits

exercise in, and I didn't have to go through the trauma of a rugby lesson or my body being scrutinised in the showers. While my maths and science teachers didn't let my lack of ability in their subjects stop them from putting me through the wringer, Mr Cox saw no value in making me struggle. He was one of the few strokes of luck I encountered at school. His behaviour sent me into adulthood released from the burden of exercise.

Up until my thirties, this was unproblematic. Nothing I ate had a truly negative effect on my body. I drank several cans of Coke each day and wolfed pizza and chocolate, eating with such a disregard for consequence you'd think I was making the most of my last meal on Death Row. Arriving home each day, I downed biscuits with the same enthusiasm some people applied to a post-work whisky. Three fingers of chocolate digestives downed in seconds, and more lined up on my kitchen counter. It seemed that nothing could touch me until, without me noticing, it did. On Facebook I would be tagged in photos that shamed me, my double chin frozen during a laugh and the buttons on my shirts straining to the point where they appeared to be actively screaming. A friend's mother would tell me 'You're like a big cuddly bear,' and I'd try to convince myself this meant I looked powerful and not as if I stole picnic baskets and had packed on a bunch of weight in advance of hibernation. I would lose count of the rolls on my stomach and before I realised what was

A Picture of Health

happening I weighed nineteen stone and was careening towards twenty with no stopping point in sight.

Concerned, I headed to the internet to work out the ideal body weight for my frame and learned that it was roughly thirteen stone, a weight I had not experienced since my late teens. Still, at a quarter inch shy of 6ft, I told myself that I could carry this off. My height and the apparent popularity of the dad bod gave me a free pass to think of myself as in decent shape. I could disregard a gym body as a passing fad, ignoring the fact that being muscular is not an entirely new standard of beauty. Greek sculptures, renaissance paintings and chapel ceilings seemed to prove that we've always had a pretty good idea about what represents a hot male body and we didn't need a Gold's Gym or a Fitness First to achieve it. But I guess it became harder to reach that kind of physical perfection the closer society got to desk jobs and the invention of Ben & Jerry's. Harder for me, certainly. And also, it seemed, for the people around me.

'My mum's worried about you,' my then wife told me. Her mother had confessed to her that she could hear me breathing from the other side of the house: 'He sounds like he's going to have a heart attack.'

I was dismissive of this, but the comment hurt. It's one thing to convince yourself that you're fine, but when other people start to notice the things you've been quietly self-conscious about, delusion becomes more difficult to

Broken Biscuits

maintain. So, I decided to do something about it before a medical event took the decision out of my hands.

At first, I tried following a British Military Fitness programme that came free with a Sunday newspaper. Several times a week I'd put myself through a series of stretches, press-ups, dips and sit-ups then head out for a run. I never felt any healthier and I didn't lose a significant amount of weight but, running along the side of the road, I did see a lot of litter. The things people threw from cars as they drove through my town. So, I'd stop to pick this up as I went, dumping it in the bin when I staggered home on my cool-down walks. Before long, my morning runs had transformed into the act of putting on shorts then mildly jogging down the street as I scanned the pavement for crisp packets and spent coffee cups, a bulging refuse sack in each hand.

Arriving home from my exercise, I'd take off my shirt and assess my progress in my wardrobe mirror, giving in as always to the small, shameful need to flex. There were faint lines of definition around my biceps. I rotated my arms a little, tensing my triceps as they came into view. They looked okay. There were pleasing cables of muscle running down my forearms. But then there was my stomach, as ill-defined and paunchy as ever. The pecs that resembled dollops of failed meringue. And my love handles, a soft feminine curve to them. The kind of shape I've always enjoyed feeling on a woman but were attached

A Picture of Health

to me, so felt repulsive. Once I started to pay attention to myself in this way, I saw problems everywhere, and knew I needed to do something a little more drastic.

I downloaded a calorie-counting app and started tracking all of my meals, trying to chop my intake down to 1,200 calories a day. It was miserable but once the hunger pains and sugar pangs subsided, it became bearable and, crucially, I was noticing a change in my body. My weight rapidly moving away from twenty stone and in the direction of that seemingly unachievable thirteen. Still, while I may have been losing weight, I still had that porridge-y, toneless body that so blatantly showed through my T-shirts they may as well have been made from clingfilm. But then my friend David sent me a link to a YouTube video, the subject line of his email reading:

Have you tried YRG?

YRG, I learned, stood for Yoga for Regular Guys, a programme of 'dynamic resistance yoga' put together by a former wrestler named Diamond Dallas Page. It promised greater flexibility, weight loss and, based on the people in the promo clip, the body of an American wrestler. So, I ordered the instructional DVD and followed the programme through routines with wrestling-related names, setting up my laptop and a yoga mat in my bedroom and sweating my way through sequences named

Broken Biscuits

The Road Warrior, The Diamond Cutter and a pose that required me to 'Hulk it up!'

What surprised me was that it worked. I was beginning to develop a level of definition I'd never seen on myself before. I didn't look great, but I didn't look terrible either. I'd always wanted to look like a wrestler, but the state of my body had always been the evidence of exactly how much I'd really wanted it. Now, here was YRG, making it seem possible and, importantly for me, relatively easy. My problem was that I got impatient, deciding that I didn't want to wait for that body. So, I pledged to do YRG every day, certain that in a few weeks I'd surely look as if I came with Mattel branding and a barcode.

A couple of weeks into this commitment, I was woken in the night by a sharp pain across my chest. It wouldn't shift and I couldn't get comfortable, so I headed downstairs and took a bunch of the super-strength ibuprofen that my mother had given me. She'd been prescribed them for her knee pain, but had more boxes than she knew what to do with, so she'd given me a few when I'd last visited her. When these didn't take the edge off the pain and it still hurt to breathe, I started to worry, so dialled the non-emergency NHS number to ask for advice.

'I can't sleep,' I said, 'I've got these sharp pains across my chest –'

'An ambulance is on its way,' the operator said before I finished my sentence, her tone brisk and efficient.

A Picture of Health

'I'm not sure I need that.'

'We need to make certain,' she said. 'It could be your heart.'

Outside of my mother-in-law's comments, I'd never really considered my heart, but now it was all I could think about. I remembered all the men on my father's side of the family who'd had heart issues. My own father had had a stent fitted, my grandfather died after his third heart attack, my great grandfather died of his first, aged forty. It didn't seem out of the realms of possibility that, given the way I'd lived, I'd already worn mine out. And at an age when I was younger than all of them.

The ambulance crew arrived, knocking on the door and waking my wife, who came downstairs to find me sitting on the sofa looking pale and embarrassed, a paramedic hooking a heart monitor to my chest. I couldn't help but notice how muscular he was and had to stop myself from mentioning YRG.

'Have you taken any medication?' the other paramedic asked. I showed her the packet and she frowned. 'Wait, where did you get these?'

'They're my mother's,' I said.

'You shouldn't be taking anyone else's tablets. Do you know how dangerous that is?'

'Yes,' I said meekly, thinking, *Please don't tell me off, I'm dying.*

Broken Biscuits

When my heart readings proved inconclusive, they decided to admit me for further checks. I got up to walk to the ambulance but was ordered to sit in a wheelchair.

'I'm not sure that's ...' I said, beginning to protest.

'It's easier,' the paramedic said, guiding me into it. 'Trust me.'

I sat down, feeling suddenly weak and elderly. Then I was strapped into the chair and wheeled up a ramp into the back of the ambulance. Arriving at the hospital a short drive later, I was rolled into a corridor and made to wait. It was the early hours, a Saturday night leaking into a Sunday morning. Before I'd arrived, a stabbing victim had been admitted, and with that had come chaos. A man was shouting. Security guards were trying to keep things under control. The paramedics chatted about what was going on, then transitioned into a conversation about dating. All of this conducted above me, as if I wasn't there.

'So, we ask for the bill, and he says, "Your profile said you were a feminist, so shall we split it fifty-fifty?" and I was like "Mate, I had a salad, you had the sirloin. It's not happening."'

This is what happens when you're not important, I thought. *This is how people behave around you when you're dying and it doesn't matter what you hear.*

Eventually the corridor was cleared of screams and shouts and I was wheeled into a room in A&E, where I was asked to lie on a gurney while I awaited a consultant.

A Picture of Health

I was there for around an hour when a doctor finally appeared, looking upbeat but exhausted.

'So,' he said, looking at my chart, 'you've got chest pains?'

I detailed what had happened and explained where the pain was located. He examined me, prodding various tender parts of my torso and asking 'Does that hurt? How about now?' until he had enough information for a diagnosis. Then he stood back from me, frowning.

'Well, it's not your heart. It looks like you've severely strained your intercostal muscles, right here,' he said, gesturing near his ribs. 'Have you been doing anything strenuous lately?'

'I've been doing this kind of ... yoga,' I said, and quickly added, 'for men.'

'And have you been doing it a lot, this ... men's yoga?'

'Every day for the last few weeks.'

'Okay, well that will be it. If you're not used to exercise,' he said, trying not to stare at the parts of my body that proved this, to draw attention to the softness he'd just methodically felt, 'then you can hurt yourself.'

I was embarrassed by his assessment of my body and on reflex found myself flexing my arms. The main part of my body that YRG had really affected.

'Honestly, I usually see this injury in older men who are ...' he paused to think of the right word, '*struggling* on the toilet.'

Broken Biscuits

Apparently concerned that I wouldn't understand what he meant, he illustrated this for me, clenching his fists and performing a brief mime that demonstrated the act of defecation. At this, I stopped flexing.

He prescribed me some painkillers, warned me off exercise for a couple of weeks and discharged me. I shuffled through to the reception of A&E, where I called for a taxi, wondering if I'd rather have had the heart attack and, what's more, died from it. Then I took my taxi home and gave up on Yoga for Regular Guys.

This wasn't the end. Over time there would be other bursts of enthusiasm for exercise. The month of running, the brief commitment to 100 press-ups a day, the self-assigned challenge to perform as many kettle-bell squats as I could manage during a single episode of *Grey's Anatomy*. All of these fads would come and go, an injury to my hip or my rotator cuff eventually giving me a blessed release from exercise. If I'd wanted it enough, I would have found a way past this. But what my body always seemed to want most of all was a way out. It did not like PE, and it was not good at it.

When I was finally able to phone up my mother and tell her that I had won something, I was forty-five years old, and it was a prize for writing. This activity I'd mostly undertaken while sitting in front a computer at my kitchen table and eating chocolate chip cookies. I had

A Picture of Health

managed to write an award-winning book using the hunched body that shamed me every time I took my shirt off in public. While writing is a job where many who do it are beautiful, it also doesn't matter if your author photo makes you look as appetising as a blob of yoghurt on the last seat of a bus. Readers like you for your brain, but they would never care to look at the actual thing.

I wrote most of that book during the COVID-19 lockdowns, a period when I could not get a haircut, ate whatever comforting trash I could get my hands on and couldn't get to a gym even if I'd wanted to. Dressing for a dinner date over Zoom with my girlfriend, I found that I could no longer button up my suit. So, it was fortunate that the prizegiving ceremony got cancelled due to the same lockdown restrictions that birthed the book itself. But a large part of me felt robbed by this, because it meant that I didn't get to head up on stage and hear the applause of an audience. To accept the glow of praise I'd always wanted. But most of all, I wouldn't get to show off my hands, so nimble and ripped from all that typing. To hold up my award in the spotlight and watch the beam highlighting the only part of my body that gets regular exercise. The only part of me that aches from effort. The only part of me that ever truly wanted it.

It's the End of the World As We Know It

December 2023

I cannot think of a day over the last eighteen years when I haven't spoken to my daughter, Effie. From the moment she could talk, we've been in conversation, and we haven't stopped since. These days she splits her time equally between her mother's home and mine, but even when she's not with me, the talking continues. She'll phone me on her walks to the bus stop before college. As she heads to the gym. To her job in a Chinese takeaway. And when we're together we'll sit in my living room, gripping mugs of tea or bowls of the soft noodles she brings home after her shifts, discussing books, politics, the guy who'd walked up to her counter and ordered 'all your prawn toast' as if he were robbing a bank. Neither of us ever reaches a point where we run out of things to say to one another and nothing really important needs to be said,

Broken Biscuits

but what is important to both of us is that we're always saying something.

My phone is linked to my laptop and when she calls while I'm writing, the words will be whipped away from my screen, replaced by a pop-up message: *Effie is calling.* If anyone else interrupted me in the middle of my work I'd be pissed off and snappy, as if the call had somehow also violently swiped my laptop to the floor. But when it's my daughter, the standard rules do not apply. And I was working on this book in the days just after Christmas when my words suddenly vanished.

Effie is calling.

'So, the chickens,' she said when I answered, getting straight to the point, 'you don't need me to clean them out, do you?'

'No, just feed them,' I said, 'and make sure they're still alive.'

'Oh, thank God,' she said.

My new wife, Emma, and I had hired a cabin in the countryside where we'd soon be heading off to spend a few days over the new year break. The two of us needing some dedicated time and space to write. And because I'm still a few years away from being the kind of man who insists on travelling with his chickens, Effie would be popping over to keep an eye on them while we were gone.

'Call me as soon as you get there,' she said, 'and send me a photo of something.'

It's the End of the World As We Know It

'I will,' I told her. 'I promise.'

Disconnecting the call, it was hard not to feel a niggling reminder of the first time I'd headed off on a writing retreat and left Effie behind. So much having changed for the two of us since then.

May 2016

'I'll call you as often as I can,' I told Effie, who stood watching me while I packed my bag, a Nerf gun held loosely in her hand, 'and I'll take lots of photos then come back and tell you all about it.'

'But why are you going away without me?'

She wasn't happy about this. Ten years old at the time, she had rarely known a day without my company. Now, it seemed, I had decided to go on holiday on my own, leaving her and her mother behind. I needed to give her an explanation for my behaviour, and I'd better make sure it was a good one.

'It's not a holiday, sweetheart.'

'But you won't be at work.'

'I know,' I said. 'But there won't be any TV or internet.'

'Oh!' she said, her eyes widening as if she'd just heard a gunshot. '*Why?*'

'Because I need peace and quiet. I'll be in the middle of

nowhere. I'll just be writing. You won't be missing out, I swear.'

She chewed this over, her thought process so obvious it could have been playing on a screen across her forehead.

'Sounds disgusting,' she said, then headed downstairs to reassure herself that on-demand TV still existed.

I was about to turn forty at the time, and what I'd wanted most of all, more than a party or a significant gift, was to get away from everything. To rent a place somewhere on my own and write. I didn't need anything fancy, because fancy is wasted on me. If the price was right, I would sleep in a murder house. Remove the police tape and mop the crime scene myself, if I had to. What was important to me was that this place should be in a remote location, away from the distractions of technology. And, just as I'd told Effie, there would be no TV, no internet and no other people. Nothing but my thoughts, my work and my greyhound, Betty, for company.

The place I'd found was an old farmhouse in Wales, enclosed by dense trees, knotty briars and, beyond that, a barrier of swooping hills that gave no indication they had ever known the disruptive pressure of a human foot. Sitting at my laptop and clicking through the photos on the listing, I could tell that it would be perfect for my needs. Isolated and twee, its whitewashed stonework and tumbledown good looks suggested the kind of place

It's the End of the World As We Know It

where thoughtful bestsellers were written. I pictured myself sitting at a desk by a window looking out into the magnificence of nature, typing away then pausing to draw fresh inspiration from the wonder of my surroundings. This image flew in the face of the more likely reality of me, feral and undignified, brushing pastry crumbs from my keyboard and wondering if I could go another day without showering. But aside from any creative benefits, I was looking forward to heading out into the countryside on my own again. Something I hadn't allowed myself to do in years.

As a child I'd often feel overwhelmed, gripped by a need to scream at everyone around me. To see no one and not be seen. The rural Suffolk town where I'd spent the first sixteen years of my life had offered me plenty of opportunities to do this. I could leave my home and within twenty minutes find myself alone in a cornfield, a river or an orchard. While hay fever sometimes made this challenging, puffed-up eyes and sneezing fits were preferable to the sight of another person. I had grown up in a house where I was one of six, on an estate that never fully slept, and at times I felt so hemmed in it was as if I couldn't breathe. But if I spent a couple of hours out in the countryside, I found that I could think clearly; the suffocating pressure would subside and I would return home as relaxed as if I'd been treated with a mild sedative. Over time I learned that if I didn't regularly

Broken Biscuits

escape our home and end up at the top of a tree or doused in the cooling depths of a river, then I'd feel distanced from myself and unbalanced. My sense of security during these solitary periods enhanced by the knowledge that any genuinely threatening creatures had been driven away generations earlier and that I was never more than a short walk away from a TV or a chiller full of ice-cold Cokes.

Now, decades later, I was putting my trust in that same process. Running off to the countryside in the hope that taking time away on my own and reconnecting with that sense of calm would prove fruitful. I would become one of those authors who wrote books in remote places and produced reflective think pieces about the nurturing sanctuary of nature, then parlayed them into an endorsement deal with Patagonia. My dreams were at once big and small: a book deal and a free pair of durable hiking trousers in exchange for an Instagram post. My retreat could take me anywhere. Anything seemed possible.

There was a knock at the front door and Effie answered it. I heard excited conversation and could tell she was talking to her friend, Reuben, who lived across the road. She called to me up the stairs.

'I'm going out!'

'Okay,' I called back, the door slamming closed before I'd finished the word. I looked out of my bedroom window and down into our cul-de-sac to see her and

It's the End of the World As We Know It

Reuben running over to his house, Nerf guns in their hands, other kids from the street waiting for them out front. While it was still only the morning, it was already proving to be a sticky, sun-roasted day. Later, I was certain, there would be water fights. A request for ice-cream money. Various concerned parents would rush outside to slather their children with Ambre Solaire or fit them with unwanted sunhats. Then there would be more running and yelling until the street finally drained of children, each of them scuffing to their respective homes in the fading light: filthy, joyous, exhausted. Days like this were the ones I enjoyed most during my own childhood, and while I was away I'd miss seeing Effie enjoy them, too. And I'd simply miss her. A feeling I knew I was soon going to have to get used to.

I set off on the morning of my fortieth, having said my goodbyes and given Effie a tight hug. The kind she was still young enough to leap up for, gripping me like a monkey and issuing a muffled 'happy birthday' into my ear as I set her back down on the ground. Then I put my bags in the boot, clipped Betty into the car and drove away, feeling as I did that I had left the most important thing behind.

Outside of commuting, I didn't drive anywhere without Effie in the back seat, and I felt her absence. I was used to her sitting behind me and pointing things out, asking that

Broken Biscuits

I turn up the radio, chastising me for swearing about other drivers.

'They can't hear you,' she'd tell me. 'But I can.'

More often than not, she'd pick up one of the *i-Spy* books she kept in the pocket of the car door then peer out of the window. She had a few of these books, little subject-specific spotter's guides designed to keep kids occupied on journeys. There was one containing lists of dogs; others about birds or things to look for at the seaside, each item assigned a different point value based on its rarity. Driving along, she'd hawkishly scan the scene outside her window, pencil at the ready to tick a box and shout out what she'd seen.

'A Doberman!' she might say. 'Twenty points!'

Encouraged by this kind of win, we'd both scour the streets, looking for more. A whippet. A boxer. A strutting, high-value mastiff. Each of us invested in racking up the tally.

'Look, a bichon frise!'

She would have loved the drive to the farmhouse, I was sure. The first couple of hours maybe not so much, since they were definitely on the bleak, low-scoring side. Nothing much to spy. There were pylons. Ribbons of featureless grey road. A single sunflower thriving, despite the odds, on the central reservation of the M6. But as multilane carriageways gave way to the winding B-roads of the Welsh countryside, I imagined her looks of wonder at the regular sight of kestrels and spring-loaded rabbits. The cloud of sheep that ambled in front of my car and slowed it to a crawl. A white horse that ran alongside me in a roadside field making me feel, for a few exhilarating seconds, as if it was joining me on this trip.

Twenty points! I wanted to shout. *Fifteen points! Thirty!*

As I got closer to the farmhouse, though, I encountered things that I would rather she didn't see. A buzzard hoisting a gashed and struggling squirrel into the air. Rats the size of Labrador pups bolting across the road in front of me. Muscular cattle that stared me out from fields, swinging their tails like baseball bats. This was not the countryside of my childhood, and it was easy to convince myself that the wildlife around me was collectively up to no good. That the benign gaze of a donkey could just as easily be one of insolent threat. Because I was out in the real country now, where my phone had no signal and I could not call for help. I'd ordered my nature served red in tooth and claw, and I'd got exactly what I'd asked for.

When I pulled up at the farmhouse, though, these thoughts were swept aside. However wild and unmanicured everything else around me might be, this little place belonged to somewhere different. A small, whitewashed refuge nestling in the comforting bosom of nature. The kind of scene you'd expect to see decorating a tin of shortbread. As I turned off the engine, Betty began making

Broken Biscuits

the keening noise she always makes when she wants to go outside to pee on something, so I let her out of the car. She squatted on the grass then sniffed around the farmhouse and its surrounding gardens, getting to know her home for the next few days. I took some photos for Effie, then grabbed my bags and headed inside. Betty followed, her nose snuffling the ground as she moved.

The place was homely and cosy, the floorboards creaking with age as I entered the living room and set down my bags. There was a cushion-stacked sofa and a pair of tired, chubby-looking easy chairs, each draped with its own antimacassar. A China tea set rested on the coffee table alongside a brick of polythene-wrapped fruitcake and a vase of wildflowers. It couldn't have looked more like they'd hired my nan to style the place if my school photo had been sitting on the mantelpiece. As I nosed through the various rooms, I noticed that each had the same pleasingly familiar smell, nailed to an indefinable comforting place in my past. Or perhaps places. There were notes of sweet tea and biscuits, woodsmoke, my grandad's outhouse, the tattered hessian on the back of my primary school's upright piano. I wanted to bottle that smell and pour it into a diffuser back home. I was certain that only good things would happen for me in this place.

'What do you think?' I asked Betty.

She looked up at me, likely wondering if I had said one of the five words she understands; walk, breakfast, wee,

It's the End of the World As We Know It

dinner, park. Assuming I'd mentioned food she began hopping excitably, her claws sounding out a desperate plea on the three-hundred-year-old floor.

I filled her a bowl of dog food then boiled the kettle for the first of what would surely be dozens of cups of tea, then took a look at the desk by the window where I planned to spend most of my time. The view outside was baking in the late afternoon sun, the scene looking so much like a painting by Jules Breton that I almost expected a barefoot peasant worker to walk through it carrying a sickle. Instead, I spotted the white-painted wrought-iron table and chairs I'd seen on the cottage's website. So, I grabbed my tea and took it outside, perching on one of these chairs and taking in my surroundings. Whatever dark detail I'd picked up on during my journey seemed absent and absurd then. There was chattering birdsong. Crackling insect noises. Nothing that suggested the imminent arrival of a homicidal falcon or a red-eyed bull with bad intentions. So, I sipped my tea and pulled out my phone, cursing the lack of reception. Wanting to let my wife know I'd arrived safely.

My wife. Two words I'd been saying for so long it felt as if they'd pressed a permanent groove into my tongue. It was strange to think I wouldn't be saying them for too much longer. Stranger still to think of the way the world would look when I'd have to start saying 'My ex-wife'.

Broken Biscuits

I had spent half of my life believing that I had so much worked out, loading my twenties and thirties with a real sense of certainty. While I didn't live in a perfect world, I at least knew my place in it and where I would eventually end up. Everything was mapped out. I had plans that reached out decades ahead of me. And that sense of certainty I was used to feeling really came from my marriage.

'You'll marry the first one that comes along,' my brother Robert told me when I was in my early teens. The way he said this felt as if he'd slapped me, but I wasn't sure what with or why. He'd seen something in me and whatever he meant by this comment, it clearly wasn't intended as flattery. So, I pushed back.

'No, I won't!'

'You fucking will.'

'I won't!'

'I'm telling you now, you will.'

That I ended up marrying the third one that came along didn't feel like I'd proved him wrong exactly, but by that point I didn't care. I was just happy to have found the person I was going to spend the rest of my life with, and so easily, too. My wife and I met in September of 1997 while I was on a visit to Manchester. I moved to the city a month later and we got engaged just before Christmas. We were both twenty-one. By the time we turned twenty-four, we were married, in love and believing wholeheartedly that this would be it for us. We'd cracked the thing that people write songs about. Poems, movies, TV shows, a whole entertainment industry was built around it. Looking for love seemed to be everyone's impossible goal but, somehow, we'd just stumbled into it. The two of us bought a house and began amassing a portfolio of pensions and insurance policies. Then, once we'd made all the sensible preparations, we had Effie. We were on the tracks and wheeling through adulthood, hitting all the grown-up achievements. Doing all of this in your early twenties was pretty standard among the generation that went before us, but none of our friends were engaged, let alone married. Instead, they were enjoying single living or cycling through partners every couple of months. A try-before-you-buy situation that seemed to work for all involved.

If I had any doubts back then about how hasty I'd been in settling down, I wasn't aware of them. Perhaps they manifested in the overly authoritative way I spoke about relationships. The smug confidence of a man who believed he'd worked it all out, but in retrospect was perhaps trying a little too hard to convince himself.

'You shouldn't get married unless you know it'll be forever,' I'd say, ignoring the fact that my mother's second marriage had been the successful one. Over time, I made my married status a part of my personality. I was the guy who'd embraced love's young dream and had gone in with both boots. Looking forward to a golden anniversary while I still had my original hips. But I was far too young to be talking about forever.

I got up from my seat and paced the grounds of the farmhouse, waving my phone in the air. Hoping to catch a signal as if it were a butterfly that could be swooped into a net. When that failed, I got back in the car and drove to the closest village, hoping to fall in range of a signal tower. As I turned onto the high street, message notifications began pinging through on my phone, so I pulled up outside a chip shop and called home. My wife and I chatted for a minute or so, then she called into the street for Effie and passed the phone over to her.

'Is it nice there?' Effie asked, her voice small and crackling. The reception as stable as chimney smoke.

'It's very pretty,' I said. 'I saw a beautiful white horse running next to the car.'

'That ...' she began to reply, but the line cut dead. I tried calling back but couldn't get through, so I texted to say that I'd try again tomorrow. Then, because the smell of fish and chips always has me floating like a cartoon dog following the scent of a pie on a windowsill, I bought a fish supper and drove back to the farmhouse. I sat at the desk by the window and opened up my laptop, eating my dinner straight from the paper and staring alternately between the steadily darkening view outside and a half-finished essay that had been open on my screen for

It's the End of the World As We Know It

weeks now. About something funny my mother had said that I was trying to put into context. I passed a scrap of battered fish into Betty's waiting mouth, wrote a few sentences, ate some chips, changed the font on my words, deleted them. I dropped the final piece of fish into Betty's mouth, balled up the greasy papers and closed the laptop.

'Come on, sweetheart,' I said, patting my thigh and urging Betty to follow me outside. Wanting to take her out for one last wee before I called it a night.

What I'd not been prepared for was the brilliance of the stars when I looked up. My view of them largely obscured by light pollution back in the city. I tried to think of ways to describe them that no one else had ever thought of, and while I did I considered *Abel's Moon*, the Shirley Hughes picture book I'd often read to Effie at bedtime when she was little. It tells the story of a father who works away, but wherever he is in the world he's always connected to his children by the same moon they're all looking up at. That night, it was a brilliant white fingernail, but I was pretty sure Effie wasn't looking up at it, too. More likely she was tucked up in bed and, if she was still awake, reading from one of the books that sat in a teetering tower on her bedside table. No longer needing me to read her stories.

There was a sudden rustling noise on the far side of the farmhouse garden, and Betty and I both sharply turned our heads to see what it was. A shrub was shaking, some-

Broken Biscuits

thing sizeable disturbing its leaves. I took hold of Betty's collar, knowing that if she followed the urge to chase whatever it was, she'd disappear into the darkness and I'd probably never see her again.

'What do you see?' I asked her. Not expecting an answer, just wanting the protection of a human voice, even if it was only my own.

Betty continued to stare intently at the shrub, one paw lifted like a pointer. Her breeding as a hunting dog always rushed to the surface in moments like this. I squinted into the leaves, faintly lit by the glow from the farmhouse window, my heart rate increasing. I expected to see a pair of eyes looking back at me. Something to pounce from the darkness. But when the shrub stopped shaking, I dismissed it and pulled Betty back inside. Then I drew the curtains, sat down at the desk and re-opened the laptop. Typed a few words at the bottom of the document I had open.

Bush shaking. Mysterious. Fox? Wolves?

Perhaps they'd be useful in the morning. Likely not, but I couldn't think straight anymore. The long journey had taken its toll, I told myself. The pressure of finally being here, having made a time and financial commitment to my work, was starting to kick in. So, I headed up for bed, vowing to start afresh in the morning, the stairs creaking in a way that matched the twinges in my back. I climbed into bed and put on a podcast where a pro wrestler was interviewing the creator of *The Walking Dead*. Then I

It's the End of the World As We Know It

stared up at the beams of the bedroom ceiling and waited for sleep, listening while men discussed the end of the world and what might follow.

I woke at around 4 a.m. – a time I had grown used to getting up. From the age she could get herself out of bed until a few years into primary school, Effie and I seemed to live in our own unoccupied pocket of time; in the gap between the night owls and the early birds. Each day I'd wake to the sound of her breathing, her face close to mine as she stood beside my bed and leaned in to check if I was awake. When my eyes creaked open, she'd slip her hand into mine and urge me out of bed. Keen for the day, our day, to begin. I'd get up and we'd creep downstairs so as not to wake her mother. Then we'd read together, draw and construct Lego villages while I sipped strong coffee and waited for CBeebies to begin broadcasting, when *In The Night Garden* would take over and I could close my eyes for a few minutes before getting ready for work. But I always knew this time was precious and would be fleeting, so I never wished it away. Never hoped that she might give me a day off.

She'd often use these mornings to press her pencil case and a wad of paper into my hands, then ask me to write her a story.

'What about?' I'd ask, letting her lead things. Working to her brief.

Broken Biscuits

Her responses to this question changed daily. These stories were almost always about a little girl, but outside of that they could go anywhere. They might feature a hot-air balloon. A robot. An alien planet. A cat with a gun. I'd draw a picture and write a caption beneath it, Effie directing me if she felt I was going wrong. If I produced something that didn't match the image in her head, she'd give me a look that suggested she was about to fire me. Then she'd take a felt tip pen and correct my mistake.

'No,' she'd say firmly, 'the robot is blue.'

'The legs should be longer.'

'There should be a bear in that cave.'

We were always discussing things, building worlds together, and now I was planning to leave the one that we had been a part of for so long. However amicable the split might be, a divorce would mean Effie and I not sharing every morning together. And not just that, I wouldn't always be on hand when she needed me. When she'd choked as a baby, I'd been there to get her breathing again, reeling from a wave of dizzying relief as she took a deep gasp and let loose a scream that sounded to me like baby talk for, *'What the fuck just happened?!'* Then there were the trips to A&E for stitches and the moments of sadness when she just wanted me to comfort her. But mostly what she needed was for me to be available. To drop everything so I could help her build a boat out of cardboard boxes or sit beside her, eating cinnamon and raisin bagels and watching back-to-back episodes of *Arthur*.

Getting out of bed in the cottage, I wondered what she was doing at the same time. Was she awake? Was she drawing alone? Writing a story? I would have to get used to this. The not knowing.

I headed downstairs, made a coffee and opened up my laptop, staring at the words I'd left on screen the previous night. The cursor pulsing. I considered typing something then took my coffee outside instead, choosing to watch the morning begin. As the sun rose over that barrier of hills, Betty sniffed around the garden, concentrating her efforts on that now motionless shrub. I thought of the words on my laptop screen.

Mysterious. Foxes? Wolves?

And as I watched the day begin, I decided that I would use some of this time away to write Effie a short story. One about a girl out in the wilds, inspired by the things I'd see on this trip and the creatures that crawled around in the undergrowth. The ones that made the leaves tremble. I sat thinking about this until my coffee went cold and the light no longer belonged to me and Effie. Then I pushed myself to my feet and took Betty for a walk, wanting to see a few more things and get some inspiration before I began writing.

I led Betty down the path from the farmhouse and onto a single-track road, walking the grass verges and trying to

Broken Biscuits

decide on a setting for the story. Thinking of the characters who'd inhabit it. I'd spotted a picturesque church from my bedroom window that morning, and it looked like a good place to start, so we headed towards it. When we pushed our way through its parched wooden gate, we found that the graveyard was neglected and overgrown. Anyone buried there was now long forgotten. But as we picked our way between the gravestones, I saw signs of life and activity. A pair of swifts flitted in and out of their nest in the eaves of the church doorway, issuing chew toy squeaks as they flew back and forth. I thought of Effie marking them in an I-Spy.

Swift: *50 points*. Tick.

Betty spotted a rabbit and pulled me away from this scene, wanting to chase it. I gripped her lead firmly, allowing her to guide me as she followed its trail around the church and through the long grasses.

Rabbit: *10 points*. Tick.

I was looking around the churchyard, taking some photos for Effie, when I skidded on something slimy and looked down to see my foot disappearing into the belly of a dead sheep. It had been concealed by the tall grasses, though watching my foot entering the torso I wasn't quite sure how I'd missed it. The bloody ribs jutting through its downy, mash-filled pelt. The dark, gooey hole where its eye once sat. The smell. I yelped and withdrew my foot, pulling Betty away from it and leading us back onto the

It's the End of the World As We Know It

road, where I wiped my shoe. I put this experience down to bad luck. This was the countryside, after all, where you'll find gross dead things once in a while. But as we continued on our walk, death became a theme. Every few minutes I was presented with another item to tick off on my growing list of countryside terrors.

A roadkill badger, a pair of crows pecking chunks of blackened meat from a grinning wound across its side: *30 points*. Tick.

The splayed remains of a pigeon, its wings held wide as if pinned to a board in anatomy class: *15 points*. Tick.

The burst and flattened corpse of a large rat, its body shivering with flies: *10 points*. Tick.

Arriving back at the farmhouse, I sat down at the desk and began writing. Trying not to focus on the grim things I'd seen. Instead, I wrote about the swifts. The blooming, hardy gorse. The grass-parting bunnies and the wheeling birds. A little girl walking through it all. Then I started a new paragraph and found that I could not stop thinking about the bodies all around me. Outside my window, on the road, in the churchyard, surely under the floors where generations of mice must have been turning to dust.

'Death is everywhere,' I wrote, then deleted it, closed the laptop and drove into the village to call home. Effie answered on the third ring.

'Hello, Daddy. Are you getting lots of writing done?'

Broken Biscuits

'A bit,' I said, 'but don't worry about that. What have you been up to?'

I listened to her talk about her day, about *Minecraft* and Harry Potter Lego, happy to be discussing something other than dead things. When she was done, she passed me over to her mother and it wasn't long before the two of us were talking about the dead things.

For the longest time, my wife and I had been perceived by those around us as a two-part jigsaw puzzle. Our lives and personalities seemed to fit together with a neat and satisfying click. As a unit, we worked and that was how other people saw us, too. In the build-up to her own wedding, one of my wife's colleagues had told her, 'I want what you and Adam have,' and that sort of statement was common, fortifying the view we had of ourselves and of each other. When Effie came along, our puzzle effortlessly expanded to three pieces, the new picture it created changing but still perfect in the way it was assembled. It still fitted with a neat click. But after almost twenty years together, my wife and I had each slowly become pieces of two different puzzles. Our lives were increasingly lived separately, and we no longer made sense in the picture we'd been a part of for so long.

I'm sure we had both noticed this, but ultimately, I would be the one to buckle under the pressure. No longer able to ignore the fact that we'd reached the end I'd never expected for us. So, when I got back home from this trip,

It's the End of the World As We Know It

we'd talk. About other dead things. It would be painful and the two of us would work it all out in time, I knew. But what had really been bothering me during the months leading up to the retreat, gnawing on me in the night as I slept in short, troubled bursts, was what the split would mean for Effie.

'You need to really think about this,' my mother told me when I called her to tell her how I'd been feeling, invoking the impact her own divorce had on my older siblings. 'Robert and Becky hated it. They were sad and angry for so long.'

I tried to picture Effie being sad and angry with me. Not just annoyed that I was going away on a trip but upset that I had decided to tear our family apart. Undermining everything she'd ever known and disrupting her sense of security. I wasn't sure I could bear doing that to her. But at some point, things would have to change and for a long time none of us was going to like it.

My days in the farmhouse quickly fell into a regular pattern. I would take Betty out on our daily walks, full of renewed purpose and fresh ideas for Effie's story, then I'd encounter something disturbing that would derail me. Soupy innards; carrion-stripped bones; a selection of small, crushed skulls. Had I wanted to write a story about a little girl trapped alone in a post-apocalyptic rural landscape, I would have had all the source material I needed.

Broken Biscuits

Wherever I looked, natural beauty seemed to be taking a back seat to the gory and the ominous. Betty was often spooked, stopping to catch random scents and stare off at threats unseen. I saw hedges scarred with flattened grass and tunnels, apparent entry and exit points for large creatures. I pictured badgers the size of mopeds darting out of these boltholes and dragging ramblers into the briars. Caught myself scanning the patchwork quilt of fields for a big cat on the prowl, possibly tiring of sheep and considering levelling-up to a dog-walking human who was out of his depth.

At night, I would glumly stir a Pot Noodle and peer out into the inky darkness, following every terrifying route my brain presented me with. I thought about the moment earlier in the week when Betty and I had discovered the top of a fox's head, just sitting there on the roadside, the ears still upright like a macabre parody of something a child might strap to their head at Disneyland. I thought about how it had ended up there. About which creature had done that. I tried to remember what I'd heard about the reintroduction of wolves into the UK. Whether it was just being considered or if the government had actually gone ahead and done it. I couldn't access the internet to check so I had to assume they were out there now, waiting for me to pop out to the bins. Hiding. Shaking the shrubs.

I had only seen one other person in the vicinity of the farmhouse. Another dog walker early one morning who'd trudged up the narrow road towards me. She was wearing pyjamas and a dressing gown and when her dog paused to crap on the road she didn't pick it up in a bag. Instead, she drew back her slippered foot and booted it into the bushes before shuffling off home. Unlike me, she was made for a place like this. An exploded squirrel or a liquefied lamb was surely nothing to her. Just another part of her day that, like a kicked turd, would be dealt with in due course by bugs and animal predation.

But I could only witness so much death before it got to me, and I started to consider my own mortality. I'd look down at Betty, snoring on the rug in the living room, her huge, glistening tongue hanging from her mouth, making her look as if she'd passed out halfway through eating a pack of bacon.

Would she defend me out here? I wondered. *Would I need her to? What if I had a heart attack or an aneurysm and died out here? Would someone get to me before she, alone and ravenous, decided to eat me?*

I once read an article about how quickly a pet starts eating its owner after death. Cats, I seemed to recall, waited hours rather than days, heading straight for the easily accessible eyeballs. Dogs held off for a slightly more respectful period before chowing down. Soft parts first. It was here, thinking about my dead body being eaten by my best friend, that I realised I was hungry. And, more

Broken Biscuits

than that, I had been on my own for too long. I saved the document containing the fragment of Effie's story, knowing that I'd never finish it out here, put Betty in the car and drove into the village, where I found a dog-friendly pub. I ordered a sandwich and a Coke then seated myself at a table by the window, listening in on a conversation between the landlord and two elderly drinkers leaning at the bar.

Each of these customers was tall and sinewy, like they'd been assembled from the same kit. I'd have had difficulty telling them apart were it not for the fact that one of them was quite obviously wearing a wig. Obvious, because he had it on sideways, as if he'd just placed it on his head that morning, given it a spin, then left the house with it sitting in whichever direction it stopped.

'Is it legal to adapt a drone to fire a crossbow?' he asked.

'I don't think the law matters,' the landlord replied, wiping down the bar with a rag. 'No one can prove you're controlling it.'

'That's true,' the other drinker said. 'Who's going to stop you?'

In remote places like this, where there is little to do but talk, these are the things that bubble to the surface. Thoughts that would have remained as just that in other circumstances. Things privately wondered. But out here they are given air and serious consideration. I listened as

It's the End of the World As We Know It

this conversation went back and forth then took Betty outside so she could pee. When I returned, the conversation had shifted to home surgery.

'People lack the very basics of human anatomy,' the landlord was saying, arranging shot glasses and beermats along the bar, each representing a different part of the human torso. What he was doing, I learned, was detailing the process for removing gall stones. 'People should know this,' he said, when he was done explaining the procedure. 'It's fundamental stuff.'

'I'm happy to remain ignorant,' the guy in the wig said, taking a deep swig of his pint. I held my breath, expecting his hair to slip off his head, hoping Betty wouldn't chase it.

'One day you might not be so happy,' the landlord told him. And there was something cold in his tone, as if he'd had a premonition of this man suffering alone in a post-society wasteland. His ignorance of a simple medical procedure leading to his death, his lower portions densely wadded with obstructive stones.

What chilled me most about this was that it was the future I could see for myself. Come the fall of human civilisation, I knew that I would be among the first casualties. Especially out here, where I had no crossbow drone, no medical savvy. I'd likely be dead fifteen minutes into the end times, having downed a fistful of poison berries or been trampled by determined looters in a

Broken Biscuits

squabble over a tin of broccoli soup. Certainly dead long before that tin had reached its expiry date.

My brother Robert possessed a set of skills that would have served him well in a post-civilisation world. He'd often disappear on weekend camping trips and return with a rainbow trout or a rabbit. I'd come downstairs for breakfast to find him gutting his catch with his camo-painted hunting knife. Spotting me, he'd fling the innards at my head, laughing as I ran squealing from the room. What this underscored was that, while I may have grown up in the countryside, I am not *country folk*. Nature has been tamed and made safe for people like me by a better, tougher generation.

I had spent most of my life holding onto the idea of my childhood self, this version of me who'd confidently wandered the Suffolk countryside, a part of it as much as I was a visitor. But the truth was I had become citified during the intervening years. My journeys to the woods now largely came courtesy of out-of-season family holidays to Center Parcs. I have no survival skills and, as much as I need to get away from people, I also desperately need to be around them. Alone, I am helpless. That's not to say I don't have skills. I could write you a story, play you a passable rendition of 'Soul to Squeeze' on bass guitar, but what good is that when you're starving, under threat or shivering without shelter? Out in the wilds on my own, I was exposed as a second-rate citizen, at best,

It's the End of the World As We Know It

and it was tough to shake the feeling that I was just one hot, crazy summer away from being caught up in something bad. One fuel crisis. One dystopian scenario. And I was not built to survive it. The top of my head destined for the side of the road.

Packing up the car on the day I had to leave, I felt like a man getting ready to outrun a tornado. This sanctuary, all this wildlife, everything I'd been desperate for, I wanted it in my rear-view mirror and shrinking away. Right then what I needed was everything I usually hated and wanted to escape from. Concrete and street lighting. Traffic noise. To be in a location where, if a wolf was stalking me, it'd be pretty easy to spot and report to someone capable of dealing with it. But as I drove away from the farmhouse and the wilds slowly gave way to Wi-Fi and twenty-four-hour supermarkets, my brain was freed up to consider what awaited me back home. I would soon be destroying the world I'd helped to create, and I hoped that we'd all survive the blast.

January 2024

When Emma and I got back from our retreat, I unpacked the car then drove over to my ex-wife's house to collect Effie. I knocked on the door and she opened it immediately, already waiting in the hall with her bags. I spent a

Broken Biscuits

while chatting with my ex, the woman with whom I had spent nineteen years of my life, listening as she proudly showed me some recent improvements to her home. It had taken us a while to get to this point, but any turbulence between us had largely subsided. We've become part of our own separate pictures now, each of us with new end points in sight. I wished her a happy new year and grabbed Effie's bags, carrying them out to my car.

'It was weird not talking to you,' Effie said, as I opened up the boot. 'I don't want to do that again.'

I refrained from mentioning the text conversations we'd had the whole time I'd been away. About a new Agatha Christie adaptation; her upcoming college trip to America; her growing interest in Tudor history. Not to mention the two phone calls we'd had, including the one where we discussed the pony I'd sent her a photo of on the day we arrived. The one that had peered through the glass at me each morning while I worked. I hadn't brought up any of that, because I'd understood what she meant.

'No,' I said, loading her bags into the car and closing the boot. 'Let's never do that again.'

'Promise?'

'Promise,' I said. 'You can even text me when I'm dead.'

She made a growling noise then. The small, frustrated one she always makes whenever I bring up the idea that there will one day come a time when I'm not around for her to talk to.

It's the End of the World As We Know It

'But you know I still will,' she added, smiling as she opened the passenger door. 'I'm burying you with your phone.'

And as we climbed into the car and I started the engine, I didn't doubt her. I just silently placed my hope in the possibility of an afterlife. Never wanting to miss out on a single word of what she had to say.

Acknowledgements

My first attempt at writing these acknowledgements was a concerted effort to thank everyone who, in however small a way, might have helped, inspired, encouraged or guided me through the writing of this book. However, it breached my word limit before I was even close to halfway through. So, while in this version I'm just going to thank a few people, do know that if you expected to see your name here, it was almost certainly in the first draft.

Thanks to Zoë MacGechan for being my friend for forty-seven years and giving me permission to write about her belly. Julie at JE Books in Hull, for the uncanny and hugely appreciated bookselling powers. David Coates, for giving me so much time on the indie wall. Jeni Honeysett, for always banging the drum. Sara and Rosie at Saraband, for keeping the *Cold Fish Soup* flowing. Lucy Nichol, for Hull College and being so generous with advice. Miranda France, for Moniack Mhor. Every member of the Northern

Broken Biscuits

Writers Salon WhatsApp group, for the constant support. Jenn Ashworth, for always having the right answers. Kate Feld, for Bernie's coffee, workshopping the subtitle and collecting me from the hospital that time. And, naturally, huge thanks to the whole team at HarperNorth.

I also need to thank my parents, to whom this book is dedicated, and my siblings, Becky and Ben, for their generosity in allowing me to write about them. My infinitely wise daughter Effie, for being so accepting of the embarrassment several of these essays will cause her. And of course, my beautiful, hugely talented wife Emma, who has had to endure so much of my agonising during the writing of this book, as well as all the times when I stood beside her while she read extracts from my manuscript and calmly dealt with me asking, 'But is it funny though?' every forty-eight seconds.

Finally, I'd like to pay my respects to Jal 'Jay' Framji, a beautiful human being who should have lived to read about himself in this book. It breaks my heart that he didn't get to. And also, to my late brother, Robert. Always to Robert.

Harper North

Book Credits

HarperNorth would like to thank the following staff and contributors for their involvement in making this book a reality:

Sarah Allen-Sutter
Laura Amos
Fionnuala Barrett
Luke Bird
Lauren Braggs
Sarah Burke
Alan Cracknell
Jonathan de Peyer
Anna Derkacz
Tom Dunstan
Kate Elton
Sarah Emsley
Laura Evans
Simon Gerratt
Lydia Grainge
Monica Green
Natassa Hadjinicolaou
Emma Hatlen
Megan Jones
Jean-Marie Kelly
Taslima Khatun
Holly Kyte
Rachel McCarron
Alice Murphy-Pyle
Adam Murray
Genevieve Pegg
Amanda Percival
James Ryan
Colleen Simpson
Eleanor Slater
Hilary Stein
Emma Sullivan
Emily Thomas
Katrina Troy
Daisy Watt
Samantha Willis
Ben Wright

For more unmissable reads,
sign up to the HarperNorth newsletter at
www.harpernorth.co.uk

or find us on Twitter at
@HarperNorthUK

Harper
North